6.95

# THE
# REAL
# McCOY

The Life and Times of Norman Selby

# THE REAL McCOY

ROBERT CANTWELL

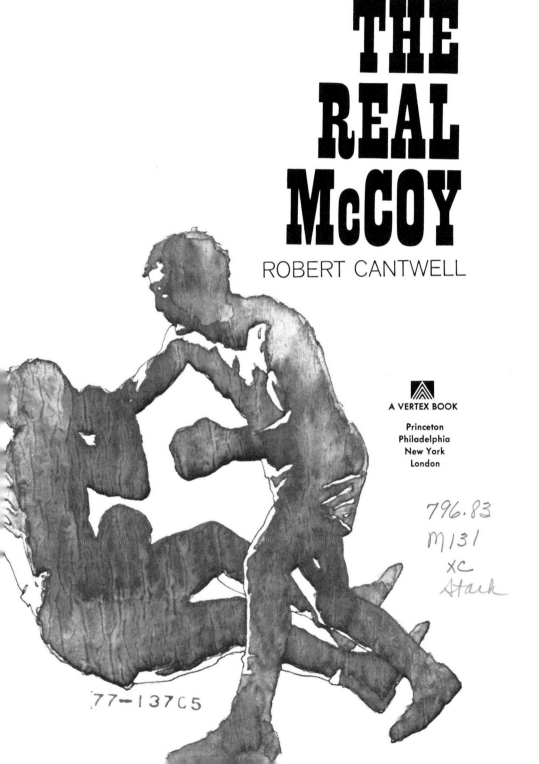

A VERTEX BOOK

Princeton
Philadelphia
New York
London

Published simultaneously in Canada by Book Center, Ltd.

Library of Congress Catalog Card Number: 70-147202

International Standard Book Number: 0-87769-072-3

First Printing
Printed in the United States of America

# Contents

THE
REAL
McCOY

# 1. The Real McCoy

Around the turn of the century celebrities became acutely conscious of something that came to be called "image." That was the public's general impression of them, a publicity-created characterization, quite apart from their real existence in ordinary daily life, and it added a new dimension to human motives when actions were controlled, not by the ideas of right or wrong, or even of financial gain, but by considerations of whether they would help or hurt one's image.

Actors and politicians were among the public figures who carefully nurtured their popular images, but in no field were celebrities so conscious of them as in prizefighting, and no fighter was ever so completely entrapped in a mythical identity as was Norman Selby, who fought under the name of Kid McCoy. Selby was the original of the phrase "the real McCoy."[1] By 1902 he was one of the most widely known individuals in the United States—as a fictional being, that is, in his public image as Kid McCoy. Norman Selby remained completely unknown to the general public. The phrase "the real McCoy" settled into common speech; it meant authentic, genuine, not bogus or contrived, "usually preceded by *the*," according to a dictionary, "as *the real McCoy*, the genuine thing, as stated, promised, or implied." Norman Selby, alias Kid McCoy, was an extremely accomplished ring craftsman, perhaps as good as any in the history of American prizefighting, but his accomplishments in this respect were obscured by the way in which his public image took hold of the popular imagination and radiated out into virtually all aspects of American life.

It is hard to understand why "the real McCoy" suddenly became so widely used. "That's the real McCoy," was a catch phrase, but it

1

was something more; it was heard everywhere, and it meant something definite; it filled a need. The real McCoy was a term of approbation, as a rule, or even of high praise, but it was praise devoted to something ordinary or everyday, like a drink of good whisky— "That's the real McCoy"—for which noble or romantic terms of approval would have seemed inflated or otherwise inappropriate. But at the same time, "the real McCoy" was used soberly to describe a genuine catastrophe such as a tidal wave or a shipwreck, as opposed to some exaggerated scare story.

In general "the real McCoy" came to mean anything genuine, a good suit of clothes, an ample meal, a tip on a horse race, a truly bad man, a full house, an expensive cigar, a no-hitter, a diamond ring, a real love affair, a winning lottery ticket, a reformed burglar, an earthquake, tornado, train wreck, epidemic, or other catastrophe, or merely an unadulterated breakfast cereal. During Prohibition "the real McCoy" meant genuine whisky as opposed to bootleg hooch. This usage was so common that in the first edition of *The American Language,* H. L. Mencken referred to "the real McCoy" only as a Prohibition term. The phrase drifted into literature: a comedy entitled *The Real McCoy* was produced in Dublin in 1928, and in the 1930s the phrase appeared in English novels and even popped up in Scotland, where it became "the real McKaye."

The real McCoy himself, that is, the fighter whose real name was Norman Selby, did not like the phrase.[2] When he acquired wealth and his name had become a household word, he tried repeatedly to recapture his identity as plain old Norman Selby. But it was impossible. The newspapers referred to him as "Mr. Norman Selby (Kid McCoy)." His wife named her yacht *The Kid McCoy.*[3] He played the part of the fighter in David Wark Griffith's silent movie masterpiece, *Broken Blossoms,*[4] in which Griffith, an old friend, billed him as Norman Selby. But no one paid attention; the reviews of the movie changed it to read "The Fighter . . . Kid McCoy."

2

The real Norman Selby was born on a farm in Moscow, Indiana on October 13, 1873.[5] His father was Francis Marion Selby; his mother's maiden name was Mary Campbell. The Selbys were among the first settlers of southeastern Indiana. John Selby was a pioneer of Rush County, having moved there from Kentucky in 1820, soon after the land was ceded by a treaty with the Delaware Indians and opened for settlement. The village of Moscow, a part of Orange Township, was only some 40 miles southeast of Indianapolis, but this corner of Indiana near the borders of Ohio and Kentucky had been bypassed by the roads and railroads; in Norman Selby's childhood it had not changed much since his grandfather's time. There was a store in Moscow, a school where Laban Selby was the first schoolteacher, a grist mill and sawmill powered by the water of Flat Rock Creek. That mill gave the village one of its few claims to the attention of Indiana historians. It was the first in Rush County. Settlers came from all over the region to get lumber to replace their log cabins. The other historical note was that two early settlers in Moscow operated old-fashioned copper stills which the history of Rush County said, "amply supplied the spiritous wants of this then notorious town and its vicinity."

John Selby had no part in this reputation; he was God-fearing, hard-working, a devout member of the Christian Church, who figures in the history of Rush County as a respected and prosperous farmer. He had three sons, of whom nothing is recorded except in the case of Charles, who had high moral principles although he was not a church member. At the time Norman Selby was born, Moscow had a population of about 100, a sizeable proportion of them members of various branches of the Selby family. Norman Selby had a younger brother named Homer, and three sisters—Jennie, Georgia, and Mabel. The family was close-knit and affectionate, and the parents were somewhat family-proud and liked privacy.

Norman Selby was never robust, even when he was a contender for the heavyweight championship. When he stripped in the dressing room for one of his first fights in New York, the sportswriters, accustomed to the battered, reddened, muscular, and hairy torsos of fighters, were shocked by his appearance. One of them wrote that he looked ghastly. He was, however, unusually fast in his movements, light on his feet, and a good athlete insofar as the town of Moscow provided any outlet for competitive sports.

By Norman Selby's time a gravel road had been built to Rushville, 10 miles north, and another due west to Shelbyville, 14 miles away. When he was eight years old a new schoolhouse was built in

Moscow on Charles Selby's farm, and a few years later a drug and grocery store opened in the town to provide competition for the general store that had operated there ever since the first settlers arrived. But that was all. To the east and southeast were rolling wooded hills with a few farm settlements like Moscow itself. Flat Rock Creek flowed southwest through nearly a hundred miles of hill country before joining the White River, which flowed into the Wabash. The region was one of immense natural springs and lost rivers—streams gushed out of limestone cliffs, flowed briefly across land, and sank into the earth, to come out again miles away in a deep pool in a river.

History bypassed the region. Nothing happened to distinguish it. The most distinctive natural feature was the blue grass. If the woods were cleared and if the land was not plowed, blue grass sprang up spontaneously, providing rich, deep, springy pastures which the local enthusiasts believed nurtured the best trotting horses in the world. If their immediate neighborhood suggested any other, it was the hill country of Kentucky, but it lacked the backwoods flavor and the legends and feuds of Kentucky; it was just farmland, noted, if at all, for the second highest per capita wealth of any county in Indiana and for being unsurpassed for the production of corn and alfalfa.

The farms were concentrated along Flat Rock Creek. As a boy Norman liked to hunt rabbits in the fields along the creek. That was all he ever said for publication about the pleasures of his boyhood. He did learn to ride. He rode well and liked horses, and when Kid McCoy became famous he was often pictured on a horse. He never learned to swim, which was not unusual for farm boys in a countryside of fast-flowing streams. Oddly enough, a lasting account of boyhood in that isolated hill country was written in Norman Selby's early years. It was *The Bears of Blue River,* by Charles Major, a prolific writer of romances whose well-written tales of medieval chivalry had phenomenal sales. Major was also the author of *When Knighthood Was in Flower,* which sold 200,000 copies a year after publication, and while that book was still going strong, with its dramatic version a hit as well, he wrote *Dorothy Vernon of Haddon Hall,* which became almost as popular. *The Bears of Blue River* was a juvenile classic, one of the best boys' stories in American literature. Major was a tough romantic writer who rigorously excluded from his books anything that might be called realism, but he had a genuine feeling for the country, and when he wrote of its pioneer past he evoked little rivers, isolated cabins, hills that were densely timbered with oak and hickory, beech and sugar maple, the friendly gleam of fireplaces on a winter night. The setting of *Bears of Blue River* differed only slightly from that of the farm country where Norman Selby was growing up, 14 miles from where Charles Major was writing his books. The houses were now frame instead of log cabins and there was a little more cleared land around them. "I hear the buzzing of the wild bees," Major wrote, "the song of the meadowlark, the whistle of the bobwhite, and the gurgling of the creek. I see the house amid the hollyhocks and trees, the thin line of blue smoke curling lazily from the kitchen window and floating over the deep, black forest. . . . I see the maples languidly turning the white side of their leaves to catch the south wind. . . ."

Norman Selby reacted to this enchanting scene in the traditional fashion of farm boys—he ran away.[6] One story of his life had it that he ran away in 1886 at the age of 13. If so, he was soon home again, where he continued to live even after he had become fairly well known in the Middle West as a fighter. The story about his running away from home at the age of 13 was part of the legend of Kid McCoy. It appeared in print after he had won a number of fights. According to it, Kid McCoy (his real name was not known to sports followers then) lived in hobo jungles all over the United States after fleeing the family farm, and learned all the tricks of dirty fighting that were needed to survive in them.[7] It was not altogether fabrication, for in his late teens Selby did wander around some; rather, it was a useful fiction designed to fill a specific need at the time he began to fight. He did not look tough. The New York *World,* which was generally favorably disposed toward him, described him coming into the ring for one of his biggest fights: "McCoy was as pale and calm and pretty as ever." Norman Selby's natural appearance was that of a sensitive, quiet, thoughtful boy, the opposite of a hobo brawler, and the story that he had spent his youth on the bum, riding the rods, fighting with other tramps, was hopefully presented to cover up his unfortunate handicap of being extremely good-looking.[8]

But he did leave home, probably at 16 or 17. He went to Louisville.[9] That great city, only 80 miles south, with a population of nearly 200,000, was hospitable and prospering. Its citizens wanted to make it a kind of New Orleans of the border states. Along with the Kentucky Derby, which had become a social event after Dom Pedro, the Emperor of Brazil, attended the second one in 1876, they promoted

the annual spring parade of the Satellites of Mercury, a more restrained saturnalia than the Mardi Gras of New Orleans, but still an
exciting festival, with a two-mile parade and as many as 493 floats.
Norman Selby had, at first, no interest in the gambling halls and the
theatres for which Louisville was then famous. He got a job in a department store and joined the Young Men's Christian Association.[10]

Another Louisville youth at the time was David Wark Griffith,
who appeared and reappeared in Norman Selby's life.[11] He was two
years younger than Selby and ran an elevator in a Louisville department store before he got a job as a reporter on the Louisville *Courier-
Journal* and then began appearing in minor roles with a stock company at the Temple Theatre. Norman had no such luck. He worked at
his job and spent his evenings at the YMCA. After monumental
struggles with community indifference, the Y in Louisville managed
in the late 1880s to raise $100,000 for its own building on Walnut
Street. It now had, in addition to night classes, a fine gymnasium and
an instructor who taught all manly sports, including boxing.

Selby began to box there and was soon so proficient that people
talked of a professional career for him. All of this side of his life was,
of course, rigorously excluded from the legend of Kid McCoy because it spoiled the image. Louisville was not a good fight town, and
there were real difficulties in getting a start as a fighter there. The
city's sportsmen were interested primarily in horses, and the pool halls
and gambling houses that made Louisville one of the few places in the
country where gambling was legal concentrated their interest on
horse racing. Sports in Louisville tended to be stratified along class
lines as well. After the YMCA opened its new building the exclusive
Louisville Athletic Club in 1889 built a handsome new structure on
Fifth Avenue not far away, a community showplace and social center
in a way the Y could hardly hope to be.

Selby never had the backing of local sports followers in Louisville in the way James Corbett in San Francisco had the support of the
Olympic Athletic Club throughout the early stages of his career. It
could hardly be wondered at. In his early years Selby actually looked
frail. But he was lithe and catlike in his motions, and extraordinarily
fast. In the days when he was still Norman Selby, he was conscious of
his ability, or of his potential ability, but he was even more conscious
of the difficulty of getting fights, or winning the attention of the sports
crowd. Lightweight fighters usually had to arrange their own fights.
The arrangements were often primitive.[12] When Jack McAuliffe

fought Jem Carney for the lightweight championship at Revere Beach near Boston, they both piled into a corner and fell during the 74th round, bringing down one of the posts and the ropes, in which they became entangled, whereupon the referee called it a draw and declared that all bets were off.

One classic misadventure came close to the world of Norman Selby. In 1889, at North Judson, Indiana, a mining town on the opposite side of Indianapolis from Selby's country, Jack McAuliffe met Billy Myers for the lightweight championship. They fought in a big hall over a saloon. The gate receipts, along with the bets deposited with the bartenders, were locked in the saloon safe when the fight started. It began in a frenzy, with McAuliffe knocking Myers down and plainly winning until, in the fourteenth round, Myers broke McAuliffe's arm, an accident that required McAuliffe to bluff, jab, fight with one hand, and conceal how badly he had been hurt for the next 50 rounds. At the end of the 64th round the weary referee called it a draw. So much excitement had been generated that while everyone was upstairs watching the fight, thieves cleaned out the saloon, taking the safe and with it the purse, gate receipts, and all the bets.

Norman Selby quit his job in the department store, or was laid off, or fired, or became ill, or otherwise found reason to leave Louisville. In Butte, Montana, in 1890 he got his first professional fight, a four-round affair for which he received five dollars.[13] This fight was not listed in the official record of his fights that appeared in his lifetime. It was mentioned in a Detroit newspaper after his death, but since his brother Homer was then living in Detroit, and supplied information on Norman's background, the fight probably took place.

Norman found fighting an easier way of earning money than farm work or working in a department store, and he became intent on getting as many fights as he could. But here he ran into trouble. He was a little too heavy to be a lightweight, then set at 133 pounds. The next class was middleweight, then including anyone up to 158 pounds. In England there had long been an intermediate category, called tenstone—140 pounds, or welterweight—but it was not used in the United States. Norman was so emaciated-looking that he did not inspire much confidence when he tried to line up a fight with some hardened veteran a decade older and 25 pounds heavier. A fighter who saw him a little later said that more than anything else he gave the impression of suffering from tuberculosis.[14]

His first fight under the name of Kid McCoy was at St. Paul,

Minnesota, on June 2, 1891, against a local fighter named Pete
Jenkins.[15] McCoy won in four rounds. The transformation of Norman
Selby into Kid McCoy began at that time, and he was never again
simply Norman Selby in the way that he had been before. In those
days there were very few fighters called "Kid." In 1891 there were
only Kid Lavigne, Kid McCarthy, and Kid Hogan; except for Lavigne,
who later became the lightweight champion, they were not prominent.
Subsequently the name became popular, but that was because of Kid
McCoy's success. It was a period in which fighters gave themselves
such names as Cyclone Kelly and Knockout Brown; "Kid" had an
element of condescension, unless it was used by lightweights or feath-
erweights or juvenile contenders.

Why did Selby pick the name McCoy?[16] One ring historian
wrote that he chose the name in honor of Pete McCoy, a respectable
middleweight and an old friend of John L. Sullivan. Pete McCoy was
no one to be ashamed of. He had fought such formidable opponents
as George LaBlanche, renowned for the savagery of his title bout
with Nonpareil Jack Dempsey, and Pete McCoy himself had fought
Dempsey. He lost to Dempsey in 1886, but that was hardly a disgrace
—Dempsey had not been beaten in 38 fights. Hence there was nothing
improbable in a beginning fighter calling himself Kid McCoy after
Pete McCoy.

On the other hand, Pete McCoy was not outstanding enough to
warrant being chosen on his own merits. Norman Selby possessed
more than an average amount of self-confidence; if he had wanted
to call himself after some other fighter, he would have chosen someone from the top rank. Moreover, he did not merely use the name of
Kid McCoy in his fights and call himself Norman Selby in everyday
life. He invented a whole new identity for himself. He said he was
Charles McCoy, a farm boy who had run away from home and become a hobo. He shifted his birth date and concealed his birthplace.
There was, of course, nothing unusual in a fighter taking a ring
name.[17] The real name of Tommy Ryan, the welterweight champion
(and McCoy's lifelong enemy) was Joseph Youngs. Stanley Ketchel
was originally Stanislaus Kiecal, Freddy Walsh was really Frederick
Thomas, Knockout Brown was Valentine Braun, and Peach Cross
was originally Dr. Louis Wallach, a New York dentist. Jack Root's
real name was Janos Ruthaly. Fireman Jim Flynn was, at one time,

Andrew Haynes and before that, Andrew Chiariglione. Selby was unusual in that he did not remain Norman Selby outside the ring, but gave the real name of Kid McCoy as Charles McCoy. There was a Charles Selby who lived in Moscow and who raised trotting horses in emulation of more prosperous Rush County farmers. And McCoy was a famous pioneer name in southeastern Indiana: the Reverend Isaac McCoy went through the region establishing Indian missions before the territory was ceded to the government, and a farm settlement near Moscow was later called McCoy.

Kid McCoy was a good ring name. It was not as challenging as Bull McCarthy or Tiger Smith. It was broad enough to encompass national groups without being limited to one, like Dutch Neal or Dago Frank, or the many fighters who were called Irish something. But Norman Selby had one problem that was to bother him all his life. He could never decide where Kid McCoy came from. When he fought in Minneapolis he said he was from Indianapolis. When he fought in Indianapolis he was billed as coming from Muncie, Indiana. At various times he was from Cleveland, Ohio, Hot Springs, Arkansas, and Fall River, Massachusetts. On one occasion, after he beat Shadow Maber in a fine fight in Memphis, he candidly announced that he was willing to make Memphis the home town of Kid McCoy if the local sportsmen would make it worth his while by lining up fights for him there. But he never said that Kid McCoy was from Moscow, Indiana. The reason was obvious: the family objection to his fighting in his early years was eased by the understanding that he did not involve the name of Selby in his fights or attract fighters and the fight crowd to the Selby farm.

In the summer of 1892 Selby had two fights in Indianapolis under the name of Kid McCoy. He met Billy Barlow on June 6, 1892, in an outdoor ring and won in six rounds. On September 14 he knocked out another Indianapolis fighter, Bob Lewis, in the first round. Two weeks later he took a 150-mile train ride to Columbus, Ohio, where he fought an eight-round draw with Herb Hall. He had now had four recorded fights, with three wins and one draw—not bad for a 19-year-old beginner.[18] But he was dissatisfied. "I had a lot of trouble getting fights," he said, in one of his few recollections of those days.[19] He could only have meant up to this time, for thereafter he averaged a fight a month for the next seven years.

3

Apart from his ability and his showmanship, there was a development in boxing itself that stimulated interest in the fights of Kid McCoy. In San Francisco James J. Corbett, from 1886 onward, demonstrated that a good, fast, well-conditioned boxer could at least hold his own against the huge, powerful, elephantine sluggers who then dominated heavyweight fighting. Corbett's fame and the subsequent scandals in Kid McCoy's life concealed the extent to which both men were once linked as ring craftsmen—scientific fighters was the phrase commonly used—in contrast to such portly and overbearing brawlers as John Lawrence Sullivan. In his recollections of that generation of fighters, William Naughton, the sports editor of the San Francisco *Examiner,* said that for some years in the new era then beginning, "Fellows of a neater build, such as Corbett and McCoy, cut a swath in the world of sport."[20]

They were not merely of "neater build." Corbett made a career of being a gentleman fighter, as opposed to Sullivan.[21] Corbett was born in San Francisco in 1866, and at his death in 1934 *The Times* of London said he would always be remembered "as the man who lifted boxing from the hands of thugs and brawlers." Corbett's father was the owner of a large livery stable, and Corbett, a tall, slender athlete who originally planned to become a professional baseball player, was a familiar figure to San Francisco sportsmen from the start. His career in the ring began with four historic fights with Joe Choynski, in a struggle that went through nearly four years of frustration before Corbett won. Corbett's brother Frank worked in City Hall, in the auditor's department, where Joe Choynski's brother Herbert also worked, and the Corbett-Choynski fights (and with them much of modern ring history) began in the arguments of Frank Corbett and Herbert Choynski as to which had a better fighter for a brother. The first Corbett-Choynski fight, which Corbett always claimed he won, was officially recorded as no decision; the second, first scheduled for an isolated quarry and eventually held in the sand hills near town with only a few spectators on hand, was stopped by the police after the fourth round; the third, which took place on a barge, was won by Corbett with a knockout in the 27th round, with Choynski followers still unconvinced. Only a fight the following

month in San Francisco, under less exceptional circumstances, finally
settled the debate, when Corbett won in four rounds.

Corbett said he had never known as many conflicting prejudices to
be aroused as did his fights with Choynski. It was Jew versus Gentile,
for Choynski was Jewish, but it was also Protestant versus Catholic,
for Corbett's supporters were Catholic. And Choynski was backed
by prominent Episcopalian sportsmen. It was also capital versus
labor, for Corbett worked in a bank, and Choynski was a factory
hand whose supporters included good union men as well as socialites.
Choynski, in Corbett's words, was "a magnificent-looking fellow with
a blonde head and great strength . . . one of the gamest and best
fighters that ever lived." He took boxing lessons, trained, and quit
his job in the candy factory to become a professional prizefighter. As
such he was a formidable contender for 20 years. One of Choynski's
historic achievements was knocking out Jack Johnson before Johnson
became heavyweight champion. Another was his fight with Kid
McCoy, which led to McCoy becoming known as "the real McCoy."

Corbett was also an actor. He began acting in San Francisco when
he was an amateur fighter, and toured the West with a minstrel company when he was known as a professional fighter. He had a few
fights in remote mountain towns, on one occasion being mistaken by the locals for Nonpareil Jack Dempsey, and on another
occasion entering the ring as a man of mystery who was rumored to
be Charley Mitchell in disguise, greatly increasing interest in the
fights, since Mitchell had twice fought Sullivan.

In everything Corbett maintained an engaging carefree air that
contrasted with Sullivan's solemn dissipations. Sullivan had not had
a real fight since he defeated Jake Kilrain in Mississippi in 75 rounds
in 1889. Each night, however, and sometimes during matinees,
Sullivan won, enjoying thousands of fantasy knockouts on the stage.
In 1890 he appeared in New York in *Honest Hearts and Willing
Hands,* in which his part called for him to knock out the villain.[22]
Sullivan entered with enthusiasm into the scene. He sometimes forgot
that it was all pretense, and hit the villain—in real life an old friend
and sparring partner—so hard that two standby actors were hired for
the role in case the first did not show up for the next performance.

Sullivan had been on a lengthy drinking spree before the opening
of *Honest Hearts and Willing Hands,* but he was able to remember
his lines and give life-like performances, or he belted actors around

the stage. Indeed, it would hardly have been life-like if he was altogether sober. On one occasion in his fighting days Sullivan appeared
for a bout at Madison Square Garden too drunk to go on with the
fight. Sullivan enjoyed the company of actors, and as a ladies' man
of legendary renown he also liked actresses and other pretty women.
He was urbane and gracious with them, while generally surly and
unfriendly with fighters and the sports crowd. As *Honest Hearts and
Willing Hands* played on the road for years and earned more than
$100,000, Sullivan became a trouper, parading after performances
in his evening clothes, black silk hat, and chinchilla-lined overcoat.
Genuine actors were awed by the money he made, his commanding
presence, and his indifference to the nuances of their art. "One likes
that bluff, hearty manner," said the Polish actress Helena Modjeska
faintly, after she had seen Sullivan on the stage in Cincinnati. But
Sullivan would not fight any genuine contender for his title, and in
particular he would not fight Peter Jackson, the great Negro heavyweight from Australia. "You shouldn't fight a nigger," Sullivan told
Corbett, demeaning himself for the moment to give advice to a newcomer in the interest of racial superiority. Corbett and Peter Jackson
nevertheless fought their historic 61-round, no-decision battle, one
result of which was that Sullivan refused to fight Corbett.

The theatre, not the prize ring, finally brought about their meeting. Corbett was a far better actor than Sullivan. William Brady, the
theatrical producer, had known Corbett in his boyhood. He hired him
for $150 a week to spar in a boxing scene in a melodrama, *After
Dark,* in New York. Corbett did well enough to justify Brady's plans
for his future—as an actor, not as a fighter. Corbett next appeared in
*Sports McAllister, One of the Four Hundred.* When it succeeded,
Brady hired Charles Vincent, a respectable hack dramatist, to write
*Gentleman Jack* specifically for Corbett to play the starring role. All
this was too much for Sullivan who had returned from Australia,
where *Honest Hearts and Willing Hands* was a flop; he accepted
Corbett's challenge in the spring of 1892 and the fight took place in
New Orleans that fall.

*Gentleman Jack* was a smart and agreeable melodrama, sophisticated Broadway fare compared to the stolid primitive art of *Honest
Hearts and Willing Hands.* It had the added novelty that the entire
third act consisted of a simulated prize fight, with the ring on the stage
and the theatre audience the ringsiders. Brady knew he had a hit, and

did not care particularly whether Corbett fought Sullivan or not. When he encouraged Corbett to issue his challenge to Sullivan he did so because he thought it would be valuable promotion for *Gentleman Jack*; in fact the opening of the play, "Starring James J. Corbett, the Heavyweight Champion of the World," was announced before Corbett and Sullivan actually fought for the title. But Brady was not taking much of a chance. The fight crowd expected Sullivan to win, but the theatrical crowd knew better. Everyone in the theatre knew how heavily Sullivan had been drinking and how paunchy and bedazzled with his own importance he had become after two years before the footlights.

The fight was in New Orleans on Wednesday, September 7, 1892. It was part of a three-day boxing festival.[23] The city of New Orleans, capitalizing on a nationwide reform movement against prizefighting, liberalized its boxing laws in a drive to become the sports center of the nation. On the Monday night before the Corbett-Sullivan fight George Dixon met Jack Skelly for the featherweight championship of the world. Dixon was a brilliant Negro boxer, knocked down only once in years of almost constant fighting (and never beaten until he lost to Terrible Terry McGovern eight years later), who put on a dazzling exhibition of skill in knocking out Skelly in eight rounds. The following night Jack McAuliffe defended his lightweight title again against Billy Myers, winning by a knockout in the 10th round.

These fights were followed around the country with a degree of interest which, if it did not equal that given heavyweights, was far greater than fighters at the lighter weights were accustomed to; a new period in ring history had begun. And a new element of people began attending prize fights, along with the old regulars seen at every fight. Corbett made no attempt to win the favor of the old fight crowd. He sauntered around New Orleans in a light summer suit and a new straw hat, in the pose of an elegant amateur, which in itself antagonized fight followers. They expected heavyweights to be saturnine gladiators. Corbett knew Billy Myers and liked him, and after Myers was beaten by McAuliffe (and on the eve of his own fight with Sullivan), Corbett went out of his way to be seen with Myers in a fashionable restaurant—alarming his own camp for it was considered bad luck for a fighter to be seen before a fight with any defeated fighter, and further antagonizing the regular fight crowd, who pointedly ostracized the loser after a fight.

The fight crowd was overwhelmingly in favor of Sullivan, growing silent when Corbett dominated the first round. The mood began to shift in Corbett's favor in the seventh round, when Corbett was sure Sullivan was beaten—hopelessly beaten—unless Corbett became careless enough to let Sullivan land a wild desperation punch. But Corbett was never incautious. By the time he knocked out Sullivan with patient efficiency in the 21st round, the fight crowd was more violently for him than it had been for Sullivan at the start. As Corbett stood listening to their cheers he experienced a numbing sense of revulsion and disgust which in itself reflected his own contradictory feelings about his role. He had transformed the public attitude toward prizefighting, but he had also, in the words of the New York *Times,* "faced the ridicule and contemptuous indifference of sports followers that would have destroyed a less intelligent individual." From now on the emphasis would be on the art and science of boxing, on speed, skill, brains, and ring generalship; a fighter of Corbett's build and manner found that what had previously been a handicap was now an advantage.

Kid McCoy benefited enormously from the charged atmosphere. Another development changed things even more in his favor when the welterweight division was established in the United States.[24] In December 1892 Mysterious Billy Smith fought Danny Needham in San Francisco and, when he knocked out Needham in the 14th round, claimed the welterweight championship of the world.[25] Smith had some justification for his claim. He had previously beaten Shadow Maber, the welterweight champion of Australia. Almost at once the new division became popular, and the title was fought for all over the country, with half a dozen contenders of nearly equal ability battling with energy, frequency and, in some cases, with a skill absent in the older divisions whose champions were less willing to risk their crowns. As a youthful middleweight Kid McCoy was hopelessly obscured by the ability of the experienced men in that class: the future heavyweight champion, Bob Fitzsimmons, then held the middleweight title. But as a welterweight McCoy was not outclassed in the field of ambitious contenders for the new championship. His normal fighting weight then was 145 pounds. In England welterweights fought at 140 pounds, but five pounds were added when the division was established in the United States; it was made for McCoy, and at the age of 19, with only four fights to his credit, he began his campaign to win the title.

4

McCoy's 12 fights in 1893 were against unknowns who played no further part in ring history.[26] Only a few were even reported in the local newspapers at the time. But by the fall of that year McCoy had become a minor celebrity. The season began with two fights in Hot Springs, Arkansas, in January. He won the first, against one Jim Dickson, in five rounds, and the second, against Jim Connors, in three rounds. From Hot Springs McCoy went to Milan, Tennessee, in February, where he won in two rounds over a fighter whose very name is lost to history, and 10 days later on February 22, 1893, he was in New Orleans, where he was credited with having beaten Frank Lamode in three rounds. The New Orleans *Times Picayune* carried no report of this meeting, which was hardly surprising: Fitzsimmons was in New Orleans training for his $40,000 fight with Jem Hall, the British middleweight champion, and in the excitement over that event, sports editors did not care whether an unknown named McCoy beat someone equally obscure.

McCoy was back home in Indiana in May 1893 when he won in two rounds from Frank Murray in Indianapolis. The following month he knocked out Kid McCarthy in Muncie, Indiana in three rounds. In July he fought again in Muncie, his first long fight, a 22-round draw with Ike Boone. A week later he put away Dick Harris at Marion, a few miles north of Muncie, in one round.

Paradoxically McCoy's quick victories antagonized sports reporters. Indianapolis newspapermen were not impressed when McCoy fought there on August 15, 1893, two weeks after he had knocked out Harris in Marion, though the occasion was more important than his previous fights in Indianapolis had been. The Indianapolis *News* carried this account:

> A number of young and old men witnessed a "fight" between "Kid" McCoy, said to be of Muncie, and Young Merritt, said to be of Pittsburgh, at Powell Hall early this morning. McCoy won in the second round with a knockout. The spectators left with considerable more experience than educated in pugilism. They were disgusted, and many called for their money back.

This was all that was published about the fight. A baffled Norman Selby read it, wondering what one had to do to win public attention.

The big sports news that day was a long account of a dull fight at
Rory, Indiana, in which Dan Creedon, the middleweight champion
of Australia, won a 15-round decision over Alec Greggains from
California before 6,000 paid fans.

Tommy Ryan, born in Redwood, New York in 1870, the son of
an English mother and French father, was to fight Mysterious Billy
Smith on August 29, 1893, and was in need of sparring partners at
his training camp in Detroit.[27] There was always a shortage of sparring partners around Ryan's training camp. He was a phenomenally
fast defensive fighter, and as a boxer was unequalled in ring history.
He had not been beaten in 25 fights. Famous for his 76th-round
knockout of Danny Needham (and for his 46-round victory in
another fight, and a 57-round draw in the next), he was superbly
conditioned and a master at pacing himself as he wore down his
opponents. He liked to demonstrate his boxing skill to admiring supporters, and he was a notorious punisher of sparring partners when
he trained. In his history of American boxing, Alexander Johnston
wrote: "When Tommy Ryan was training for his fight with Mysterious
Billy Smith, he took on as a sparring partner a youth who called himself Kid McCoy. The boy was just beginning, but he showed signs of
unusual cleverness, and Ryan took a fancy to him and taught him a
bit about boxing."

Ryan's way of showing his fondness for anyone was to beat the
tar out of them. *The Ring* magazine reported McCoy's experience with
Ryan differently: "Ryan was not a pleasing sparring partner, and
McCoy and others who were supernumeraries in his camp grew to
hate him because of the relentless manner in which he slammed them
around in practice. McCoy, because of the terrible mauling he received at Ryan's hands, was most pronounced in his antipathy for the
champion. . . ."[28]

McCoy was not only mercilessly slammed around by Ryan; he was
stunned, humiliated, and made to look ridiculous in the eyes of the
knowledgable fight followers who watched Ryan's workouts. He was
expected to remain with Ryan until after the title fight with Mysterious
Billy Smith. Instead he dressed, walked out, and did not return. The
courtly phrase used in fight journalism—"he was most pronounced in
his antipathy"—was an understatement. He went down the road burn-
ing with a deadly hatred of Ryan so strong it would have been more
accurate to say that he wanted to kill him.

Ryan went on to fight a dull but highly publicized draw with Smith. McCoy returned to the obscurity of fights with opponents scarcely better known than himself. If he was going to be beaten up in the ring he could at least be beaten up in genuine fights. In spite of his failure to get anywhere with name fighters he was gaining a kind of regional attention because of his record of quick knockouts. He thought that record perhaps was a factor in his difficulty in lining up fights, and when he met George Bennett in Akron, Ohio, on September 30, 1893, he slowed down, expecting to win by a decision, and had to be satisfied with a draw. But his performance was good enough to make him known among fight followers in Ohio River towns; a match with any reasonable opponent could draw a fair crowd.

The first to take advantage of it was a Wheeling, West Virginia promoter named Jimmy Rowan who had devised an ingenious scheme for getting around the laws against prizefighting there. Rowan spread the word that the fight would be held with McCoy matched against Jack Welch of Chicago, but kept its location secret.[29] People who were interested were told to meet at the railway station at eleven o'clock on the night of the date set.

The last Baltimore and Ohio Railroad train left Wheeling at 11:15 p.m. It was made up in Wheeling; by eleven on October 13, 1893; there were more than 400 people on hand. The autumn night was cool and pleasant. Most of the crowd had come to see the sports celebrities on the train, but the animation and excitement affected them, and one group after another detached itself from those on the platform and boarded the train. They looked like any passengers, except that there were more of them than had ever taken the 11:15 before, and they differed from any other passengers in that they did not know where they were going.

Norman Selby was among them. He had put on his boxing trunks before leaving his hotel room and wore them under his ordinary clothes and dressed as he usually did, neatly and inconspicuously. His appearance was that of a tall skinny farm boy with long thin arms and bony shoulders. He had gray eyes, black wavy hair and thin regular features that suggested a more rugged and more thoughtful John Barrymore. It was his 20th birthday. He had little to say, and spoke softly when he said anything. He looked younger than his 20 years, and appeared to be lighter than the 145 pounds he claimed as his fighting weight. He looked more like a student than a fighter, and in fact was referred to by the fight crowd as the boy from Indianapolis, though no one really knew where he came from. There was a boyish solemnity in his manner, an occasional friendly smile, and a careful suppression of any outward sign of nervousness or excitement. He was on his way to his first important fight.

Jack Welch was a good Chicago middleweight—shorter, stockier, heavier, more experienced, and the favorite in the betting. Neither McCoy nor Welch knew where they were going. The organization of the McCoy-Welch fight was one of the best-kept secrets in that period of illegal prizefights. Wheeling, which was then a city of about 32,000, was an ideal take-off point for secret fights. It stood on the Ohio River about midway up the narrow panhandle (50 miles long, north and south, and from five to ten miles wide) between Ohio and Pennsylvania, so that only a short trip was required from any stop on the railroad to bring a fight crowd into any one of three states, or into half-a-dozen different counties—an impossible problem for the county sheriffs responsible for preventing fights. Wheeling was a good sports town in itself, and it was only 66 miles from Pittsburgh, which was a sports center. A sizable crowd of sports from Pittsburgh had in fact arrived in Wheeling and stood around on the platform waiting for the 11:15 to leave for its unknown destination.

The only person who knew where the fight would be held was Rowan, the promoter, who kept his plans entirely to himself. To be arrested for promoting a prizefight at that time was not as serious as arrest for other forms of law-breaking such as robbery, but it could be more than troublesome, and it was always expensive. In addition, a fight that was raided and stopped by the police made it almost impossible for a promoter to attract a crowd to another fight. If the authorities were tolerant the arrangements were scarcely secret, no more so than the location of speakeasies during Prohibition. But even in those cases police raids were not uncommon, especially if a local man appeared to be losing. And occasionally promoters vanished during the raids, taking the gate receipts and the purses promised the fighters. Over much of the United States fighters met in barns, on barges in rivers between state lines, in the woods in summer, or in closed summer hotels in winter, in warehouses, abandoned quarries, dance halls, theatres, or, in one famous case, on an isolated shore of Long Island, in a ring pitched so close to the water's edge that the tide came in and covered it, leaving the fighters battling in water up to their knees by the fourth round.

Jimmy Rowan took no chances of anything of the sort happening. He must have been a born military strategist, for he organized the fight as carefully as a plan for a surprise attack in a war. His planning began with his choice of the fighters. McCoy had been fighting only two years, but in 12 fights had not been defeated. His opponents up to this time had not been nationally known fighters; they were local boys, but he had fought widely, in St. Paul, Hot Springs, New Orleans, Akron, and in and around Indianapolis. His name was beginning to be known. What aroused interest in Kid McCoy was that his fights were brief in that time of marathon ring battles. McCoy jumped into action at the bell as though he had to catch a train. Of the 10 fights he had won, two were by one-round knockouts. In two fights he put away his opponents in two rounds, in three fights, in three rounds, in one fight in four, one in five, and one in six rounds. He had fought two draws, one of eight rounds and the other, his only long fight, of 22 rounds.

Sometimes McCoy really did have to catch a train. A quick knockout was not regarded as a sign of ring mastery if he knocked out a popular local fighter. Jimmy Rowan had picked as McCoy's opponent one of the few fighters whose style of fighting was like that of McCoy himself, and who also rushed into action determined to get the business over with as quickly as possible. Consequently it appeared that the fight would be brief. If it went for more than a few rounds Welch was expected to win.

People going to the fight were instructed to get tickets to Moundsville, but no one expected the fight to be held there. For one thing, Moundsville was the county seat of Marshall County, West Virginia, and known Marshall County deputy sheriffs (in disguise) were on the train. There was no bridge across the Ohio at Moundsville, so that destination was considered to be a ruse. There was a new steel bridge across the river only a few miles south of Wheeling, leading to the village of Bellaire on the Ohio side. It was a reasonable assumption that the passengers would leave the train before they reached Moundsville and cross to Ohio on the Bellaire Bridge. The deputy sheriff of Belmont County in Ohio, where Bellaire was located, was at the Wheeling station with his assistants. Everyone was so convinced that the fight could only be held in or near Bellaire that the deputy and his men left the station before the train filled up, and hurried to the Ohio side to intercept the fighters when they crossed the bridge.

The 11:15 left on time. A number of prominent Wheeling citi-

zens, not regulars of the sports crowd, got on the train at the last moment, infected by the general excitement and the prevailing belief
that Rowan had found a way to get around the anti-fight law without
risk. But in general it was a pretty rough crowd, with most attention
given the visiting Pittsburgh sports. With them was a giant Negro who
fought under the name of Othello, and who had once lasted a round
with the former heavyweight champion, John L. Sullivan, and once
stayed two rounds with the heavyweight contender, Peter Maher, before being knocked out. He was a more notable ring figure than either
McCoy or Jack Welch. In the midst of tough fight followers of this
sort, the Marshall County deputies aboard prudently refrained from
doing anything to prevent the fight.

The train stopped at the Bellaire Bridge, but Rowan gave no in-
structions for anyone to get off. As it clattered off again into the dark-
ness, past the farms along the river, the Wheeling citizens began to
get nervous. The strain was increased when the train pulled into
Moundsville at midnight. McCoy and Welch were hurried away while
the other passengers milled around the station trying to find out where
they were supposed to go. Under Rowan's plan the only risk was in
getting the fighters to the scene of the fight. Promoting a prizefight
was a felony in Ohio, and he intended to *act* only in West Virginia.
So McCoy and Welch and their handlers were hurriedly rowed across
the dark river. The Ohio was nearly a quarter of a mile wide at this
point. On the Ohio side, back from the shore, there was an abandoned
amusement park, long dark, known as Lee Anschutz's Famous Belmont Park. Rowan had fixed up a ring on the dance floor, hidden
away among the boarded-up booths and rides. The fighters took off
their outer clothes and punched and shadow-boxed to warm up.

But now a snag developed in Rowan's careful planning. An
essential part of his plan was that he was not going to sell tickets to a
fight in Ohio. All he did was sell tickets in West Virginia, entitling
the purchasers to ride across the Ohio River. If they wanted to go to
the fight on the other side, that was their business; there would be no
admission charged at the amusement park or the ringside. The trans-
portation that Rowan provided consisted only of several flatboats
propelled by large oars and poles. After one look at the arrangement
a number of Wheeling citizens protested that they did not want to
take a chance on them. Here in the middle of the night they were expected to pay $5 for a ride across the Ohio River, with no guarantee

that they would get to see a fight, or even that they would get to the other side. They insisted they should be taken across the river for nothing, and pay their admission at the scene of the fight itself, when they were sure it was going to take place. "There were several pretty prominent citizens in the party," said the Wheeling *Intelligencer,* "who, if they had known officials were on the track"—on the track of the fighters that is—"and that prize fighting, abetting or witnessing a fight was a felony under Ohio's law, would have been elsewhere."

The officials who were on the track of the fighters were still in Bellaire. As the hours passed and they realized they had been duped they tried to get to Lee Anschutz's Amusement Park, but found that all the horses and rigs in Bellaire had been hired, so they were stuck there. They attempted to order a locomotive of the Wheeling and Lake Erie Railroad, which ran along the west side of the river, to take them to the fight, but the railroad officials were unwilling to provide one. Meanwhile, in Moundsville itself arrangements were finally straightened out, and the ferrying of the fight patrons across the river began. But by this time the scenes of confusion and controversy on the river bank had aroused the sleeping town. Many of the towns-people owned rowboats or other craft, and when they learned there was to be no admission charge at the fight itself, the only charge being the flatboat fee for crossing the river, they got out of bed to row people across for less than Rowan charged and, after the business ended, to rush to the fight scene. It was estimated that more than 500 Moundsville citizens were on hand when the fight started.

The Wheeling *Intelligencer,* a morning paper kept its press open, planning to run a front-page story on the fight. But at 2:40 a.m. its sports editor telegraphed from Moundsville that people were still crossing the river in flatboats. With that information the paper went to press. The frustrated reporter hurried back to the ring. Torches had been lighted to illuminate it. When everything appeared to be ready another problem arose in connection with the choice of a referee. That was settled, but then it was discovered that something had happened to the stopwatch and a search had to be made for one. Some time after 3:15, the bell rang for the first round.

Ordinarily both McCoy and Welch rushed into action at the bell. This time they were both cautious, understandably so, or perhaps they were merely cold, but the first round was a tame sequence of feints and dodges. McCoy had a distinctive style of fighting that he later perfected with Fitzsimmons' help. His reach was longer than that of most fighters of his weight. He usually bounded into the ring, practically jumping there from his corner, and moved fast, clockwise or counterclockwise, almost on his toes, rather than with the usual fighter's shuffle, using his longer reach to land overhand jabs. Almost invariably the reports disparaged these jabs as light, or faint, or tame; they did not seem to do the damage a punch on the jaw was expected to do.

At the beginning of the second round Welch rushed the fighting, landing a hard punch on McCoy's ribs. McCoy staggered Welch at once with the first real blow he had landed in the fight and got in another one almost immediately. "It was in this round," said the Wheeling *Intelligencer* reporter, "that McCoy's superior length of reach began to be noticeable." Both fighters again became cautious and the round ended quietly.

They rushed to the center of the ring at the start of the third, McCoy landing an uppercut and following it with a punch that landed on Welch's neck. But Welch, while he was struck repeatedly, did not seem hurt. "Then followed a hot exchange to which Welch had the best of the inning. From this time on Welch pushed the fighting. Welch gave a good swing on Kid's ribs that sounded like a pistol shot. They were hard at it at the call of time." It was Welch's round.

In the fourth Welch rushed the fighting, McCoy keeping out of the way. He landed a hard left to Welch's face, but again it did not seem to slow Welch, who bore in and did more damage in the infighting than he had previously done during the fight. The pro-Welch crowd at the ringside became wildly enthusiastic by the end of the round and the uproar increased when the fifth round began with a violent exchange. "Kid's long reach was used to advantage," said the *Intelligencer*, "but his blows seemed to lack force, and did not do a great deal of damage." Significantly, however, "clinch followed clinch. Both men were winded at the close of the round. This was a hot one from start to finish and at the end McCoy had much the best of it."

When both men came on fast for the sixth round "it looked as though the fight would be a long one." This was, in itself, expected to be to Welch's advantage. He kept away from McCoy's long jabs, clinching and pounding on McCoy's ribs. Breaking away from one clinch Welch landed a hard shot on McCoy's jaw that visibly jarred him. At the break from another clinch Welch landed another punch to McCoy's face just as the round ended.

At the start of the seventh round McCoy hit Welch low. The *Intelligencer*'s reporter, who was a Welch partisan, wrote that McCoy deliberately fouled Welch. If so, the referee ignored it. Welch did not claim a foul, and Welch was not injured, for he "forced the fighting fast and furious. This was the best round of the fight."

It was now nearly four in the morning. Both men were badly winded, and at the eighth round Welch rushed the fighting to try to end it. He landed two hard blows to the body without a return blow by McCoy; an instant later, however, McCoy landed a hard punch on Welch's neck. They clinched, and "this was another round marked by almost continuous fighting. Repeated clinches and hot infighting aroused the enthusiasm of the crowd. . . ." And now, suddenly, Mc-Coy was able to hit Welch almost at will. "He played with his man," said the *Intelligencer* reporter indignantly, "though no very hard blows were struck. . . . McCoy's reach was to Welch insurmountable."

Welch again rushed to the center of the ring in the ninth and tried to trade punches in the hammer-and-tongs fashion of the earlier rounds. But McCoy "seemed to be able to hit Welch wherever he pleased." Neither fighter was marked, there had been no knockdowns, and neither had drawn blood; it was just that Welch "seemed to be somewhat dazed. He was struck repeatedly, but he did not receive near the punishment that should knock a man out. . . . The blows he received were not knockout blows." Near the end of the ninth round Welch "went down in a heap on the floor and was counted out."

The sky was growing light. The torches were extinguished; the spectators awoke belatedly to the problem of getting back to Wheeling. The *Intelligencer*'s sports reporter watched Jack Welch suspiciously. When he noted that Welch got to his feet unassisted and walked away without difficulty after being counted out, he decided the fight had been fixed. The proceedings left everyone irritated. The mystification about where the fight would be held, the mixup over crossing the river, the high cost to the Wheeling spectators, while the Moundsville people got in for nothing, the long wait for a northbound train—all left the crowd with a sense of having been defrauded. Much of the hostility was focused, irrationally, on McCoy. He was a different kind of fighter than the regulars had seen before. There was something stylish and scientific about his way of fighting that they did not like. When they went on these night adventures they expected a wild one-punch fight-ending knockout. The *Intelligencer* said McCoy's fighting seemed tame "compared with some of the other fistic encounters that have taken place recently."

Actually McCoy's victory over Welch was one of his best fights. It moved him from the status of a minor barnstorming battler into the ranks of possible contenders. "McCoy was wonderful," said James J. Corbett. Corbett was generally sparing in his praise of other fighters. "McCoy was clever to wizardry," said Alexander Johnston, the historian of boxing, "a close second to Corbett in that respect, and he had a knockout punch in either hand." Nat Fleischer, founder of *The Ring* and the authority on such matters, knew McCoy when he was fighting in the heavier divisions; he ranked McCoy as the best light heavyweight of all time. But the best appraisal was made by Damon Runyon, then a young sportswriter at the beginning of his career. He called McCoy one of the greatest fighters in ring history, exceptional particularly because of his intelligence—"One of the cleverest, craftiest men who ever put on boxing gloves."[29]

McCoy's fight with Welch was a masterly demonstration of his ring intelligence. It revealed his ability to size up a situation, accurately appraise his own ability and limitations, and revise his tactics when necessary. Everything was going against him during the fight. He was a newcomer; he was only 20 years old; he was known only for his habit of rushing a fight. The hostile crowd, the long hours of prefight confusion, his own past record of quick victories, could have been expected to make him rush into this fight as he had with others. But he did not do so; instead he relied on the cumulative effect of those long jabs that seemed light to watchers at the ringside. But they were not light. He had a knockout punch in either hand, and the steady if limited bombardment went on until, as the *Intelligencer* man said, "he seemed to be able to hit Welch whenever he pleased." A cold intelligence, a certain restraint, and a kind of snobbishness that made him indifferent to the opinions of the fight crowd characterized McCoy after the Welch fight. It was a decisive point in the transition from Norman Selby to Kid McCoy.

But these qualities left him unpopular in Wheeling. The story persisted that the Welch fight was fixed. (A comparable reaction dogged McCoy throughout his career. The fight crowd did not understand him, and one victory after another was dismissed as tainted in one way or another. But *85* fixed fights?) McCoy never fought in Wheeling again. One of the strangest results was that his fight with Welch, one of his most intelligent victories, was never credited to him. It went down in the record books as a draw, though all newspaper accounts at the time of the fight reported that he had won it by a knockout.

# 2. Solid Ivory

McCoy's image had begun to take shape as a cloudy and still insubstantial second personality akin to that of Norman Selby, yet with more sharply pronounced individual features or more heavily accented qualities. The most conspicuous of these was a reserve in Selby that hardened in McCoy into an almost challenging candor. Norman's reserve and lack of pretense were natural. He was a farm boy with elemental notions of propriety, committed by the world in which he lived to a sense of the right kind of life that included marriage, a family, a good livelihood, and a due regard for the opinions of mankind. But Kid McCoy was becoming a citizen of another world, that of illegal fights, grafting promoters, inquisitive gamblers, brutal ringsiders, quick money, and feverish alternatives between hysterical adulation and indifference. "Solid ivory," F. Scott Fitzgerald once wrote of sports figures.[1] He was discussing the work of Ring Lardner, and trying to explain Lardner's myopic view of human nature. He believed that Ring Lardner as a sportswriter had spent too much time among the thick-skulled and shallow-eyed celebrities in the sports world to retain much faith in the resources of the human spirit. "Remember it was not humble ivory," Fitzgerald wrote. "It was arrogant, imperative, often megolomanical ivory."

McCoy's reaction to the arrogant ivory of the fight crowd was a pose of unsparing self-honesty. He did not volunteer information about himself, but if he was questioned he answered with a civil flat candor that was frequently shocking in its avoidance of any claim to lofty or unselfish motives. This was particularly the case if he was asked about the women in his life, as he often was. McCoy was married 10 times, three times to the same woman.[2] He was believed, in that era, to have been married more times than anyone in America. In McCoy's later years a reporter from the Columbus *Journal* interviewed him in New York and, finding him in a reminiscent frame of mind, persuaded him to philosophize about his wives and the reasons for his many divorces. "Only one of them married Norman Selby," McCoy said. "The others all married Kid McCoy."

The one who married Selby was Lottie Piehler, a nice quiet girl who worked in a millinery shop in Middleton, Ohio.[3] The time of his meeting with her was obscured in his accounts. After his defeat of Jack Welch in Wheeling he knocked out a fighter known only as Deaf Mute in Pittsburgh in four rounds. He then went to New England for three fights in the first three months of 1894.[4] He was reported in the newspapers to be in love with some unidentified seamstress. He went into the ring "wearing black trunks supported by a green belt upon which the name of Kid McCoy had been daintily embroidered by his sweetheart." No doubt inspired by this proof of affection, he won three fights in quick succession.

The first was with Pat Hayden in Providence on January 8, 1894. McCoy tore into action with the opening energy that had become his trademark. When the bell rang for the first round, one sportswriter said, "he started to split kindling." He knocked out Hayden in the second round, but the fight was really decided in the first few moments. On February 12 he repeated the performance when he knocked out Joe Burke in Fall River, also in two rounds, the second being unnecessary. In a later period, a fighter on the ascent, carefully schooled and managed, ordinarily disposed of small-town or small-city contenders, charitably called opponents, to bolster his credentials for entering the big time. In McCoy's day it was generally the other way around. It was a period of strong local patriotism, when local fighters, like baseball teams and bicycle racers, were supported by whole towns against the favorites of other towns, and hometown fighters in particular were backed with local money and fattened on beginners from distant places. McCoy was accused of cruelty, or at least of a lack of sportsmanship, in eliminating so quickly so many fighters who might have gone on to good careers if he had not knocked them out in a round or two and thus ended their interest in prizefighting. He said he was doing them a service. "A quick knockout could be construed as merciful," he said. "I always tried for one."

The New England fight crowd had seen him in action for only a few minutes in two fights. A group of Fall River fans worked up a fight they were sure would last longer. In Woonsocket, Rhode Island there lived Jim Scully, a veteran of countless fights, experienced, battered, sagacious enough not to be clobbered in a first-round fiasco and renowned for his ability to take punishment and come back.[5] Scully was old; he had "the appearance of a typical old-time pug." He was in virtual retirement and had no enthusiasm for the fight. But he was broke; the grocery store had cut off his credit for not paying a $45 bill. The build-up for the McCoy-Scully fight began after McCoy knocked out Joe Burke, and continued for a month. McCoy was presented as a discovery of the Fall River crowd. He was suddenly transformed into Kid McCoy of Fall River, a local idol.

The fight was held in the New Bedford Athletic Club on Saturday night, St. Patrick's Day, March 17, 1894. A special train carried 150 McCoy supporters from Fall River to New Bedford. About 50 additional McCoy fans joined them at the New Bedford Athletic Club. They were still in the minority; all 500 seats in the club were taken; with standing room occupied, the crowd was predominantly for Scully. The amateur featherweight champion of the United States was reported to be present, along with unidentified sports from Boston, New York, and Newport. It was the biggest fight crowd ever assembled in New Bedford.

Scully was the favorite in the betting, with the odds 7 to 5. The preliminary fights of the evening were dull cautious encounters between local boys who had met each other before, and there was no animation in the crowd until, at ten o'clock, Scully came into the ring. He was cheered, with the cordial enthusiasm given an old war-horse. Scully wore only a white breech clout, and his tough, heavy, muscular frame looked powerful. One acute observer thought he looked overtrained. He was determined and casual, with the natural dignity of a seasoned professional, impassive and expressionless and thoroughly prepared for whatever lay ahead.

The shock came when McCoy arrived at the ring, pallid, thin, and unnaturally white, wearing his black trunks and green belt, seeming boyish and thin compared to his mature and hardened rival. Yet compared to Scully, "he was lithe and supple." The shock was not in McCoy's appearance, it was in the unexpected and hysterical reaction of his Fall River supporters. They began cheering, the cheer grew to an ovation which went on and on.

At the bell both men jumped for the center of the ring. Scully's reach was equal to McCoy's, and in the first exchange they both landed heavily. McCoy was faster, and when they backed away and sparred he jarred Scully, who closed in and punched in sharp in-fighting, the round ending in a flurry of short-arm punching with Scully on the offensive. He continued it when the second round be-gan, going after McCoy in the evident belief that if he was to win he had to win quickly. He landed a hard punch that missed McCoy's jaw and hit his neck; in an instant McCoy landed two hard jabs on Scully's jaw, and then drew blood with a punch that split Scully's upper lip. But the round was even.

When the bell rang for the third round Scully drove forward with an air of solid determination. McCoy met him with a confident smile. They collided in an exchange too fast to follow, Scully apparently getting in his share of punches in an almost continuous give-and-take in the infighting in this fast round. But at the bell Scully "showed the effects of the cyclone pace."

At the end of the round both men were winded. They came out cautiously at the start of the fourth. McCoy began jabbing, keeping at a distance and, finding Scully weakening, closed in and delivered a terrific series of punches on Scully's head and body. Scully recovered momentarily, came back weakly and, as the round ended, sank to his knees.

At the opening of the fifth round McCoy "went at his man like a tiger." Scully's nose and mouth were bleeding; he was dazed and al-most helpless, and as McCoy swarmed over him, hitting him at will, he went down in a heap. Incredibly, he got to his feet at the count of nine, and tried to retaliate. Knocked down four times, Scully was still on his feet at the end of the round. At the start of the sixth round he came back in surprisingly good shape, jumped to the center of the ring, and tried to carry the fight. McCoy knocked him down. Scully took the count and tried to keep fighting and was knocked down again. This time he got up and started for McCoy, who again knocked him down. Scully staggered up at the count of nine, and "McCoy gave him a left-handed swing which sent him down, limp and lifeless."

McCoy's backers from Fall River rushed to the ring. They wanted to carry McCoy on their shoulders in triumph. There was a struggle at the ropes as the police guard prevented them from reaching McCoy. It was perhaps just as well. There was not a mark on him; he was scarcely winded; and he evidently had no sense of satisfaction in his victory, for he never included it in his recollections of his good fights. He was becoming Kid McCoy. But he was not going to be Kid McCoy of New Bedford; his ambitions went beyond that. He never returned there, despite the fact that the McCoy-Scully fight was recorded in New Bedford's sports annals as "one of the best contests ever seen in this city."

2

When McCoy turned up in Cleveland two months after the Scully fight he was alone, and the reports of his stay there did not mention his bride, or bride-to-be.[6] An anonymous writer for *The Ring* called him a "youthful hobo who said he was a fighter. He did not look the part. He was tall and skinny. His face was pale; those who became acquainted with him were sure he was on his way to a quick death because of tuberculosis, or even a victim of anemia."

He worked out in Al Rumsey's gymnasium on Vincent Street. In spite of his appearance of ill health, or perhaps because of it, he attracted the attention of three Cleveland sportsmen, Colonel Jim Buckley, Jimmy McGlade, and Frank Penny, who were powers in Cleveland's boxing world, such as it was. McCoy's reputation for rushing a fight and winning by a quick knockout had preceded him. He had now had 19 fights, had never been defeated, or knocked down, for that matter, and had won 16 fights, 11 of them first, second, or third-round knockouts. Also, he looked good in his workouts and received the restrained praise given by the regulars at gymnasiums—"a pretty clever boy."

But his appearance was not impressive enough to warrant a match against an opponent with a standing that his record might seem to warrant. In fact it was suggested that he get out of boxing into some more healthful line of work. In later years Jimmy McGlade recalled that McCoy said, "I am going to stick to the fighting game, if for no other reason than to get even with Tommy Ryan. I can beat him, and I will beat him the first time I meet him in the ring."

McGlade arranged a fight at the Cleveland Athletic Club with Billy Steffers, a beginner McCoy regarded as far below his own stature. The fight game as such, fight-club personalities, the vast importance attached to subtle gradations in the standing of opponents, meant little to McCoy, however; fighting was a means of making money, and he was known for his willingness to fight anyone. But he told his Cleveland friends that Steffers was a set-up.

The fight took place on the night of May 10, 1894. There was only one blow struck. McCoy jumped to the center of the ring as he ordinarily did, to start the action at whirlwind speed. Steffers hit him on the point of the chin and knocked him out. It happened so suddenly that McCoy's few supporters thought at first it was a gag, and that he would get to his feet as rapidly as he had gone down. But, said *The Ring,* "he really had been kayoed." He was counted out and, recovering consciousness, left the ring and left Cleveland. *The Ring's* reporter said McCoy was so overconfident he actually stuck out his chin, daring Steffers to come at him.

If so, it was the most foolish action ever reported of McCoy in the ring, and he never did anything of the sort again. A week after the Cleveland fiasco he was in Minneapolis, where he was billed to fight 10 rounds with James Barron. He was now Kid McCoy of Indianapolis; Barron was referred to as "an Australian champion." Barron was part of the invasion of Australian fighters that began when Peter Jackson arrived in San Francisco in 1888, and which included Bob Fitzsimmons, Dan Creedon, ranked by Corbett as one of the best of all middleweights, Young Griffo, sometimes called the fastest of all fighters—"a marvel," in Corbett's words—an eccentric who never trained and who refused to sit in his corner between rounds, standing at the ropes and making speeches to the crowd; George Dawson, a close friend of Fitzsimmons, a promising middleweight who became a boxing instructor after a ring injury, Joe Goddard, who was, briefly, a contender for the heavyweight title, Steve O'Donnell, Tom Tracy, and half a dozen others. William Naughton, the San Francisco *Examiner's* sports editor, wrote that the influence of the Australians was all to the good; they were skilled boxers, and their success stopped the wild roundhouse swinging that had characterized American prizefighting.

Barron was a promising recruit to the Australian colony. He began his career in the United States with a three-round knockout of Bobby Dobbs, an indestructible Negro middleweight who was reported to have had more than a thousand fights before he retired in 1914 at the age of 56—and Dobbs was still a formidable contender when he and Barron met. Barron's span as a title contender was brief, which his fight with McCoy did not help. They met at the Twin City Athletic Club in Minneapolis on the night of May 18, 1894, with only a handful of spectators on hand. McCoy was cautious, using his longer reach effectively, Barron taking the initiative through the first four rounds without noticeable effect. "It looked like McCoy's contest," said the Minneapolis *Star,* which dismissed the fight in two brief paragraphs on a back page. "It was the general opinion of the sports crowd that Barron had been much over rated, and that he would be whipped in this country as soon as he met any good men."

In the fourth round Barron missed with a hard punch that landed on McCoy's shoulder, and broke a bone in his right hand.[7] The remaining six rounds were desultory jabbing sessions, with neither fighter showing an inclination to end it; the result was declared a draw. That McCoy had failed to knock out an opponent with a broken hand was a remarkable departure from his normal fighting pattern; nevertheless, the boxing skill he showed was more impressive than Barron's skill in concealing the extent to which he had been hurt, and insofar as there was any discussion of this fight, it was to the effect that the decision should have been given to McCoy.

In any event the fight, or perhaps the restraint he had shown, after his defeat by Billy Steffers, made it easier for him to get fights than it had been at any time in his past. Two weeks after the Barron fight he beat a local boy, Charles Maxwell, in Akron in six rounds. McCoy then returned to Cleveland.[8] The recollection of his previous performance there was still strong. He had two fights with unimportant aspirants in the summer of 1894, knocking out Harry O'Connor in three rounds on July 2, and winning from one Jack Grace in seven rounds on August 12. *The Ring* said, "The stranger won. They put him on again. Again he won. Such was the introduction of Cleveland fistic fans to Charles Kid McCoy, who soon developed into one of the country's greatest fighters. . . ." On August 29, 1894, he was again matched with Billy Steffers, who had knocked him out so ingloriously three months before. "This time McCoy did not attempt any jokes," said *The Ring.* "He went after Steffers from the start, and when the tenth round was ended McCoy was the winner by several hundred meters and Steffers was literally cut to pieces."

3

At some point in his wanderings McCoy met Fitzsimmons, the middleweight champion. Fitzsimmons liked and befriended him and taught him some measure of ring generalship to add to his natural ability.[9] Fitzsimmons arrived in San Francisco from Australia in 1890, a tall, knock-kneed, awkward-looking fighter, a former blacksmith, uneducated, with a curious mystical and religious streak in his makeup. Fitzsimmons was so simple and direct in his manner that he was ridiculed as a simpleton by the livery stable wits who hung around boxing clubs; his friendliest supporters called him a child of nature. He was so susceptible to slights and insults, real or imagined, that opponents tried to play on his nerves before a fight. Even Corbett, far more gentlemanly than most, in an attempt to unsettle Fitzsimmons, refused to shake hands with him, and admitted that he hissed in Fitzsimmons' ear whenever they met: "I never saw a Protestant I couldn't lick."

Fitzsimmons went on the stage, as did all champion fighters, but as he was unable to sing or dance, and was not ranked as star material as an actor, his act consisted of working at his forge as a blacksmith, shaping horseshoes, perhaps the least enthralling form of theatrical entertainment ever presented prior to the appearance of masters of ceremonies at television shows. But Fitzsimmons had survived worse terrors than operating a forge in vaudeville. For that matter, vaudeville acts were often so bad that an honest blacksmith working at his forge was a welcome change. A part of Fitzsimmons' vaudeville company was the song-and-dance man, Joe Howard, the composer of "Hello, My Baby" and "I Wonder Who's Kissing Her Now," whose distinction in vaudeville was the rendition of a melodious tear-jerker, "Stick to Your Mother, Tom."

On September 26, 1894 Fitzsimmons met Dan Creedon at the Olympic Athletic Club in New Orleans, and Kid McCoy was part of Fitzsimmons' entourage. New Orleans had always been hospitable to Fitzsimmons. He fought Nonpareil Jack Dempsey there in 1891 for an $11,000 purse, the largest boxing purse in history up to that time, and won the middleweight championship. The next year at the same club he met Peter Maher, the leading heavyweight contender (to whom Corbett gave the title when he retired), survived an early

knockdown by that dangerous but uneven fighter, and won by a
12th-round knockout. Fitzsimmons was still a middleweight. In 1893
Fitzsimmons knocked out Jem Hall, the English champion, at the
Crescent City Athletic Club in New Orleans, in the midst of the civic
excitement in New Orleans previously mentioned in connection with
McCoy's fight then with Frank Lamode. It was a remarkable forward
step in the progress of Kid McCoy to be associated with Fitzsimmons
at the time of the Creedon fight; the St. Louis *Post-Dispatch* remarked
that McCoy was said "to have learned many of the foxy Australian's
tricks."

However beneficial it may have been professionally, close association with Fitzsimmons was often difficult socially. He had recently
married a famous acrobat, Rose Julian, whose brother Martin became
his manager, and he had a well-nigh fanatical belief that the homely
pleasures of domestic life, large family dinners, served in precise
order on fine silver and china, followed by the singing of hymns, was
as attractive to visitors and to members of his entourage as they were
to him. Fitzsimmons was also extremely superstitious. Even more
than Sigmund Freud he believed in dreams as a clue to human dis-
orders and destiny; in fact, he said, he believed in dreams as he believed in the Gospels. But he was also a determined practical joker.
Essentially kindly, even toward his opponents in the ring, he said he
never had a fight in which he did not feel sorry for the man he defeated. He was also generous, and enjoyed giving people expensive
presents they did not want. He once gave Tom Sharkey, the candidate
of the Neanderthals for the heavyweight championship, two magnificent peacocks on the eve of an important fight, not knowing that
peacocks were an ancient Irish symbol of bad luck. (Sharkey lost and
always blamed his defeat on the peacocks.)

But Fitzsimmons was a magnificent strategist, particularly ex-
celling in bringing down opponents who outweighed him by as much
as 50 pounds. He was better in that respect than Corbett, and better
than Kid McCoy, who likewise made his reputation fighting men out
of his own weight division. It was impossible for anyone as sharp and
ambitious as Kid McCoy not to have learned from close association
with him. The fight with Creedon was a minor episode in Fitzsimmons' career. The fight was in defense of his middleweight title, but
he was already challenging Corbett for the heavyweight crown. It was
a dull contest, almost the only excitement being provided by Joe

Choynski, who accidentally shot himself in the right hand "while fooling with a 44-calibre revolver" (New Orleans *Times-Picayune*). Fitzsimmons knocked out Creedon early in the second round.

McCoy left New Orleans for Cincinnati, where he had had a 10-round drawn fight with Al Roberts on October 12, 1894, the day before his 21st birthday.[10] (Fitzsimmons went on to fight an exhibition bout with Australian-born Con Riordan in Syracuse; when Riordan died after the fight, Fitzsimmons collapsed with remorse.) McCoy's second fight with Al Roberts, on January 19, 1895, also in Cincinnati, marked the opening of what turned out to be a brilliant year. He won it easily, knocking out Roberts in the fifth round. He had now had 27 fights and, except for Billy Steffers' never-to-be-forgotten one-punch knockout, had never been beaten. The New York *World* said, "McCoy is certainly one of the most promising young men pugilism has known in a long time."

4

But what of Lottie Piehler? Unlike the woman who married Kid McCoy, the one who married Norman Selby never appeared in the news. She was never mentioned in the newspaper accounts of his fights or his travels or in the paragraphs that ran at the time in the newspapers under such headings as "Items of the Ring." McCoy's fights were now generally covered at length in the newspapers, together with discussions of his appearance, how he dressed, the hotel where he stayed, and quotations giving his opinion of the city and the sporting club involved and his estimate of the fighters in the forthcoming big heavyweight fight. But there was never a reference to his wife; Lottie kept out of the limelight so successfully they might never have been married at all.

A quiet domestic life with a girl who worked in a millinery shop did not square with the growing legend of Kid McCoy. Yet McCoy was still notably quiet and retiring in contrast to the fighters of the time. When he arrived in Memphis for his fight with Shadow Maber on March 14, 1895, he created a kind of reverse sensation: he was not flashy, loud, arrogant, boastful, or otherwise sensational. The *Commercial Appeal* said he "indulged in none of the bluffing that characterizes most of the stars of the fistic arena." He stayed at Luehrmann's

Hotel, lived quietly, and when he spoke, which was rarely, expressed himself with a rather self-conscious, schoolteacherish precision. He was a different kind of fighter than had been seen in Memphis before, and his pleasant, quiet manner and politeness won him a following that he had not received in other towns. The only flaw in his popularity was that he was not expected to win.

Inwardly, as he later admitted, McCoy was more intensely worked up than he had ever been in his life. Maber was considered one of the best fighters for his weight (140 pounds) in the country.[11] The former welterweight champion of Australia, he lost a 26-round battle in Portland, Oregon, to Mysterious Billy Smith, a fight that marked the opening phase of the establishment of the welterweight division in the United States. Maber was amiable, experienced, able to take punishment, and famous for his quick, clever recoveries when he seemed to be beaten. He was the best fighter McCoy had met.

Maber was a headliner and the favorite in the fight that was the biggest sports event in Memphis history up to that time. Although there was considerable friendly money bet on McCoy at the last moment by people he had come to know in Memphis, the general feeling was that Maber's experience would be decisive—"Class will tell," said the *Commercial Appeal*. Maber had, however, been ill; the fight was his first since his recovery from an operation several months earlier.

The arena of the Pastime Athletic Club was filled to capacity, all 500 seats sold, and standing room was at a premium. Maber and McCoy arrived during the preliminaries. To get to his dressing room McCoy had to pass by the ring. He wore dark trousers and a black turtleneck sweater. McCoy looked astonished when a cheer rose as he was recognized; a pleased smile crossed his features. He had been telling himself that he had to win. "I realized the fact that I was to meet the best man of my career," so he later admitted, "and that my future depended on the outcome."

He wanted to stay in Memphis, a wish that revealed how tired he was of being from nowhere and of how pleased he was at his friendly recognition. He told himself that if he won he would become "Kid McCoy of Memphis." McCoy thought about staying there as long as he was undefeated. He was young and more impressionable than he seemed to be. He told himself that he would win, and make himself and Memphis famous, until—if he finally lost—he would simply disappear, saying nothing to anyone. He dressed in his black trunks—the green belt embroidered with his name had been replaced with a red, white, and blue belt—and at nine o'clock vaulted over the ropes into the ring.

At the start of the first round he jumped to the center of the ring, feinted with his left, as did Maber, then led with his left for Maber's jaw. But the jab was short, and in an instant Maber landed the first blow of the fight with a left to his chin. It was a clean punch, but light, and McCoy moved in fast, countering with a right to Maber's jaw that he thought jarred him, and following it up with a hard punch to Maber's body that he knew landed solidly. Maber shot a dangerous left to his head. He ducked back and escaped its full force, and drove in, landing a left that connected with some force on Maber's jaw, and another that hit Maber on the mouth, but without drawing blood. He wanted to keep away from Maber's left, and crowded in again, again landing fast on Maber's jaw and mouth. He led with his left, and Maber ducked and clinched. When they broke he hit Maber awkwardly in the mouth again, and Maber again clinched. He was surprised at how easily he hit Maber, and suddenly remembered he was fighting the best and trickiest fighter he had ever met. McCoy grew cautious, feinting with his left as the bell rang.

He thought he had won the first round easily, and came out fast at the start of the second. He was smiling when he met Maber in the center of the ring, but the smile quickly vanished. He landed a few punches and took a few in a fast exchange that was going on when Maber slipped and fell to the canvas. McCoy was startled and stepped back, and as he did so Maber jumped to his feet in an instant and landed a hard left on his mouth. He bore in and shook off the effect of the blow during hard infighting in the middle of the ring. Maber was breathing hard and seemed dizzy, backing off as he landed a right hook to Maber's mouth. He tried to pull away when Maber clinched, and was startled but not hurt when Maber tried to knee him in the clinch. He was dimly aware of the uproar in the hall and the cries of foul when the referee pulled them apart and warned Maber. He was dumbfounded at a man of Maber's standing trying to foul him, and told himself that he was not hurt. But he became cautious and feinted with his left, suddenly taking a hard punch on the jaw that came from nowhere. He countered with a jab to Maber's mouth, and a right that landed squarely on Maber's jaw, and was puzzled and alarmed that

neither seemed to have any effect. McCoy led with his left. Maber
ducked and planted a straight left that hit him flush on the mouth as
the bell rang.

He was seeing stars and flashes of light as he got to his corner. It
was Maber's round, and he knew it. Maber knew it, the crowd knew it.
"Class will tell," a ringsider quoted in the *Commercial Appeal* said.
He paid no attention as the second the Pastime Club had assigned to
him talked about Maber's obvious foul. At the start of the third round
he rushed Maber to the ropes. He pounded on Maber's ribs and
Maber clinched. When they broke they traded punches in close infighting and he worked his right on Maber's ribs. He saw Maber break
clear and led with a hard left, but Maber ducked and he missed, and
Maber planted a hard left hand in his face. He laughed and led again,
Maber backing away. He followed, jabbing with his left. He missed a
left jab as the round ended, Maber swinging with his left as he did so,
but McCoy saw it coming and pulled his head back out of the way.

There were all those stories of the effects of Maber's illness, so
McCoy decided to work on Maber's ribs, and rushed matters during
the next two rounds, Maber keeping out of his way, almost sprinting
around the ring. He reminded himself of Maber's reputation for
cleverness and followed him cautiously, sparring for an opening in
the periods after a clinch. He was sure he had won every round after
the third, and he was sure he was going to win, uneasy only because
he could not believe Maber's retreat and the lightness of the few
punches he landed were all he could do.

At the start of the sixth round Maber crowded him in the center of
the ring in a return to the rapid exchanges that marked the start of the
fight. But Maber's punches now landed harmlessly, and he got in a
right to Maber's jaw, a left to his face, another right to the jaw, and a
left that landed on Maber's neck as Maber raced away again. He
pounded on Maber's midsection when they tangled, and landed two
hard punches to the face, without retaliation, as the round ended.
Maber looked sick.

McCoy started the seventh round with a hard left jab that caught
Maber in the face, and followed up with body-punching. He was closing in when he took a right under the jaw that startled and nearly
staggered him. He crowded Maber to cover up how hard he had been
hit, punching on Maber's ribs. Maber clinched. As they broke Maber

landed a hard right uppercut that sent his head back. The referee yelled a warning to Maber about fouling. Maber nodded.

In the eighth round he bore in on Maber at the bell, and as they met in the center of the ring Maber slipped and fell. He was up at once, but appeared to be dizzy, and when he led with his left Maber, in trying to avoid it, again slipped and fell. He landed two hard punches to Maber's face when Maber got to his feet, and crowded him to the ropes. He poked a left to Maber's jaw. Maber tried to get off the ropes and again slipped and fell.

He started to end it when Maber got to his feet for the third time. Maber had been on the canvas three times without being knocked down once. He was measuring Maber for a knockout when he thought: I don't want to take the chance. Maber could not be as badly off as he seemed to be. He told himself that here was the trickiest man in the ring he had ever seen. It was too open an invitation. And there was too good a chance of a wild punch that could change everything. He said to himself, "I have been forcing the fight. The decision can't go against me." Why win by a knockout?

At least that is what he said he thought, when a reporter finally got to him in his hotel room after the fight and asked him why he had not knocked Maber out in the eighth round when he could easily have done so. It was just caution. But his restraint in not knocking out Maber, in view of the reports of Maber's reported operation, was considered in Memphis to be a remarkable example of good sportsmanship. It was all the more remarkable because of McCoy's own reputation as a fighter who always went for an early knockout, and doubly so because Maber had twice tried to foul him. At almost any moment in the eighth, ninth, and tenth rounds McCoy could have kayoed Maber; instead he fought carefully, content to win by a decision, and with an art that was in itself a sign of respect for a wary and dangerous opponent. There was an ovation when the referee announced his decision—"not a man present did not concur"—and he was unhurt, while Maber, dazed and bleeding from repeated blows on the mouth, was lucky to be on his feet. Yet Maber had given a demonstration of resourcefulness in putting up a fight against an opponent who outclassed him, and the result was "the most satisfactory event of the kind ever undertaken in Memphis," an opinion that boiled down in the *Commercial Appeal*: "Everyone agreed that the fight was one of

the best that ever took place. That McCoy is a rising star no one
doubts. . . . While McCoy was known to be a fighter of no mean
ability, he surprised even his best friends by the phenomenal showing
he made. He is very shifty on his legs, and is a wonderfully hard hitter
with both hands. As McCoy is only twenty-one years he has a most
brilliant career in the ring before him. By his easy victory over one of
the foremost fighters in the country he, at one leap, bounded into
fame."

# 3. The Idea and the Image

McCoy confidently expected to be nationally famous after his fight with Shadow Maber, and was surprised and disappointed that promoters did not rush to sign him up for future bouts. Offers to fight went out from Memphis, which was now billed as his home town, under dignified letterheads identifying him as the middleweight champion of the Middle West. But the best he could do was a fight with Jack Wilkes at the Suffolk Athletic Club in Boston on April 19, 1895, a month after his victory over Maber.[1] Wilkes's only claim to fame was that he had twice fought Tommy Ryan, who was now the welterweight champion, losing the first fight in 1892 and getting by with a draw in the second in 1894.

McCoy originally was slated to meet Tom Tracy, a good Australian middleweight and a partner of Dan Creedon, who a week before McCoy's fight with Maber had fought a six-round draw with Ryan in Chicago. But Tracy broke off the negotiations because of illness, and Wilkes was substituted. Before the fight there were rumors that McCoy was also ill. One published report said McCoy, "tall, slender and pale faced, looked to be a fit subject for a hospital." A persistent story was that McCoy fostered the story of his ill health himself, with the intention of making Wilkes overconfident. He reportedly coughed hollowly and gave indications of being at the point of collapse, so much so that Wilkes was afraid to hit him. "One good punch will kill him," Wilkes said, "and I don't want to be arrested for murder."

The first round, accordingly, was very tame, with Wilkes trying to avoid striking his "lethal" blow and McCoy wobbling about the ring like a man barely able to stand. At the start of round two McCoy jumped to his feet in an amazingly instantaneous recovery of good health and knocked out his prudent opponent, hitting him so hard that Wilkes was unconscious for 10 minutes. Such was the story.

Contemporary accounts of the fight did not quite bear out the legend, although, in view of the importance McCoy attached to Maber's reported illness, there may have been something to it. Wilkes was a St. Louis fighter, and the St. Louis *Post-Dispatch* (which before the fight ranked him as very near the top rank of contenders) reported nothing of the sort, saying that Wilkes was clearly outclassed from the start. "It took about seven minutes of actual fighting to finish Wilkes, and the ringing of the gong at the end of the second round saved Wilkes from certain slaughter. When time was called for the third round McCoy went at his opponent and soon had him at his mercy. Referee Watkins then stopped the fight." McCoy was unmarked and had scarcely been hit; Wilkes's face "resembled a raw beefsteak." Wilkes quit the ring after this fight.[2]

McCoy remained in Boston where he fought Dick O'Brien the following month.[3] O'Brien's credentials were as good as those of McCoy. He had a 10-round draw with Mysterious Billy Smith to his credit, and in 1894 had put up a 12-round battle with Joe Walcott before Walcott knocked him out. Both McCoy and O'Brien were cautious, and the fight went through 25 tame rounds before ending in a draw.

The rewards of fame were not as great nor so satisfying as McCoy had expected them to be. Going back to the Middle West, he happened to have $300 left from his last fight when he met Lottie Piehler in Middleton, Ohio. "I met her on Thursday, and we were married the next Wednesday," he said.[4] "We took the $300 and went shopping in Cincinnati and stayed there until we were broke."

McCoy decided to go to Louisville and get a job—"to go back to work," as he put it. On the train he and Lottie traveled in the same car with a theatrical troupe, a road company on its way to put on an old melodrama, *The Pacific Mail,* in Louisville. Two roughnecks began annoying the actors, and McCoy stepped in and stopped them. Perhaps in gratitude, or perhaps because they appreciated the advantages of having a prizefighter in their company, the actors suggested that McCoy appear with them in their performances, in an additional act in which he would fight any challenger on the stage.

This form of theatrical entertainment had become fairly popular; Corbett, after appearing in *After Dark,* put in three weeks at the Central and Lyceum Theatres in Philadelphia in a vaudeville act in which he fought anyone from the audience who challenged him. A good deal of stagecraft was required in selecting likely looking challengers who were certain to lose and in avoiding ambitious and unknown aspirants who might really be able to fight. Corbett and his manager spent much of their time between shows privately interviewing the contestants for future appearances, and in trying to avoid a powerful and excited amateur named McGuiness who loudly proclaimed his willingness to get into the ring night after night and who was always bypassed in favor of less formidable-looking opponents who understood that they were not supposed to win. When McGuiness could no longer be avoided and actually got on the stage, Corbett was alarmed at his colossal size and obvious strength, but was reassured when McGuiness missed with a roundhouse swing and, plunging from the ring, knocked down the scenery.

Nothing like this was reported of McCoy's theatrical ventures in Louisville. He appeared each night during the three-week run of *The Pacific Mail*. His record for the time lists, rather mysteriously, two victories over Charles Siefert, and two over Joe Sheers, each won in three rounds, followed by a six-round knockout of one Dick Moore. For his theatrical labors McCoy received a total of $750. He and Lottie saved their money, planning to go east to line up fights with more prominent ring figures than those found in the audiences at performances of *The Pacific Mail*.

Trouble began at once between Norman Selby and Kid McCoy. There was no problem with Kid McCoy; all *he* had to do was win enough fights. He was the hobo brawler, sickly appearing but tough, pleasantly surprising people with his good manners when they came to know him. It was true that no one knew where he came from, but that was part of the legend. He was now 21 years old and no more robust that he had been when he began to fight. He did not smoke or drink and was a firm believer in fresh air, simple food, and plenty of exercise.

It was hard to reconcile the life of this self-contained, aggressive, and tireless fighter with young-husband Norman Selby settling down to a quiet domestic life. (In such cases it appears to be an inflexible law of public relations that the private life has to adjust itself to what will help or hurt the public image. "Every image corresponds to an idea," said the novelist Honoré de Balzac in an essay on Stendahl, "or more exactly, to a sentiment which is a composite of ideas. The image is essentially popular, is easily understood. . . . It will not live in the human memory unless it conforms to principles and the laws of form . . . comparable to what we call design and color in painting."[5]) The myth of Kid McCoy ran up against the emotional reality of Norman Selby's life with Lottie, and the two sides of his character never really came together after that. He treated her badly, with a callousness he admitted—another violent departure from his own standards, for he held to a courtly code of conduct toward his wives and ex-wives even during the trials of his many divorces and the financial problems they involved.[6] It was not that marriage in itself ran counter to a fighter's image; marriages and love affairs were an essential ingredient, provided they were with glamorous or well-known women. Every fight McCoy won widened the gap between his image and the home life Lottie provided.

McCoy began his eastern trip with a 13th-round knockout of Abe Ullman in Baltimore.[7] A few months earlier it would have been a major event in his life, for Ullman was a middleweight of some standing. But now McCoy had beaten Maber and was impatiently working for a chance at the title. On October 13, 1895, he fought a three-round exhibition in Jersey City with one Arthur Walker—another theatrical appearance.[8] His dissatisfaction with this uncertain way of earning a living increased.

Then unexpectedly he got an offer to fight in England. His opponent was to be Ted White, the former amateur welterweight champion of England, who had recently turned professional. There was a condition (or understanding) attached to the offer. White's backers in England were unfavorably impressed by McCoy's record of one-round knockouts. They did not want to pay the expenses of his trip to London only to have him knock out their man with the first punch. McCoy, in turn, was finding his "killer" reputation a handicap in lining up fights. He wanted a fight with Tommy Ryan for the welterweight championship; a victory over an English champion in that division would be an added credential in his challenge to Ryan. He agreed to a 10-round fight. His "understanding"—or so he later said, after he left the ring—was merely that the fight would go 10 rounds; there was no implication that he agreed to lose. He was confident that he could beat White without knocking him out, as he had beaten Shadow Maber. For White, who subsequently became one of the half-dozen top-ranking English welterweights of all time, his fight with McCoy was an important event in his early career. The details were agreed to and the fight was set for London on November 23, 1895.

McCoy sailed from New York on the first of many trips abroad. One contemporary reported that McCoy made 66 trips abroad between 1895 and 1912, an almost unbelievable figure, since it would mean nearly three of the 15 years were spent on the water. McCoy himself put the figure at 22, but there may have been reasons for not wanting to enumerate all of the trips. More likely, the figure of trips meant 66 transatlantic crossings, going and coming, a total of 33 trips abroad.[9]

McCoy left Lottie at home when he sailed to meet White. (Lottie didn't accompany him on any transatlantic trip.) The trip was brief. McCoy carried the fight to White, won every round easily, at least in his own opinion, and was dumbfounded when after the 10th round the decision was awarded to White.[10] A British boxing historian, R. A. Haldane, wrote: "White had one unusual distinction; he defeated Kid McCoy. . . . He was no doubt lucky in striking him off color, but the feat was none the less remarkable."

It was McCoy's second defeat in 38 fights and a shattering blow to his plans to build up to a challenge to Tommy Ryan. Back in New York he got some encouragement in the form of a fight with Tommy West, who had a drawn fight with Ryan to his credit. McCoy met West at the Manhattan Athletic Club on January 31, 1896, in a fight that might have added to his standing had it not been obscured by ridiculous events in the preliminaries that received so much attention that the feature bout was dismissed in a paragraph.[11] In the semifinal a huge fighter named Frawley lost the decision and, after expostulating with the referee and calling on Heaven to witness that he had really won the fight, broke down and sobbed. His grief so impressed his handlers that the ring was presently filled with weeping men, in a scene that resembled an act in grand opera; the emotions involved, together with the embarrassment of the referee, left the reporters thoughtful. "The Pugilist Sobbed," ran the headline in the New York *World,* which devoted a column to Frawley's tears and a paragraph to McCoy's victory over West. After the crying scene, "the so-called star bout was short and sweet. In the first round Kid McCoy appeared to be nonplussed at West's savage and uncouth style of fighting, and contented himself with light jabbing and keeping out of danger. In the

second round, seeing that West knew absolutely nothing about fighting, McCoy cut loose and soon had West bleeding and groggy. Six
times McCoy sent his man down with straight arm smacks, West getting up within the 10-second limit. He was willing to continue after
the last knockdown, but Charlie White threw up the sponge."


## 2


When McCoy had money he lived at such midtown hotels on
Broadway as the Ansonia, the Dunlop, or later on, at the Cumberland, his favorite; he eventually moved into a comfortable apartment.
But the official residence of Kid McCoy was still Memphis, though he
never lived there, and he was often referred to as the Tennesseean. His
note paper carried his address as Memphis and his title as the middleweight champion of the Middle West.

A note bearing this letterhead went to Tommy Ryan, who read it
with amusement. Ryan remembered McCoy as the sparring partner
he had tried to befriend by giving him boxing lessons. McCoy offered
to put up a forfeit of $1,000 for a 15-round fight. Ryan did not believe
McCoy had backers who would put up the money and, remembering
McCoy as the youngster who could not take punishment as a sparring
partner, dismissed the offer as a joke.

According to *The Ring* McCoy met Ryan personally to repeat the
offer, while concealing the hostility he felt. He reportedly gave Ryan
the impression that the fight would be no more than a boxing exhibition—a report that rang true, incidentally, coming so soon after Mc-
Coy's experience in England—from which they would both profit.
McCoy was quoted as having said: "You have forgotten more about
boxing than I ever knew, but there is a chance for us to go and get the
money."

Ryan was surprised when the Empire Athletic Club of Maspeth,
Long Island, was willing to put up the purse. But he had made a remarkably good business of being the welterweight champion in the
two years he held the title. Since Fitzsimmons had outgrown the middle weight of 152 pounds which he himself had set, Ryan also claimed
the middleweight championship. At that time he was undefeated in 44
fights, in a career that had started in 1887 when he was 17 years old.
The marathon ring battles that characterized his early years—one of

33 rounds, another of 46, and one of 57 rounds, climaxing in his 76-round knockout of Needham—ended after he won the title. His nine fights as the welterweight champion were all short, except for an 18-round victory in a return match with Mysterious Billy Smith.

Ryan was a consummate boxer in addition to being a civic hero in Syracuse, New York. He scarcely trained for his fight with McCoy. The betting on the fight was heavy, and according to the *World,* "there was plenty of money on both sides," a lot of it at 2 to 1 in favor of Ryan, with many bets of $200 to $100. At the ringside the odds dropped to $100 to $75. On the night of the fight—March 2, 1896—a near blizzard swept New York, without discouraging a capacity crowd that struggled through the storm to Maspeth. One reason was that James Kennedy, the promoter, while a small operator compared to the major sports figures in New York, had made a reputation from staging honest and well-managed fights, generally between first-rate boxers whose skill appealed to discriminating fight fans. Another reason was that a special train brought a crowd from Syracuse to back Ryan. But a deeper reason was that McCoy's reputation was growing. He was becoming recognized as a polished boxer, perhaps Ryan's equal in that respect, who also had a fast aggressive style, in addition to a drive to make a quick end to things, which Ryan lacked.

Ryan climbed into the ring at 9:55 p.m., his second the light-weight champion Kid Lavigne.[12] McCoy came in a few minutes later. His second was a surprise: he was Steve O'Donnell, Corbett's old sparring partner, who claimed the middleweight title that Ryan also claimed. The accounts of the fight are contradictory. Alexander Johnston called it "a magnificent example of the double-cross"—that is, McCoy's deception lulled Ryan into not taking him seriously. Instead, he now found McCoy a good, mature fighter, and while Ryan's beautiful boxing helped, "he began to wilt under the pace. McCoy was trained to the minute, and never showed the slightest sign of tiring." Recollections of the fight published later had it that "not until the second round was well on did Ryan actually realize what he was up against. He then saw he had been tricked, and did the best he could to win, but it was no use."

Contemporary reports were less charitable to Ryan, or, for that matter, to McCoy. When the first round opened Ryan tapped a left to McCoy's face and followed that with an exhibition of sparring that went nearly half the round and ended when McCoy landed a hard left to the face, and after a brief flurry, landed again. Ryan rushed McCoy, crowding him to the ropes, but got a hard right to the face and resumed his long-range defense until the round ended. The second round was largely spent "in a lot of fiddling," until McCoy closed in, landing a heavy body punch, followed by a right and left to Ryan's face and neck. Ryan backed away, and "McCoy was chasing him around the ring when the gong stopped the race."

In the third, Ryan started fast, crowding McCoy to the ropes and landing a left and a right on McCoy's face. But he took a hard left to the jaw in doing so, and thereafter kept out of the way. The *World's* reporter said that at one point it was a genuine race, with McCoy literally chasing Ryan and hitting him on the back of his head.

Ryan was too expert a fighter to suffer that indignity, and the fourth round and most of the fifth passed in very fast infighting as they traded punches in the middle of the ring. After a melee toward the end of the fifth Ryan swung a terrific right to McCoy's head; McCoy ducked, and it missed, and at the same moment he landed a right on Ryan's jaw. As Ryan retreated, McCoy crowded after him, connecting with a right and a left as Ryan went to the canvas. But Ryan was up in an instant and they were trading punches to the bell.

The fight had been all McCoy's, and at the start of the sixth the crowd was wild. In backing away Ryan fell, McCoy falling on top of him. They got to their feet exchanging punches, an exchange that ended when McCoy landed three hard punches in succession on Ryan's face. Ryan rushed in, but met a hard left jab that stopped him, backed off, and rushed again, taking a straight left to the mouth as the bell sounded.

In the seventh the action slowed down, McCoy jabbing his left to Ryan's face, until, in a sudden return of strength Ryan landed a hard left to the body and a right to the face, almost the first such punches he had landed in the fight. McCoy slipped to one knee, taking the count of nine before he got up and clinched. At the start of the eighth Ryan came out fast and they traded punches in two fast exchanges. In the second of these Ryan landed a hard left to McCoy's jaw, but took a left to the chin and as he backed away McCoy landed another left to the jaw and Ryan sank to the canvas. He got to his knees as the count began and the gong sounded to end the round.

In *Ten—And Out!* Alexander Johnston called McCoy "clever and somewhat cruel." It appeared that he could have knocked out Ryan at any time during the ninth, tenth, eleventh, and twelfth rounds. During the ninth McCoy "fought Ryan all over the ring." He sent Ryan to the canvas again with a left to the head and, when Ryan regained his feet, landed rights and lefts almost at will on Ryan's face and body. Ryan was bleeding at the mouth and ear at the end of the round. In the tenth McCoy limited himself to long jabs at Ryan's face. "It looked as if McCoy could put Ryan out with right and left hard head smacks," said the *World*'s reporter, "but at the end of the round Ryan was still on his feet." McCoy was repaying Ryan for that beating he had taken in private two years before.

By the 11th round Ryan's face was puffed up and he was bleeding profusely from the mouth; McCoy was unmarked. There was no hard fighting in this round, McCoy jabbing lightly, and Ryan landing only one punch that missed McCoy's jaw and landed on his neck. Near the end of the 12th round, McCoy moved in with a right and a left to the head, a left to the chin and another right to the head, in a very fast succession that ended with right and left to Ryan's face. Ryan hit the canvas, but was up at the count of nine, out on his feet. He threw his arms around McCoy's waist, holding on until the bell.

In the 13th and 14th rounds the action was light, McCoy punishing Ryan with left jabs to the face as Ryan covered up and backed away. At the start of the last round McCoy landed three hard body blows in succession, and then swung a right to the head and a left to the jaw and knocked Ryan out. Ryan had to be carried to his corner. "McCoy Was A Surprise," said the headline in the *World*. "The Tennessean was a revelation with the swift pace he set."

3

The speed with which McCoy made money as the welterweight champion of the world—a division not even in existence five years before—also astonished his contemporaries.[13] Both Norman Selby and Kid McCoy liked to have money, but Selby liked to earn it and save it, and McCoy liked to make it fast and either spend it or carry it around. One of the first noticeable idiosyncracies of McCoy, as the fictional character began to take over from Norman Selby, was that he kept his money in cash—coins, bills, and gold. After one successful series of fights he added up the money he carried on his person and found it totaled $40,000.

"He has become," said *Broadway Magazine,* "a notable figure on the street." A reporter from the Buffalo *Enquirer* described him as quiet and retiring, with large gray eyes, even white teeth, and gentle speech. "His movements are quiet and cat-like," said the New York *World*. "He does not look the prizefighter, nor is he built like one."[14] The transformation of Norman Selby into Charles Kid McCoy was not quite a Jekyll-and-Hyde affair, accomplished in an instant with a potion of publicity; it went on slowly over a period of about three years.

The first requirement of Kid McCoy was to get rid of Mrs. Norman Selby, which was accomplished coldly and efficiently.[15] A short time after his defeat of Tommy Ryan he persuaded Lottie "to go west and get a divorce." Those were his words, as he told something of his life story to Edward Smith of the Columbus *Journal* several years later. He was surprised that she made so little trouble about it; none of the marriages of Kid McCoy were dissolved so quietly, and it was possible that she was as glad to get away as he was to see her go, or that relief, or perhaps contempt, had a part in her swift departure. In any case she vanished, never reappeared in his life, and, wherever she lived in the West, no trace of her turned up.

One reason why her departure was necessary, apart from her inherent inability to be the suitable wife of a fictional being, was Julia Woodruff.[16] Julia was a handsome young actress, an intellectual, a blue-stocking, who was beginning to make a name for herself as a supporting star in light comedy roles. She had been briefly married to a Mr. Crosselmire before she went on the stage. She was attractive rather than beautiful, with thin features, an aristocratic nose, and an air of elegance unexpectedly combined with a rough-and-tumble candor—the sort of actress often cast as a scheming society heiress who tries to lure the hero away from his poor but devoted sweetheart.

Julia appeared with Marie Dressler in several shows. Miss Dressler, later known to moviegoers as Tugboat Annie, was then at the start of her career, a marvelously gifted comedienne whose forte was a salty and earthly feminine humor and common sense directed impartially at the pretenses and hypocrisies of both the masculine and feminine worlds. Julia absorbed some of Marie Dressler's manner, but in an intellectual rather than natural fashion: she liked to shock people. After she left the stage Julia became a writer and a lecturer—"She always did like to lecture," McCoy recollected grimly—skirting the edges of subjects considered daring with an arch and high-toned manner, suggesting that she knew much more than she was saying, that persisted even in her later years when she married to a New York gambler and underworld figure.

Lottie disappeared from McCoy's life sometime before 1897, and he married Julia, who thereafter was listed on theatre programs as Julia McCoy, which remained her professional name. After a few months of marriage she divorced him, charging desertion, only to re-marry him a few weeks after the decree became final. She was then appearing with Marie Dressler in a comedy of newspaper life called *Miss Print*. The news that McCoy was remarrying the actress (called his first wife at the time, so completely had Lottie faded from the pic-ture) was a major topic for New York gossip columnists.

Some of the newspaper items were sentimental, having to do with the remarriage being on again, off again, after attempted reconcilia-tions and heart-to-heart talks, but at least one account went into de-tail which by any rigorous examination appeared to be libelous. This report stated that in the divorce settlement McCoy found that he had to pay more alimony than he had anticipated, and asked Julia to re-marry him in order to save money. She refused, but after thinking it over, agreed to remarry McCoy for a cash payment of $10,000. He was offended, and broke off the "courtship." But after more alimony payments he, too, "thought it over" and began courting Julia again, this time bearing a certified check for $10,000. The reason there was no libel suit over the scandalous story was that it may have been par-tially true. "The first time I let her divorce me she got $500 a month alimony," McCoy told the inquisitive Edward Smith of the Columbus *Journal,* "so I remarried her." But by the time McCoy spoke so frankly to Smith many other things had happened between him and Julia; other marriages had come and gone, and he was undoubtedly deliberately trying to counteract the newspaper stories which implied that as far as women were concerned, the real McCoy was a sentimen-tal boob.

When Julia divorced him he was still, at least part of the time, Norman Selby, an Indiana farm boy who could neither fit into the Broadway world or leave it alone. Marie Dressler remembered him in those days as a good-looking stagestruck youngster. He sometimes had ambitions to go on the stage himself. He had liked the company of actors since his days with the *Pacific Mail* troupe; his life apart from the ring was spent in the theatrical area that ran north on Broadway from 34th Street to Times Square. When he had a connection of sorts with the theatre through his marriage to Julia he did not want to lose it, especially after a marriage that ended—twice—about as soon as it began. It was characteristic of Norman Selby to try to make a marriage last and characteristic of Kid McCoy to picture himself acting from motives of hard self-interest in matters commonly associated with love.

Kid McCoy's struggle to find domestic happiness with Julia was a subject of much Broadway small talk, and interest was increased when shortly after their second marriage Julia divorced him again, only to marry him for the third time soon after doing so. McCoy tried to keep the third marriage a secret; there were no leaks of preliminary financial negotiations or scenes of romance and reconciliation this time. But alert reporters spotted the couple exchanging vows at the office of a justice of the peace in Union Hills, New Jersey, and entertained their readers with accounts of catching McCoy trying to marry secretly a wife he had married twice before.

The ups and downs of his home life occupied McCoy, apart from his career which went on in a surprisingly successful manner. During the years in which he divorced Lottie and repeatedly married Julia (and was repeatedly divorced by her), he had 26 fights, winning them all (except for a draw in his second fight with Tommy Ryan) in an amazing display of nerve for his opponents included such dangerous men as Gus Ruhlin and Peter Maher. On April 22, 1896, six weeks after he won the title from Ryan, he returned to his synthetic home town of Memphis to meet Frank Bosworth in what was scheduled to be a 10-round fight.[17] He was greeted with enthusiasm (*McCoy is a great fighter. He is gentlemanly and clever and a popular favorite . . .*) and the Grand Opera House was packed to capacity. But the fight was a fiasco; Bosworth, aging and out of condition, was battered in the first round and knocked out in the second. (*Those who know McCoy do not believe he knew what an easy time he would have. . . . The audience greeted the end with jeers, hisses and some applause. The McCoy-Bosworth fight will result in the destruction of local interest in future events. . . .*)

A month later (March 21, 1896) McCoy met Joe Choynski in New York.[18] The fight was in the old Broadway Athletic Club building, with 5,000 spectators ($7 each the top price) reaching the arena up a flight of narrow stairs and packing the hall nearly to the point of suffocation. Betting was heavy on McCoy, largely because Choynski, sometimes called the best in the world by eminent boxing historians, had been consistently unlucky in every big fight. His fight with Corbett had been stopped by the police, as was his fight with Fitzsimmons.

His fight with McCoy should have been. It was scheduled for 25 rounds, with the odds that McCoy would knock out Choynski within 10 rounds. In the first round McCoy landed a left to the jaw and forced Choynski into a corner where he slipped to the canvas. He was up in an instant, hitting McCoy with a left to the jaw. They traded punches throughout the round, which at least ran its proper length. This could not be said of the other rounds. In the second round McCoy was knocked down four times. The first time he fell at the ropes in a sitting position, his features relaxed in the silly, lost, hopeless expression of a man almost unconscious. His brother Homer got near him and yelled to him. McCoy struggled to his knees, and stood at the count of nine. Choynski, overanxious, was wild, missing a knockout punch that hit McCoy's shoulder blade and knocked him down in the middle of the ring. He got to his feet, staggering, but still trying to punch, and took a right to the mouth that felled him as if he had been shot. The bridge of his nose was gashed and his mouth was swollen and bleeding.

The referee counted nine seconds. Before he could count 10 the timekeeper, Joe Dunn, rang the gong, later explaining that he had been counting with the referee and rang the gong at 10. But there was still a lot of time—perhaps 40 seconds—left in the round, and in any event the timekeeper had no business counting anyone out. McCoy's seconds dragged him to his corner. Choynski, puzzled, went to his corner, spoke to his seconds, and then went to the referee and demanded an explanation. He listened, scowling, but the explanation seemed unnecessary. He could easily knock McCoy out in the next round, so he returned to his corner.

The minute and 40 second rest between rounds restored McCoy. When Choynski rushed him to end it McCoy hit Choynski in the mouth and knocked him down. Choynski was up at once, and met a left hook. McCoy, appeared to be dazed, was swinging like a crazy man. But Choynski was equally·erratic. In this melee of two madmen, said the New York *Herald,* McCoy had the better of it. Choynski slipped and fell. After a clinch he swung a left to McCoy's jaw, and McCoy went down, taking the count to seven. When he got up Choynski rushed him but fell down. Again he was up at once, but McCoy landed a right to his jaw. Choynski now as completely covered with blood as McCoy, stood motionless, shaking from head to foot. McCoy rushed him blindly and he went down with a left to the jaw, but was up immediately, landing a right to the jaw that sent McCoy down for the count of six. Out on his feet, McCoy blocked Choynski and caught him with a left to the jaw. This time Choynski went down for the seven count. When he got to his feet McCoy got him with a left and right to the jaw that spun him around. He fell over backwards, taking McCoy with him. They both sat on the canvas. They both rose very slowly. They both swung heavily. The gong sounded. After it sounded—or at the same moment, according to McCoy's supporters—McCoy slammed a hard right to Choynski's jaw as he turned to go to his corner. Choynski fell as if he had been clubbed.

In the top row of the gallery a prosperous dealer in dental supplies named Byron Sabin dropped dead. He was yelling "Foul!", as were most of the 5,000 present. His death went unnoticed in the excitement. Down in the ring Choynski's seconds dragged him to his corner and worked over him, apparently with some success until, an instant before the fourth round began, he pitched forward off his stool and lay motionless on the floor. Meanwhile McCoy had stumbled to the center of the ring in bewilderment, puzzled at not finding anyone to fight. When he finally located Choynski lying at his feet he helped lift him to his corner. The referee gave the fight to McCoy amid a shower of seat cushions and cries of Fraud! Thieves! Fake! Robbery!

The second round had been too short, the third one at least a little too long. George Siler, formerly the leading referee of New York, who had moved to Chicago, said for publication: "The Broadway Athletic Club is crooked." The *Herald* demanded that boxing be outlawed. The *World,* consistently friendly to McCoy, evaded the question the fight had raised and wrote its story around the man in the gallery who died from excitement. McCoy said, "I am sorry there was a misunderstanding about the time. I was not out, but I was pretty weak. If a mistake was made it was not mine. The punch I knocked Choynski out with was started before the bell rang. I fought fairly. I thought I could whip Choynski. I did, and I think I can whip him again."

There were no such questions raised about McCoy's next 25 fights. On May 7, 1896 he knocked out Jim Daly, a heavyweight, in three rounds. Three weeks later he fought Billy Smith (not to be confused with Mysterious Billy Smith), a rough-and-tumble Boston brawler, the pet of Boston fight fans, and won by a foul in the sixth round, after repeated fouls: Smith knew he was being beaten and tried increasingly flagrant fouls to end it. (*It is high time fighters like Billy Smith were forced out of the boxing business and made to go to work,"* said the *World.*) In Brooklyn two weeks later, McCoy won a 10-round decision over Dick Moore, a fighter he had previously beaten in Louisville. And at the end of 1896 he sailed on his second trip abroad to fight Billy Doherty, the middleweight champion of South Africa, in Johannesburg.[19]

Along with his fondness for carrying large sums of money with him, Kid McCoy was fascinated by gems as another tangible form of wealth, and the diamond boom in South Africa was on. He traveled incognito and did not use the name of Kid McCoy, or otherwise identify himself, until the fight. The legend of Kid McCoy was that he cleaned up in a number of fights against locals who did not know who he was, one ring historian saying that McCoy's South African trip, during which "he had many a battle as an unknown, was filled with romance." No details of the romantic episodes were supplied, but one part of the growing legend of Kid McCoy was that he fought a huge Zulu who never wore shoes and who was so tall McCoy's punches could not reach his chin. The legend had it that he won by scattering carpet tacks over the ring. McCoy denied the legend, saying, "How could I throw carpet tacks while I was wearing boxing gloves?"

Doherty was a stately old-fashioned English fighter, with a huge handlebar moustache and the classic fighting stance that was no longer seen anywhere except in old English sporting prints. McCoy made a good show of the fight, knocked him out in the ninth round, received an ovation, and was hailed in South Africa as the middleweight champion of the world. Ryan claimed the middleweight title, but since McCoy had beaten Ryan (and since he had put on weight, and no longer fought as a welterweight), there was some logic in the claim. Doherty, who later settled in Australia where he lived to great old age, was always filled with wonder about his fight with McCoy, not because he lost, but because McCoy carried so much money with him.

McCoy did not fight again until the end of May 1897, when he met Dick O'Brien in New York.[20] The year since May 1896, during which his only fight was with Doherty, was the longest period of inactivity he had since he entered the ring. This was the year in which he got rid of Lottie and started on the merry-go-round of marriage and divorce with Julia. But another demand on his time was his first business venture. The Casino Theatre at 40th Street and Broadway had been closed for some time.[21] When it reopened there was space available for a bar in the theatre building. With some financial backing (reportedly that of the promoter James Kennedy) McCoy emerged as a saloon-keeper and restaurant operator.

The Casino was a classy showhouse devoted in an earlier period to Gilbert and Sullivan, German light opera, and heavy European dramatic imports. It was the most elegant theatre in the city, an elaborate Moorish structure with 1,300 seats. It was revived as a home for brilliantly staged musical comedies. McCoy's place was an innovation. Jim Corbett's saloon on 34th Street and Broadway (later the site of Saks) was a meeting place for horseplayers, gamblers, bookmakers, promoters, and sporting types who generally avoided the limelight.[22] Corbett's partners were George and John Considine, owners of the Hotel Metropole. Tom Sharkey's saloon on 14th Street, within easy staggering distance across Union Square from Tammany Hall, was a dark, sawdust-floor establishment favored by politicians, early filmmakers, and underworld figures.[23] When the killers of the gambler Herman Rosenthal set out on their deadly errand they first fortified themselves with $35 worth of Sharkey's food and liquor. Sharkey's saloon had a ragtime piano player and, on the walls, paintings of the trotting horses in which the fighter invested his winnings; it also had a steady patronage of surly Sharkey partisans who believed that the owner had really defeated Jim Jeffries the heavyweight champion, deserved the world title, and was the champion of everything. And they were always willing to take on anybody who denied it. The bar of the Hotel Metropole at Broadway and 43rd Street was another meeting place for sports followers. Race results telegraphed from all over the country were posted in front of the hotel, and all night bettors and bookmakers appeared at the long bar and checked their winnings and losses. Another saloon that catered to a segment of the sports crowd was the Delavan Hotel bar operated by Sharkey's manager, Tom O'Rourke; O'Rourke's partner there was the gambler Jack Rose, who was also a part-time fight promoter and who acted as Lieutenant Charles Becker's go-between in arranging the murder of Herman Rosenthal.

But all of these establishments were for men only, and McCoy's restaurant and bar was intended to appeal also to women, along with theatrical figures and sports celebrities. Instead of the smoky and shadowy atmosphere favored by people who wanted to keep out of public attention, McCoy's place had huge plate glass windows through which passersby could see the famous people inside. Above all, the Casino Theatre was famous for *Floradora,* which went through 505 performances around the turn of the century and invested the theatre—and McCoy's bar and restaurant—with some of its legendary glamor.

Julia McCoy was a close friend of Jessie Taylor, who had married Corbett in 1895, a month after his divorce from his first wife.[24] In spite of their competitive positions in business and in the ring Corbett and McCoy were, in a sense, linked in the public mind; both represented a more civilized or intellectual side of prizefighting, with pretensions (and with some valid claim) to artistic skill and science, as opposed to brawlers and roughnecks. Both Corbett's and McCoy's establishments prospered. Except when he was preparing or traveling for a fight, McCoy was unobtrusively at the Casino Theatre bar. *Broadway Magazine* reported that the restaurant was crowded every day. Rather than taking an active part in the operation of the bar, McCoy was simply on hand. He talked with old friends such as De-Wolf Hopper and provided companionship for Lillian Russell. He still did not drink, ate sparingly, and continued to assert, whenever he tactfully could, the virtues of a good night's sleep and plenty of exercise. At one time he even persuaded *Variety* to publish a column, *How to Take Care of Yourself,* to the bewilderment of *Variety*'s readers searching for items of gossip and encountering instead McCoy's earnest advocacy of fresh air. "McCoy is a gentleman," said *Broadway Magazine,* "who attends his own business in a serene and unselfconscious fashion. His manners might well be copied by other prominent men of the ring."

4

One result of the legend of Kid McCoy was an amazing proliferation of fighters calling themselves Kid. Soon there were Kid Ferns, Kid Graves, Kid Doll, Kid William, Kid Hubert, Kid Carter, Kid Cutler, Kid LeRoy, Kid McPartland, Kid Aspinall, Kid Abbot, Kid Victor, Kid Morse, Kid Little, Kid Casper, Kid Kelly, Kid Broad, Kid Stein, Kid Harris, Kid Bennett, Kid Sullivan, Kid Abel, Kid Leavitt, Kid Dodson, Kid Bush, Kid Delaney, Kid Parker, Kid Purdy, Kid McFadden, Kid Ryan, Kid Hogan, and Kid Jones.[25] In addition there were a number of fighters who called themselves Kid McCoy. The legend of Kid McCoy was that he would fight anyone, anywhere. It was a factor in his popularity at a time when Fitzsimmons and Corbett, or even lesser stars like Tommy Ryan, debated, made conditions, issued statements, and broke off negotiations repeatedly before getting into the ring. They were called orators, and McCoy was praised because he was not an orator. In one sense, however, McCoy's willingness to meet unknowns in out-of-the-way places created difficulties when he read in the papers that someone calling himself Kid McCoy had fought someone he never heard of in some place he had never been. He subscribed to a newspaper clipping service and studiously followed every item about Kid McCoy that he could find, carefully preserving the clippings.[26] The practice became a habit with him; he had packages of clippings, not only about himself and his fights, but about his wives, divorces, business—everything. There was still a remnant of Norman Selby in Kid McCoy, and Norman, the country boy, followed with intense interest the doings of that remarkable composite figure, at once real and unreal, who had taken over from him.

McCoy himself was to blame for the ease with which fighters impersonated him, if only briefly. He could be expected to turn up anywhere. He had nine fights in 1897, none against fighters of any standing, except for an exhibition with Tommy Ryan in Syracuse, officially called a draw,[27] and a 15-round decision over Dan Creedon in Long Island City at the end of the year. The others were nonentities: Jack Bonner, defeated in Philadelphia five days after McCoy's fight with Dick O'Brien; Dick Moore (whom McCoy had beaten twice before) knocked out in Buffalo in 10 rounds in July; Jim Hall, fought in a six-round, no decision affair in Philadelphia in October; George La-Blanche and Beach Ruble, both fought on November 12 in Dayton, Ohio; and Texas Billy Smith knocked out in Chicago in 10 rounds three days later. The fight with LaBlanche might have been important had it taken place earlier, for LaBlanche was a savage fighter. He was famous for his 22-round knockout of Nonpareil Jack Dempsey with a blow that was subsequently outlawed. But that had been 11 years before. This time McCoy knocked out LaBlanche in one round and, to give the patrons their money's worth, also knocked out Beach Ruble in one round on the same occasion.

In 1898 McCoy had 11 fights, 10 of them during the first five months of the year.[28] He moved around so much that Julia indeed had reason to claim desertion—if his absence on professional business could be called that. In January he knocked out Doc Payne in Louisville in four rounds. The meeting was a fortunate one. Payne became McCoy's sparring partner and business associate. The next month McCoy knocked out a local fighter named Long in Dayton, Ohio, and two weeks later was in Hot Springs for what was supposed to be a crucial fight with a promising newcomer, Nick Burley. It wasn't. McCoy landed heavily in the first round and knocked Burley out at the beginning of the second. McCoy had plenty to read when he got back to 249 West 44th Street. The New York newspapers devoted full pages to the fight, but the only interest in the fight was that the governor of Arkansas had been unable to stop it; he even failed in an attempt to commandeer a special train to take him to Hot Springs.

Meanwhile, McCoy's brother Homer was promoting a "fistic carnival" in Indianapolis, a small-scale model of those in New Orleans, intended to elevate the standards of the ring and attract respectable citizens, along with the fight crowd.[29] His main attraction was Kid McCoy, and his referee was the famous, honest and outspoken George Siler. McCoy hurried to Indianapolis after knocking out Burley, stopping only to referee a fight in St. Louis, and elevated the standards of ring on March 7, 1898 by knocking out an Indianapolis fighter, James Blackwell, in 10 rounds, and on the same evening knocking out a newcomer from Terre Haute, John Tierney, in three rounds. While he was about it, McCoy stopped at Fort Wayne, Indiana four days later and knocked out Jim Boles in one round, and the following week popped up in Springfield, Indiana, where he knocked out one Bert Bolty in one round also.

It was now time for the second showing of Homer's fistic carnival in Indianapolis. Oddly enough, the effort to attract the respectable element was succeeding. Tomlinson Hall was packed with businessmen, lawyers, and city officials, along with the usual fight crowd. There was also an unexpected added attraction. The Akron giant, Gus Ruhlin, the persistent but unsuccessful contender for the heavyweight title, repeatedly rebuffed in his attempts to get fights with Corbett and Fitzsimmons, appeared at the ring and formally challenged McCoy to a fight. Homer was taken by surprise and evaded answering. McCoy himself got to Indianapolis in time for the feature of the evening, which was his battle with Dan Molson, the middleweight champion of Indiana. Molson was so dismayed when he found himself in the ring with McCoy that he was visibly trembling—"it looked as though he would drop on the stage from sheer fright." When the bell rang Molson went to the center of the ring but retreated before a blow was struck and backed against the ropes, where he covered his face with his gloves. McCoy did not hit him, but kindly urged him to come out of his corner. Not a single blow was struck during the first round, Molson backing away and shaking his head and McCoy patiently arguing with him. In the second round McCoy hit Molson lightly, whereupon the champion of Indiana reeled as if struck by a sledgehammer and sprinted away until stopped by the ropes, along which he made his way with an expression of deep sorrow on his features, like someone struggling through a snowstorm, stopping when McCoy approached him and burying his face in his gloves. In the third round McCoy sternly ordered him to get out of the ring.

To try to salvage something from the evening McCoy and Doc Payne sparred for three rounds, after which McCoy left hurriedly. He had to catch a train, as he was fighting Tom Shea in Dayton, Ohio the next day. He knocked out Shea in two rounds. In the meantime Homer had accepted Gus Ruhlin's challenge, so six weeks later—May 20, 1896—McCoy was in Syracuse, always notorious for racketeers, and the home of his archenemy, Tommy Ryan, to fight a heavyweight contender who outweighed him by nearly 40 pounds. Ruhlin was slow, awkward, and powerful. He had knocked out Peter Maher, Tom Sharkey, and Joe Choynski (though he was in turn knocked out by each of them) and nearly outroughhoused Bob Fitzsimmons. He pounded after McCoy with a ponderous, steady attack, failing to find him round after round, and was badly beaten, in each of the 20 rounds. William Naughton, sports editor of the San Francisco *Examiner* and the best known sportswriter in the country, saw this fight and never forgot the spectacle of Ruhlin "taking a terrible drubbing while endeavoring to land a knockout punch on the nimble kid."[30] Alexander Johnston echoed Naughton: "McCoy was one of the most skillful boxers that ever climbed through the ropes. Barring Corbett, he was probably the most artistic fighter we have ever produced, and he cut Ruhlin to pieces without himself carrying a mark out of the ring. It was a triumph of boxing mind over matter." It was McCoy's last fight of the year, except for a meeting with Joe Goddard, the aging Australian heavyweight in December in Philadelphia, won by McCoy when Goddard fouled him in the fifth round.[31] (Goddard was the man who ended Joe Choynski's championship aspirations; he twice knocked out Choynski in the great fighter's early days.) McCoy had now piled up a record of 66 fights, with two defeats, in seven years.

In the meantime, on November 22, 1898, Corbett met Tom Sharkey in New York at the Lenox Athletic Club in Harlem in one of the great ring scandals of all time.[32] It was surpassed by another scandal involving Sharkey—the extraordinary fight with Fitzsimmons in San Francisco in 1896—in which Wyatt Earp, acting as referee, with a pistol in his hand, awarded the fight to Sharkey on a foul invisible to everyone else after Fitzsimmons had apparently knocked Sharkey out—"a carefully planned conspiracy," Naughton wrote, "in which Fitzsimmons was the victim." The Sharkey-Corbett fight was almost as brazen. It was so stupefying that all bets were called off. In Corbett's account he was felled by a haymaker in the second round and wrenched his ankle getting to his feet, so hobbled that he was unable to fight effectively from then on. Whatever the truth of that, Sharkey was probably winning until in the ninth round in scenes of confusion and near riot, Corbett was accused of a foul and his second, Con McVey, jumped into the ring to mix in the action, automatically awarding the fight to Sharkey. Corbett regarded the whole episode as a dark stain on his career, but claimed he had not been hurt by Sharkey's punches. The hardest blow, he said, came from his old friend Bill Naughton, who was outraged by the spectacle and wrote a savage denunciation, saying the whole fight "had been rehearsed blow for blow." In the audience, McCoy watched Sharkey's windmilling tactics and decided he could beat him.

It was a time of unparalleled confusion in McCoy's married life with Julia.[33] The stack of clippings was mounting every day, with amused, malicious, sardonic, or fabricated gossip column items about their marriage and remarriages, their quarrels over money, and their disputes as to which one was entitled to their dog. In one case a gossip columnist confused the argument over the dog with McCoy's offer of $10,000 to Julia to remarry him, and had it that McCoy was being held up to pay $10,000 for the return of a bitch.

The timing of McCoy's marital troubles was unfortunate. He was to meet Sharkey on January 10, 1899; on January 6 the papers blazed the news that Julia had left Marie Dressler's company to rejoin her husband.

Ridicule was one thing the image of Kid McCoy was not flexible enough to meet. There was no real reason for McCoy to fight Sharkey. Like Corbett, McCoy was a target of abuse from Sharkey's followers, ridiculed for what were regarded as his airs and affectations and social pretensions, as opposed to the honest uncivilized toughness of Sharkey himself. But he was far more vulnerable than was Corbett to Sharkey's battering-ram assaults in the ring and to the hostility of Sharkey's followers outside the ring. Sharkey, born in Ireland in 1873, made a name for himself while serving in the United States Navy and fighting in the Hawaiian Islands.[34] He had a sun-bronzed, brine-pickled look; he was short, stocky, broad, with powerful arms and shoulders framing the huge battleship tatooed on his chest. "You couldn't hurt him," Corbett said. "All he wanted to do was belt. You couldn't miss him, for he kept pouring in." Even the most generous sportswriters were hard put to find reasons for praising Sharkey. Joe Williams remarked in his obituary of Sharkey that Sharkey had a delightful brogue. Among the intellectuals only Paul Armstrong, who was the author of sports dramas and the man who persuaded Raoul Walsh to a stage and movie career, admired Sharkey and then only for his blind, heads-down slugging persistence. "Round after round," Armstrong wrote, "Sharkey came in like the surf."

Sharkey indeed came in like the surf in his fight with McCoy.[35] In the first round McCoy knocked him down three times. But that was all of the fight that amounted to anything. Sharkey seemed unhurt, and "took everything that McCoy had." In the early rounds McCoy wasted enough punches to have knocked out a dozen small-town fighters without stopping Sharkey's bull-like rushes. By the eighth round there was little force in the blows he was still able to land almost at will; in the 10th round McCoy was knocked out.

History had reversed itself—science had lost to brute strength, brains were defeated by brawn. It was as if Sullivan had defeated Corbett in New Orleans. Trade fell off at McCoy's and Corbett's saloons and picked up at Sharkey's place. The press clippings McCoy studied with hypnotized interest carried a new note, along with the many pictures of the beautiful Julia McCoy: McCoy had no staying power, he had beaten only beginners and nobodies, he had no real punch, as evidenced by his harmless pummeling of Sharkey and, if he had ever been any good, he was now only a Broadway playboy.

In San Francisco William Naughton, fresh from the outrage of the Corbett-Sharkey fight, was further outraged by the antics of an unknown Pacific Coast fighter far below the stature of McCoy, Choynski, or anyone in the top ranks. Naughton was an anomaly in sports history. He gave the impression of being a scholar, a scholar who had strayed into William Randolph Hearst's newspaper empire, where he was respected only because no one knew what to make of him. He was a very fine writer, not in the jerky style of sportswriters—which involved the twist of some slang phrase, or a grotesque and exaggerated image—but in the classic English sense of an accurate description or characterization. Naughton was also without racial prejudice. He supported Peter Jackson when the Negro heavyweight arrived in San Francisco from Australia and acted as Jackson's advisor in arranging his fight with Corbett. In fact, he bore Jackson's power of attorney to make the arrangements by which Jackson got $10,000. Naughton had been close to Corbett in his early days, gradually drawing away as Corbett became increasingly theatrical, and finally breaking with him over the scandal of the Sharkey fight. Yet Naughton was not demanding or exacting in any unrealistic sense. He was the first writer to appreciate the wonderful genius and oddity of Fitzsimmons, for example, and was equally appreciative of Fitzsimmons' peculiar personality when Fitzsimmons was fighting and when, as an evangelist, he was full of eloquence in his gratitude to the Almighty for being on the wagon.

In his concern about the low state of fight promotion after the Sharkey-Corbett fight, Naughton decided to go into fight promotion himself. His first promotion was a fight in San Francisco between Kid McCoy and Joe Choynski.[36] If there was one fighter (other than Jim Jeffries) McCoy did not want to fight, it was Joe Choynski. He had beaten him, to be sure, but in a fight as bad as that of Corbett and Sharkey. Choynski had fought Fitzsimmons to a standstill; he had a 20-round draw with Jeffries to his credit; he had drawn a fight with Sharkey shortly before Sharkey knocked out McCoy. Choynski was, in many respects, similar to Sharkey, though less of a roughhouse champion and with none of Sharkey's underworld connections. Like Sharkey, he had unlimited courage and was able to take punishment almost as much as was the sailor; nevertheless, he was a good boxer, marking a kind of halfway point between the old school of rough-and-tumble fighters and the modern ring craftsmen like Corbett and McCoy.

This was the opponent that Naughton, in his hatred of sham and his concern for McCoy's good name, lined up for a match with McCoy after McCoy's defeat by Sharkey.

They met at Mechanic's Palace in San Francisco on March 24, 1899. Choynski was favored, so rapidly had McCoy's standing declined since the Sharkey fight. McCoy tried to rush the fight, as he always did and Choynski knocked him down. When he came back, Choynski knocked him down again. In all, McCoy was on the canvas 16 times in 20 rounds. He had unnatural grimace on his features, the result of a bent bridge on his teeth, a broken nose, and three broken ribs. But Choynski was in no better shape, and in the 20th round McCoy knocked him out. It was a revelation of how badly McCoy's reputation had suffered in fight circles at the hands of imposters that Naughton ran the headline, NOW YOU'VE SEEN THE REAL MC-COY! People had seen the real Joe Choynski in that fight also, but, then, there were no imposters going around the country calling themselves Joe Choynski.

## 5

The phrase caught on with extraordinary speed. "The real Mc-Coy" was heard everywhere. Perhaps the moment was one of more than ordinary pretense. The most popular play in the United States at the time was *Little Lord Fauntleroy,* in which the leading character was an insufferable little boy wearing a wig of golden curls and a lace-trimmed black velvet suit. The most popular song was "Only a Bird in a Gilded Cage," about a woman who was pitiful because she sold her soul for an old man's gold and was only a bird in a gilded cage. The literary celebrities were Oscar Wilde, carrying his green carnation, and Ella Wheeler Wilcox, reciting her poems of passion amid clouds of incense and swirls of her purple robes. Presidential candidates were plumed knights or silver-voiced orators from the Platte. They did not advocate measures; they crusaded to prevent mankind from being crucified on a cross of gold or—among more modest Republicans—advocated the full dinner pail. The United

States was becoming a land of blatant imitation and outrageous pretense, of synthetic flavors, watered stock, salted gold mines, counterfeit bills, sawdust-stuffed sausages, artificial colorings, preservatives, sweeteners, patent medicines, cures, frauds, and confidence games so numerous that some simple phrase was needed to express the ordinary citizen's approval of whatever was genuine in a world of high-pressure unrealities. But for McCoy, whose wife had left him again, "the real McCoy" was an embarrassing title to live up to.[37] To begin with, he was not the real McCoy; he was really Norman Selby. And however much amusement his marriages gave the public, he did not enjoy the sensation they caused. Except for Lottie, all his wives married Kid McCoy. "They wanted to reform him," he told Edward Smith. But nine marriages?, said Smith; they all wanted to reform Kid McCoy? "None of them had any children," said McCoy bleakly, "Maybe that had something to do with it."

No human being could be expected to serve very long as a synonym for whatever was authentic or genuine. There were too many opportunities to lie, exaggerate, deceive, admire swelled heads, or indulge in whatever insincerities or other deceptions might be to one's advantage, for anyone to remain such a paragon. But in McCoy's case, while the phrase "the real McCoy" remained in common speech, he himself almost instantly lost his reputation for honesty. Within a few months he was commonly regarded as one of the most notorious frauds in the fight game—a reputation that has persisted, somewhat unjustly, in ring history—and incidentally one of the biggest phoneys in New York City. The transformation was sudden and overwhelming. Fortunately it was limited to fight followers and Manhattan sophisticates. The public as a whole went right on saying "the real McCoy" for the real thing without knowing that the real McCoy was now regarded by all but his closest friends—and by some of them also—as a crook.

McCoy was at first flattered to find himself the real McCoy, a national symbol for honesty. In one sense he came to believe in his own legend, but only in a negative way, in that he tried to adopt a pose of absolute honesty or of complete lack of pretense. In many respects McCoy in this period of his life suggested the later career of Ernest Hemingway, who was also trapped by his own legend and who felt obligated to live up to, or to write up to, the public image of a great writer and a daring, adventurous, and honest man. But the body of experience that Hemingway, as a successful writer and a public figure, drew upon in his later fiction had to conform to the rigorous requirements of the image: it differed in character from the more honest or at least more innocent and less self-conscious experience Hemingway had drawn from in the works that made him famous and a legend.

It wasn't that McCoy dramatized himself or thought of himself as a hero. On the contrary, he was merciless in his self-judgment. But the mythical "real McCoy" was an elusive and powerful abstraction that pulled human motives out of their natural orbit and made them subject to the fluctuations and changes in the legend. He returned to New York after the fight with Choynski driven by a need for action, intense and concentrated action, as though he recognized that the period in which he was to be regarded as authentic or genuine was bound to be brief. And brief it was—in the summer of 1900, a year and a half after the Choynski fight, McCoy was disgraced by his fight with Corbett, which became celebrated for being conspiciously not authentic.

Some lingering trace of the influence of Norman Selby was evident when McCoy used some of his new wealth to buy a farm, a substantial property near Saratoga that overlooked Saratoga Lake, which he called Cedar Bluff.[38] For the former Norman Selby the farm was an ideal retreat, a link to his outdoor childhood and a simple life. But for Kid McCoy, now a national celebrity and one of the most popular figures on Broadway, life there was impossible. It was at Cedar Bluff that the conflicts of the legend and the reality collapsed into a general chaos—senseless and foolish chaos, but certainly genuine chaos, as well as authentic disorder, real bankruptcy, and honest pain.

Boxing had little to do with it. Notoriety, fame, the legend of the real McCoy—these were more influential. McCoy had never been discriminating in his choice of opponents; after the Choynski fight he became less discriminating than ever. In the summer of 1899 he set out on a hurried barnstorming trip through the Middle West.[39] In Dubuque, Iowa, on August 10, 1899, he knocked out Tim Dugan in two rounds and Jack Graham in four. He hurried on to Joplin, Missouri where he knocked out a local hero, Jim Carter, in five rounds on August 14, 1899. From Joplin he went to Chicago where on August 18, 1899, he was to meet Jack McCormick who, Alexander Johnston said, was "a big strong boy who knew little about boxing, and had no business being in the same ring with the clever and somewhat cruel

McCoy."[40] Johnston said McCormick "had been hired as a chopping block to give the customers a chance to see the clever Kid work up a perspiration and administer the knockout."

Instead, McCormick swung a mighty punch in the first round that seemed to come up all the way from the floor to McCoy's chin, and knocked him out. McCoy was undisturbed by the knockout—or pretended to be; it was a lucky punch. McCoy was fighting so much that there was always a chance he would run into one. Also, a return match with McCormick was immediately booked for New York.

Augustus Thomas's hit melodrama, *In Mizzoura,* with Lionel Barrymore and Theodore Roberts in the cast, was playing at the Grand Opera House only three blocks from the fight. Thomas recollected in his autobiography, *The Print of My Remembrance*: "McCoy had many admirers in our company, . . . and as I remember, the odds were some four to one on him." Thomas had two tickets. While the company was dressing in the dressing rooms under the stage they were talking about McCoy and McCormick, and offering fine odds on McCoy. Thomas did not take any bets then, but he and Harry Hamlin, a member of the staff, walked to the arena to watch the main event. They had barely taken their seats when it was over. It happened so quickly that Hamlin, who was looking through his pockets for a match, never saw the fight at all. Thomas and Hamlin walked back to the theatre—"We seemed to have been only walking from one dressing-room to another," Thomas wrote. Barrymore and most of the cast had not yet gone on the stage. Theodore Roberts and the others came off-stage from the opening scenes of the first act. Thomas and Hamlin took all the bets they could get on McCormick (at excessive odds) and hastily left.

They met the losers at dinner after the show, confessed they had seen the knockout, and repaid the bets. But neither Thomas nor Lionel Barrymore ever forgot McCoy's defeat. While McCoy went back to New York and more fights, Thomas began work on a comedy about a prizefighter. McCoy resumed fighting as vigorously as ever. On September 5, 1899, he met Geoffrey Thorne in New York and knocked him out in three rounds, and two weeks later fought Steve O'Donnell and knocked him out in six.[41] He was now ready to meet McCormick again, and did so on September 27, 1899 at the Lenox Athletic Club.[42] The place was packed, as it certainly would not have been if McCormick had not previously beaten McCoy. Johnston considered McCoy's second fight with McCormick to have been disgraceful, something far below McCoy's natural ability and temperament. What the audience saw "was a massacre." McCoy patiently refrained from knocking McCormick out while he had administered "a horrible beating . . . McCormick's face scarcely looked human at the end." In the eighth round, when McCormick was no longer putting up a fight, and was at the point of collapse (New York referees rarely stopped fights at the turn of the century) McCoy knocked him out.

How much money McCoy actually made in these encounters, and how badly he needed money were hotly debated questions. He had few big purses.[43] For instance, he won $2,000 in his fight with Nick Burley in Hot Springs; the loser got $500. But McCoy fought so often that he made more cumulatively than did his rivals who fought only major opponents for large purses. The contemporary reports of McCoy's fights reported big, usually capacity, crowds. Even Homer's promotion of McCoy's fight with Dan Molson in Indianapolis made a profit of several thousand dollars. Tom McMahon, a Detroit newspaperman who knew McCoy in his later years, wrote that when McCoy was only 22 years old he had accumulated $100,000, which he liked to carry around with him. It was not unlikely; by 1900, when McCoy was 26, he had—or should have had, by any reasonably honest method of bookkeeping—several times that amount.

But McCoy continued to fight as though faced with destitution. On October 6, 1899, a week after the McCormick fight, he took the train back to Chicago and fought a draw with Joe Choynski, both fighters understandably wary at the sight of each other in the same ring.[44] From Chicago McCoy went on to St. Louis to fight Billy Stift, aa promising middleweight who had lost a 20-round decision to Tommy Ryan.[45] McCoy knocked out Stift in 13 rounds. Two weeks later McCoy was in Buffalo, where he put away Jack McDonough, a young hopeful, with a clean knockout in the fourth round.

McCoy wanted a chance at the heavyweight title. When Corbett retired he gave the title to Peter Maher, and while Maher never actually held it (Fitzsimmons beat him too decisively) he was still a leading contender. Maher had given Fitzsimmons a terrific fight; he had knocked out Joe Choynski; and in a savage battle with Tom Sharkey at the Palace Athletic Club in New York the end was inconclusive because the fighters kept on slugging after the bell rang for the end of the seventh round, and the police stopped the fight. McCoy met

Maher at the Coney Island Athletic Club on January 1, 1900, and knocked him out in the fifth round.[46]

Only 12 days later McCoy met Joe Choynski again in New York and knocked him out in four rounds. Then he gave himself a rest of four months, only to go through three major fights in three weeks in May and June. On May 18, 1900 he was awarded a decision over Dan Creedon in six rounds in New York, followed by a victory over Tommy Ryan in Chicago on May 29. Two days later he was back in New York, fighting Jack Bonner.[47] He defeated Bonner in 13 rounds. There were no set-ups in this list of opponents. Except for Bonner they were first-class contenders, the best in the country—in fact, just short of Fitzsimmons and Jeffries. No other fighter of his time (except the Negro welterweight Joe Walcott) fought so frequently against fighters of comparable strength.

What possesed McCoy to take the risks involved? His home life was in highly publicized disorder. Julia had returned to him, but she had also published a magazine article which purported to reveal secrets of the ring he had confided to her. The original article apparently disappeared, or had a very small circulation, but excerpts or digests of it were widely published, along with Julia McCoy's photograph, with captions like the one in *Broadway Magazine*: "Accuses Husband of Faking in Ring."[48] It seemed that McCoy had confessed to Julia such deceptions as that involved in his fight with Jack Wilkes, when he pretended to be on the verge of collapse in order to lull his opponent into a sense of false security. The impression spread that McCoy's wife had disclosed his confessions that his fights were fixed.

He was the real McCoy; there hadn't been the slightest question of his integrity in any fight since he defeated Choynski in San Francisco. And he had very little time to work toward a title fight. The Horton Law, which regulated prizefighting in New York and permitted 25-round fights, had been repealed, effective September 1, 1900. Thereafter only club fights, amateur fights, and no-decision exhibitions would be legal. It meant the end of the fight game as it had previously been played. It also meant a heavy blow to fighters like Corbett and McCoy, whose business was related to their fame as fighters.

New York promoters intended to have prizefighting end in a blaze of glory (they also planned to start agitation to repeal the anti-boxing law). The Sharkey-Fitzsimmons fight was widely advertised as the last fight to be held before prizefighting vanished. But the fight attracted only a handful of spectators, and its two rounds of savage slugging could not be called a demonstration of art and science.

The Corbett-McCoy fight was scheduled for 25 rounds on the night of August 30, 1900 at Madison Square Garden.[49] It was the last fight before boxing ended in New York, on August 31. The response was favorable; the anticipated gate was $75,000. The fighters were to get half the gate, divided 75 percent to the winner, 25 percent to the loser. The New York *Times,* which had crusaded against prizefighting, called Corbett and McCoy the two cleverest fighters in the ring, barred from the heavyweight championship by their lack of weight and brawn. Corbett weighted 190, McCoy 170. It was well known that the two men were old enemies.

The betting favored Corbett. A $100 bet would get $60. Three weeks before the fight rumors spread that the fight was fixed, and betting fell off, as did interest in the fight. One rumor had it that Corbett and McCoy had agreed privately to divide the fighters' share of the gate 50-50, instead of the official 75-25 percent. Another contributing factor was that Mrs. McCoy had disclosed Kid McCoy's past deceptions in the ring, and it was said McCoy and his wife were quarreling. The magazine *Vanity Fair* reported that Mrs. McCoy and Mrs. Corbett, formerly friendly, were no longer speaking.

None of these matters seemed important enough to generate stories of a fix, but the stories persisted. The notion became established that the fight, in the words of the *Times,* was to be "a bold fraud." The crowd was disappointing. The $35 box seats were not filled. The gate reached about $50,000, and in all respects—as a demonstration of boxing skill, as an affirmation of honesty in the ring, and as a dramatic end to boxing in New York—the fight was a disaster.

The reports from ringside did not suggest fraud. The first round was extremely fast, but with no real punches landed by either fighter, a matter of fast footwork, feinting, and speed. Corbett said he was cautious because of the rumors of the fix, and assumed that McCoy was also. In the second round Corbett landed a hard punch to McCoy's jaw, but McCoy slipped away. Corbett thought the audience was disgruntled at that point, and implied that its suspicions increased because McCoy kept out of his reach. But, he said, he was learning that "McCoy was far more clever than Fitzsimmons."

In the third round, astonishingly, both fighters began slugging, turning what had been intended to be a demonstration of art and science into a ferocious melee, compounded alternately of hard exchanges and rough grappling. Corbett denied this, and said that while it was slugging, it was pretty scientific slugging. It seemed to him that McCoy suddenly threw caution to the winds and "fought like a crazy man." Corbett tried to keep inside his swings and pounded on McCoy's stomach. In the fifth round McCoy went down under what the *Times* reporter called a merciless punching and a clean knockout. *The Times* added that the savagery of the fight contradicted the rumors that it had been prearranged, "or, if it was, McCoy took needlessly severe punishment."

McCoy's punishment had barely begun. Almost all ring history calls the fight a fraud. Alexander Johnston wrote: "McCoy dropped to the floor and gave an excellent imitation of a man in distress." Samuel Hopkins Adams, the novelist and popular historian, who saw the fight, said: "While the house shrieked and McCoy writhed on the floor in a touching representation of *The Dying Gladiator* the referee tolled out ten with his arms and it was all over. Eight thousand-odd happy suckers, including World Champion Jeffries and my humble self, departed in the fond illusion that we had witnessed one of the great events in ring history. So we had, but what we had been watching was not a supreme fight. It was a supreme fake." The most restrained comment was William Naughton's in *Kings of the Queensbury Realm,* written the following year. "A scandal arose in connection with this affair," Naughton wrote, "it being charged that McCoy had sold himself to some bookmaker. This may have been the case, but there is no gainsaying the fact that the punch that finally sent McCoy to the floor was a wicked one."

During the week following the fight the muttering about the fraud increased.[50] McCoy had intended to go to his farm with Julia for a rest, but in view of the gossip he decided to stay in his place of business during its regular hours. The muttering was still only whispers of something crooked; no one had come forward with any definite charges and no names of any accusers were mentioned in the newspapers.

On Friday after the fight Corbett disappeared from his home at 215 West 34th Street. About four o'clock on Saturday morning he appeared at the Delavan Hotel's bar with George Considine, prepared to sail secretly on the *Campania* for England that day. Also sailing on the *Compania* was Marguerite Cornille, a vaudeville singer and a beautiful woman whose friendship with Corbett was no longer a secret. John Considine, who was present at the hotel meeting, was sworn to secrecy. Corbett left two notes to be delivered by messenger, one to his wife and the other to a friend and business associate after the ship was at sea.

Mrs. Corbett got Corbett's note early Saturday afternoon. She went at once to his saloon. The crowd at the bar was startled when she burst in, agitated and confused, and demanded to know where Corbett was.

No one could tell her anything. She became increasingly excited and angry, questioning bartenders, waiters, and customers without learning anything. Spotting John Considine, she demanded that he deny or confirm that Corbett had sailed away. John said he knew nothing about it.

Returning home, Mrs. Corbett got in touch with the famous law partners, Howe and Hummel, and conferred with them until that evening. About eight o'clock she called in a reporter from the New York *World* to tell her story. Now calmed down, she explained that Corbett had foreseen the charges of fraud in his fight with McCoy and had run away rather than face the consequences. Corbett had said nothing to her about leaving. He left a note which she received four hours after he had sailed. In his note, she said, Corbett said he was going to England and would never return to the United States.

On her part, she wanted to give the complete story. "The fight was a joke," she told the *World* reporter, "as every sport in the city knows. . . . It was fixed up in this very room." Her story was that Corbett met with a representative of McCoy's and agreed to throw the fight—"to lie down." Corbett, she said, gave the agent a sum of money—she did not say how much—to bet on McCoy to insure that the agreement would be adhered to. As a result McCoy did not train. Half an hour before the fight Corbett decided on a double cross, which was why there was a lot of late money bet that McCoy would be knocked out. "That's why Corbett left," she said. "I'm not sorry he's gone."

McCoy was in his bar when the reporter arrived after seeing Mrs. Corbett. He said, "I knew Jim intended to go to Europe. But I didn't know the reason." McCoy said Mrs. Corbett's story was ridiculous. He had made no deal with Corbett and no agent or representative of his had met Corbett at any time. "The fight was on the square," McCoy said, "and the best man won."

The following day the scandal grew to sensational proportions. It would have been even greater, but a tidal wave swept over Galveston, Texas, taking more than 5,000 lives, and greatly reduced the fight's importance. Mrs. Corbett collapsed. She did not believe Corbett had sailed away with Marguerite Cornille on the *Campania*. She thought he was in hiding somewhere in the city. John Considine was tracked down by reporters and asked whether Corbett had sailed, but Considine evaded the questions. He was more concerned about Mrs. Corbett's story that Corbett had agreed to fix the fight. He said that she did not believe her own story. He was in the Corbett house before the fight. Corbett came in late from his training quarters and slept for a short time. When they left to go to the Garden, he heard Mrs. Corbett say, "Jim, I hope McCoy knocks your block off." Now, asked Considine, if she had really believed the fight was fixed, would she have said that? As to Corbett's whereabouts, he knew nothing.

McCoy issued a formal statement, saying Mrs. Corbett's accusations were absolutely false, had no foundation whatever, "and are simply the hot answer of a jealous woman. . . . I did not, and I had no representative, enter into negotiations with Corbett, or any representative of his, to have him lie down on me, as I would not take his or any other man's word on any such agreement. I am unable to see how either of us would have gained any prestige by being defeated. I fought a bad and wrong kind of fight. It was my intention to tire Corbett out. I want to state now, as I did immediately after the contest, that I was defeated fairly and squarely, and have no one to blame but myself. But I still believe I can beat Corbett, and I hope sometime in the near future to have another chance to prove it. I did intend to leave the city for a few weeks' vacation, but owing to the false rumors now afloat I have decided to remain in the city, and can be found at my place of business every day."

The following day the affair flared to new heights as simultaneously Mrs. Corbett sued Corbett for divorce and Mrs. McCoy sued McCoy for divorce. The firm of Howe and Hummel represented both women. McCoy's case was more melodramatic. Julia accused him of going to a safe deposit box at the New Amsterdam Bank, with the intention of disposing of all his property and leaving the country, and in the process taking $10,000 in jewels that belonged to her.

Mrs. Corbett's suit charged Corbett with desertion and cruelty. She alleged that he neglected her, struck her, on one occasion burned her cheek with a lighted cigar and on another drew a pistol and threatened to shoot her, being stopped by George Considine, who grabbed the gun. Mrs. McCoy charged McCoy with adultery with two young actresses, Beulah Cameron and Lilly O'Neill. McCoy, in turn, filed a countersuit for divorce, the papers being served on Julia by his brother, Homer. Julia then secured a warrant for McCoy's arrest, alleging that he had stolen the jewelry belonging to her, and asked that he be placed under bond to insure the payment of alimony —in the event, that was, that his countersuit for divorce was denied.

McCoy spent a day dodging arrest. He was reported to be on an excursion boat with a crowd of Big Tim Sullivan's supporters. He was said to have evaded a deputy trying to serve papers on him by trading hats with a friend and sprinting through the streets of the lower East Side until he managed to get on a Second Avenue elevated train that pulled out of the station before the deputy could board it. In the meantime his lawyer informed Mrs. McCoy's lawyer that McCoy would surrender himself the following morning.

This McCoy did, but the reason why he needed the free day was never explained. At three o'clock in the afternoon of the next day, McCoy, accompanied by a witness, went to his apartment at 243 West 44th Street. The street door was unlocked, but the apartment door was locked, and no one answered the bell. McCoy rammed the door with his shoulder, and the door burst open. Inside, Mrs. McCoy was holding a press conference. McCoy went to the dining room and began opening drawers. He said he was looking for some letters. Not finding any, he picked up a small oil painting of himself and started to leave. Julia said the painting belonged to her. McCoy said it was his.

"You shall not take that!" Julia cried.

"I will," said he. "I will take all that is mine!"

She grabbed for the picture, but failed to get it away from him. Seizing a decanter filled with whiskey, she swung it at his head. He raised his arm to protect his face, and the decanter, striking his elbow, broke at the neck, drenching the McCoys and the dining room with whiskey. McCoy grabbed Julia by the arms and shook her vigorously. Her glasses flew across the room. She later said he struck her. He denied it, though he admitted shaking her so hard her glasses were knocked off. McCoy and his witness hurried away, McCoy carrying the picture in one hand and in the other the broken neck of the decanter. Julia and her witnesses went to the police. She demanded protection, and two patrolmen were accordingly stationed to prevent McCoy from coming back.

Meanwhile the *Campania* reached England, and Corbett and Considine moved into the Hotel Cecil in London. Miss Cornille settled in a private hotel in the West End. In an interview Corbett adopted a tone of deep mystery. Regarding his sudden departure from New York, he said, "I had good reasons. . . . I am liable to leave London at any moment. If I do, you may be sure that no one will know where I go." He asserted that he and his wife understood each other. "If I had eloped with Miss Cornille," he said earnestly, "I certainly would not leave her go to a separate hotel as soon as I arrived here."

6

Such was the way the scandal of the Corbett-McCoy fight appeared at the time. In *There's No Fraud Like an Old Fraud,* Samuel Hopkins Adams quoted George Considine as having said that McCoy made a full and frank confession to him, admitting that he had accepted $5,000 to throw the fight.[51] Since the loser's share of the purse amounted to about $5,000 the arithmetic here was puzzling. Considine was in London, not New York, during the height of the scandal, and he was not McCoy's manager, as Adams believed, but Corbett's partner. At the time the only concrete charge made against McCoy was Mrs. Corbett's story, and within days after she told it, the rumors that the Corbett-McCoy fight was fixed were forgotten in the remarkable scandals in the domestic lives of both fighters. If these scandals had been deliberately fomented to distract attention from the fight itself they could hardly have succeeded more.

Photographs purporting to be pictures of McCoy and Corbett stalling in the ring were widely printed. They continued to be published more than half a century later, substantiating accounts, like that of Adams, of the fraudulent nature of the event. No film of the Corbett-McCoy fight was copyrighted in the Library of Congress. What *was* copyrighted was one of Siegmund Lubin's (a Philadelphia moviemaker) ingenious "impersonations," in which actors hired to play the parts of McCoy and Corbett went through the motions of fighting each other as the newspapers described the actual fight. In this synthetic rerun the fight looked like a fake, as indeed it was, with the two actors portraying Corbett and McCoy, and in the many photographs published in ring histories the two men did not seem to be fighting very hard. The only trouble with these photographs as evidence of the crookedness of the event was that the two men shown in the pictures were not Corbett and McCoy.

The Corbett fight was McCoy's last important venture in the ring. During 1901 he did not fight at all, except for an exhibition in England in December, during which he knocked out three fighters in one evening.[52] What added to the unreality of the Corbett fight scandal was that the wives of the fighters, who really started the talk, soon resumed their lives with their husbands as though nothing had happened. In the case of Mrs. Corbett this was perhaps not so remarkable—for she and Corbett remained together, though it was going too far to say, as did Corbett's obituaries, that there was never any scandal in his life—but that Julia and McCoy could again make a go of it, after the lawsuits, arrests, and decanter-smashing, was baffling.

But reunited they were. One mutual interest was McCoy's farm in Saratoga. They spent an increasing amount of time there. The atmosphere of Broadway had changed since prizefighting had been outlawed; though McCoy's saloon was still prosperous (at least according to *Broadway Magazine*) a good deal of its glamor had faded. There was still a meeting point between Norman Selby and Kid McCoy in their missionary zeal for physical fitness, and at some point (not long after the Corbett scandal had died down) Cedar Bluff became a health farm.

McCoy really believed that he could restore hard-drinking, saturated playboys and sportsmen to a life they had never previously known or enjoyed. In later years unfriendly accounts, similar to those that accused McCoy of throwing the Corbett fight, called Cedar Bluff a roadhouse, but it was, at least at first, a true rest home and reconditioning sanitarium.[53] McCoy wanted to build it up to something like William Muldoon's famous health farm, which was used by boxers for conditioning as well as by hard drinkers who were in need of drying out.[54]

Two of McCoy's first clients were a pair of wealthy young Yale graduates, Edward Ellis and his friend Ralph Thompson. Ellis's grandfather was the founder of the Ellis Locomotive Works in

Schenectady, and one of the major manufacturers of railroad locomotives in the country.[55] Thompson had been the coxswain of a famous Yale crew; he belonged to a banking family, and had a job in a bank, although he did not work at it.[56] Ellis and Thompson were inseparable. In his earlier years young Ellis had associated almost constantly with his first cousin, known as Bud Ellis, also a Broadway playboy. Bud died, leaving Edward the only surviving member of the Ellis family, and the heir to the family fortune. He and Thompson continued the high-living partnership he previously had enjoyed with Bud.

In 1902 Ellis was 25 years old. His athletic achievements included serving as coxswain of his class crew at Yale in 1896 and as a substitute quarterback on the Yale football squad. But his sports interests were fanatical. It was said that "he exercised too much" and came down with a severe illness. He went to McCoy's health farm for convalescence, and then came down with typhoid fever and nearly died, creating ghoulish amusement among Broadway wits about McCoy's health treatments "for overworked and overplayed men."

Julia McCoy had a young actress, Lillian Estelle Earle, usually called Estelle, visiting her at the farm.[57] McCoy, who was not always well-informed about Julia's doings, was under the impression that Miss Earle had not known his wife before the visit, but, as an old friend of Edward Ellis, had arrived to nurse him back to health. Estelle was a good-looking, fair-haired, blue-eyed, sociable young woman with a comfortably rounded figure, the daughter of a Utica hotel-keeper. Her career on the stage had only begun, if it could be said to have started at all, but she was pleasant company and a good nurse and, as the *World* put it: "Thanks to her incessant care the young millionaire recovered his health." In August 1902 the Reverend Herbert Gesner of Saratoga married Lillian Estelle Earle and Edward Ellis.[58] Mrs. McCoy then ran off to Japan with Ralph Thompson, leaving McCoy alone at the farm with his punching bags, diets, and health hints.

# 4. Seven Million Dollars

Edward Ellis began his married life with some magnificent gifts to his bride: a large estate on Lake George, a beautiful house on West End Avenue in New York, two automobiles, and a steam yacht.[1] The Ellis Locomotive Works were much reduced from their original importance, but the property was still very large, and while there were difficulties involved with Ellis's mother's estate, he was, as the sole survivor, in charge of a fortune.[2]

Ellis and Estelle did not lead an active social life. They were in seclusion much of the time, though Estelle came to know some of the family friends in Schenectady, including a Mr. Walker who handled Ellis's affairs there. They approved of the marriage, if society did not, because Ellis's dissipations had stopped with his marriage.

The newspapers reported that he had become a model husband, no longer engaged in a night life of strenuous gaiety, and was deeply devoted to his wife. There were contradictory accounts of Ellis's mother and the marriage. The *Times* reported difficulties between the bride and her mother-in-law that later complicated the settling of the estate. The *World* said the marriage was at first kept secret from Ellis's mother (who was still living at the time), but that she became reconciled to it and left almost all of her own fortune to her son, in addition to the fortune he had inherited from his father and grandfather. At what time this reconciliation took place was uncertain; within months after the marriage, however, Ellis was described as the only living member of the family.

Japan was fashionable at the moment. The treaty with England in 1902, intended to check Russian hostility, opened up a period of hospitality to Western visitors; good relations with official and un-

78

official visitors were earnestly cultivated as the war with Russia grew closer. Japan was a lively topic of discussion, it was *the* place to visit. Julia and Ralph Thompson were following the up-to-the-minute fashion when they chose Japan to run away to.

McCoy dropped out of sight.[3] He was drinking heavily, the first time anything of the sort was said of him. He never admitted it, however. He said only that he was studying. McCoy could not admit to being taken by surprise by anything, least of all by the flight of his wife to Japan. But he was uneasy over what he felt was an awareness among educated and sophisticated people of matters about which he knew little. Frequently he felt that things they were talking about, however commonplace or remote they seemed to him, were charged with significance or of immediate practical importance to them, so that they were somehow talking over his head even when he took part in their conversations.

When McCoy was with educated people, even people who had taken their college training as lightly as had Ellis and Ralph Thompson, he was conscious of the way in which they referred to matters entirely outside his own limited education. He began to read what he thought were highbrow books, including the poetry of Longfellow and Tennyson. In the meantime he got a divorce from Julia, and while he was about it, sued Ralph Thompson for $100,000 for "alienating the affections of his wife."[4] Julia was offended; according to her, there were no affections to be alienated. She married Thompson when McCoy divorced her, but in view of McCoy's suit, which she said would ruin her husband, she permitted Thompson to divorce her at once without contesting his suit, remaining on close terms with him despite their divorce, under the impression that in divorcing Thompson she would destroy the basis for McCoy's legal action. She testified later on that Thompson, while a rich banker, was actually a lamb among wolves.

Early in 1903 McCoy emerged from seclusion to fight a six-round bout with Jack McCormick in Philadelphia, where no-decision fights were still legal.[5] He had put on weight and was out of condition, but no particular effort was required of him to make him look good against McCormick. But his next fight, on April 22, 1903, had more historical importance. A Chicago sportswriter, Lou Houseman, had taken on the task of managing Janos Ruthaly, a young Hungarian who was in the unfortunate position of being a little too heavy to be

a middleweight and too light to fight on equal terms with heavy-
weights. Houseman, accordingly, created a new division which he
called light heavyweight, for fighters up to 175 pounds. He gave Janos
Ruthaly the name Jack Root and arranged a 10-round fight between
McCoy and Root in Detroit to establish the light heavyweight title.[6]
"McCoy fought well, with some of his old skill," said Alexander
Johnston, "but the steam had departed from his blows." Root was
awarded the decision.

It was perhaps just as well, for had McCoy won the title he would
have had to defend it, and he was "not thinking fights any more."
What he was thinking of, aside from Longfellow and the chance of
collecting from Ralph Thompson, was Indianola Arnold.[7] She was an
actress, younger and prettier than Julia, and more prominent and
promising on the stage than Julia had been. She played in *The Wizard
of Oz* and in Victor Herbert's hit, *It Happened in Nordland.* Neither
McCoy nor Indianola appeared quite so eager for the publicity connected with this affair as did their mutual friends. On several occasions the friends told the newspapers that McCoy and Indianola were
already married, and on one occasion, when they were discovered together in a hotel in Providence, they admitted that such was the case.
But Indianola continued to live in her apartment at 108 West 47th
Street and McCoy continued to live at 160 West 47th, a few doors
away.

McCoy was virtually bankrupt.[8] He still had the Cedar Bluff farm
and a share in the Casino Theatre bar, but he could no longer pay his
bills. He continued to subscribe to his clipping service, even when he
fell behind in his rent, and still carefully read and saved his press
clippings even when they related nothing except failures. At this low
point in his fortunes one of the most curious and inexplicable blows
made him a comical figure on Broadway.

Augustus Thomas[9] (he was referred to familiarly on Broadway
as Gus) had been bemused by McCormick's one-punch knockout of
McCoy. He was further impressed by the fact that Lionel Barrymore,
especially when people tried to stop him from drinking too much by
taking away the bottle, "grew argumentative, and his attitude and
gesture suddenly recalled what many persons had often noticed—a
singular physical and facial resemblance to Kid McCoy, the champion middleweight pugilist."[10] Charles Frohman wanted Thomas to
write a play starring John Drew and Lionel Barrymore. Thomas had
carried around with him for years a clipping about a clergyman who

had to resign his pastorate because of his sense of humor—he could not keep from bursting out laughing during sermons, weddings, baptisms, confirmations, and sometimes even funerals. Since Drew looked like an Episcopalian minister no matter what part he was playing, Thomas wrote *The Pug and the Pastor,* with Barrymore the pug and Drew the preacher. It was renamed *The Other Girl,* and though Drew withdrew from the part, as being beneath his dignity, Lionel Barrymore entered into his role with zest.

Barrymore's study for the part required him to spend hours in McCoy's bar. The hero in *The Other Girl* was Kid Garvey, the middleweight champion, and the plot involved a romance with an heiress whose town house overlooked the gym where the fighter trained, an elopement, an arrest for speeding which prevented the marriage of the Kid and the heiress, the false arrest of the Kid's chorus-girl girl friend for jewel theft, and the Kid's return to her and a happy ending as the heiress returned to her admirer in her own social sphere, and the Kid and the chorus girl made up. The action involved sparring matches between the athletically minded minister and the Kid in the back yard of a gym. "The girls constantly watched them," Thomas wrote. "The pugilist in gym costume was attractive. One of them fell in love with him. That was wrong on Fifth Avenue, but it was prolific in comic story."

Besides Barrymore, the cast included Elsie de Wolfe and her beautiful young sister-in-law, Drina de Wolfe, Richard Bennett, the father of Constance Bennett, and others nearly as distinguished. Drina was chosen to play the girl friend because she and her sister-in-law were at odds, and it amused Charles Frohman to cast them in roles that required them to be on friendly terms, at least on the stage. As the rehearsals went on, Barrymore spent more and more time with Kid McCoy. Up close, they did not resemble each other very much, but at a short distance one could easily be mistaken for the other. Kid McCoy's hair was curly, and Barrymore's was straight, but before the first night and throughout the six-months run of *The Other Girl* Barrymore had his hair curled. He imitated McCoy's walk, gestures, and speech, and did such an expert job of imitation that McCoy himself seemed to be playing the part. To bring the satire closer to home, the girl friend who tries to prevent the romance of the Kid and the heiress was named Estelle, the name of the actress, Estelle Earle, who married Edward Ellis.

Thomas said McCoy didn't mind Barrymore's parodying him on

the stage, and "came often to see his counterfeit presentment." But McCoy could not have greatly enjoyed the satirizing of himself. In *The Other Girl* the Kid is a wise guy. He meets people under his "real" name—Garvey Sheldon—without letting them know he is Kid Garvey, middleweight champion, an advantage in case he has to knock someone down. "My saloon's worth $500 a week," he boasts to his new society acquaintances, "and I can turn ten thousand clear with a 'dub' knockout." He likes the preacher, but, "It was preachers mostly that backed the Horton law here in New York." Defending his social position, he says: "I've come out of the ring in nothing put a pair of shorts and a G string and shook hands with some of the best men in the country." Reading a libelous newspaper story about himself and a short skirt dancer at a pleasure palace, he says: "I ought to kick on that. Myrtle's at *Keith*'s. She hasn't done a turn at the Pleasure Palace in two years. They don't care what they say, these newspaper guys." He admits that his emotional life is a little involved, and in a very clear reference to Kid McCoy's real name, Selby, the fighter in the play says: "My real name *is* Sheldon. That's the name I arrive at a hotel with and the name I put on a contract. The girl that goes with me is *Mrs. Sheldon*."

*The Other Girl* was funny, and Barrymore as Kid McCoy was a great performance, but the Kid in the play, boasting of his fixed fights, was hardly a representation that did McCoy any good. Several theatrical columnists suggested that McCoy himself should play the part, and at one point, in what may have been an in joke in theatrical circles, the story was printed that McCoy was studying the lines and preparing to take over Barrymore's role. If Barrymore could imitate McCoy so perfectly, why couldn't McCoy play himself?

The line about his saloon being worth $500 a week was especially bitter. *The Other Girl* opened in December 1903, and on January 24, 1904, the courts declared McCoy legally bankrupt. People were still saying "That's the real McCoy!" over some memorable event, but nobody could lend the real McCoy himself any money.

The shooting of Stanford White by Harry K. Thaw was the real McCoy. No exaggerated Sunday supplement society scandal there. White was dining with his son at the Madison Square Garden restaurant when Pittsburgh millionaire Thaw, a wilder (and richer) version of Edward Ellis, approached the architect's table drew a revolver, and shot White in the back of the head. Thaw had recently married Evelyn Nesbit who had been White's mistress. (Incidentally, Siegmund Lubin, in another of his movie impersonations, hired actors to reenact the shooting, and promptly produced a film called *The Unwritten Law,* which was falsely exhibited as the real thing, and gave unsuspecting moviegoers the impression that Lubin was there with a camera when Thaw shot White.)

That was one example. The fight of Joe Gans and Battling Nelson in Goldfield, Nevada for a purse of $30,000 and the lightweight title was the real McCoy; it was no fake. This was the first fight promotion of Tex Rickard, a former Alaska honky-tonk operator, an unforgettable fight that ended when Nelson lost by a foul in the 42nd round. "The real McCoy" still meant real fights, or real emotions, but for McCoy himself there were neither.

Debts, though, were real. McCoy tried to meet them by going back to the ring, but he was too late to avoid bankruptcy. Three months after the bankruptcy proceedings, he made a ring appearance of a sort, but it was fantastic. He fought a monstrous balloon-shaped German heavyweight named Herr Plaache in Philadelphia.[11] Plaache was six feet five and weighed 245 pounds (*Ring* magazine said 350). McCoy knocked him out in the second round, and Plaache sailed the next day for Germany, never to return. In May McCoy fought a six-round no-decision bout with Philadelphia Jack O'Brien in Philadelphia that the New York *Times* dismissed as an outrageous fake.

Meanwhile the married life of Edward and Estelle Ellis went smoothly on, in sharp contrast to the emotional and financial disorder of McCoy's affairs. McCoy visited them; he said he felt like an older brother to Ed, and that he admired Estelle. Near the end of August 1904 Ellis promoted a great amateur rowing regatta on Lake George, where his summer home was.[12] Scullers, rowers, and crews came from all over the country to compete and to be entertained at Ellis's summer home. Less than a month later, on Thursday, September 16, 1904, Ellis gave a dinner at the Hotel Belleclaire in New York for the entrants in the regatta. The diners were seated around a centerpiece model of Lake George with mechanically driven diminutive boats moving over its blue waters. Many figures of social prominence, if not very well remembered in sports history, were present; the society columns mentioned John Mulcahy, Sutton Titus, James Pilkington, and William Varny, among others.

The dinner was a success, with much gaiety and considerable

drinking. Ellis, becoming overheated, left the crowd and sat at an open window to cool off. The following day he had a bad cold. He thought little of it and did nothing to treat it, but on Saturday morning he was unable to leave his bed. On Sunday, September 19, 1904, his condition changed suddenly for the worse; only then did he call his physician, Dr. Bingham, who said Ellis had pneumonia. Meanwhile, his wife telegraphed Walker, the Ellis family's friend in Schenectady, who rushed to New York, arriving that night. He got to Ellis's bedside in time to be there with Estelle when Ellis died.

Ellis had not left a will. The various published accounts of the fortune Estelle inherited ranged from $3 million to $5 million and gradually increased to $7 million. She behaved with a discretion that might have indicated fear. Reported prostrate with shock, she kept to her bed for some time and lived in almost complete seclusion.

McCoy was in Los Angeles where on September 27, 1904, he fought Twin Sullivan and won a 20-round decision.[13] When he returned to New York he visited Estelle. At her insistence, on Christmas 1904, he stopped drinking. "She was the most down-hearted woman I ever saw," he said. "She couldn't go near a theatre or anything like that." Some business of an undisclosed nature took McCoy back to Los Angeles. When he returned to New York in the early spring of 1905, Mrs. Ellis got in touch with him, one result of which was her moving out of her West End mansion in mid-April and taking an apartment in the Dunlop Hotel, where McCoy lived.[14]

This move, and their friendship, did not go unnoticed, and McCoy's reputation suffered another hard blow which might have discouraged a less confident woman than Estelle. On the night of April 26, 1905, the police raided McCoy's bar and restaurant in the Casino Theatre building.[15] The Casino had entered another period of prosperity. Jean Schwartz, a tireless young songwriter (he later became famous for *Chinatown, My Chinatown*) had written a brilliant score for a musical comedy, *Paff! Paff! Poof!* The show, starring Fred Mace and Eddie Foy, was beginning its long run. The police raid on McCoy's bar, which was because of a failure to observe the legal closing hours, was as surprising as it was trivial. Nevertheless, on the front page of the *Times* was the story that the police had raided McCoy's place on Broadway. At the same time, the police raided Tom O'Rourke's bar in the Delavan Hotel. *That* was the surprise: both sides of the street were raided—Tammany and anti-Tammany. O'Rourke was arrested and locked up in the "Tenderloin Station," that is, the 47th precinct station, which was later famous as the station involved in the Herman Rosenthal murder case. McCoy escaped arrest, but his manager, George Grant, went to jail. The warrants were issued by magistrate Charles Whitman who later became famous for his crusading work as the district attorney who prosecuted Lieutenant Becker for the murder of Rosenthal, and who still later was governor of New York.

Mrs. Ellis was undeterred by a new wave of bad publicity for McCoy. Immediately after the raid she and McCoy decided to marry as soon as possible. It appeared, though, that that might not be very soon—there was the matter of McCoy's marriage to Indianola Arnold to be considered, as well as his suit for damages against Ralph Thompson. This last was settled out of court, with no cash settlement to McCoy. But the marriage to Indianola was not so quietly disposed of, and while it was being straightened out—eventually by an annulment, since it appeared that there was some question whether they were ever legally married—the world at large, or at least the part of it that followed the Broadway scene, discovered that McCoy was petitioning the courts to release him from Indianola so he would be free to marry Mrs. Ellis.

On May 27, 1905, the news leaked out: she and McCoy were engaged to be married.[16] "I know I'm not getting any angel," she said, "but I'm satisfied." She also said, somewhat mysteriously, that if anyone had any knocks to register against the Kid they should do so at once; after their marriage they would be null and void. "I don't suppose there's any use in knocking him, though," she added. "I've known him for several years." McCoy never called her Estelle; her full name was Lillian Estelle Earle Ellis, and he called her Lillian.

After the newspapers appeared on the morning of May 28, McCoy's telephone began to ring. By breakfasttime he estimated that old friends had asked him for loans totaling a million dollars. After breakfast he and Lillian took a walk through Central Park to escape the attention, then drove to White Plains in one of her automobiles. "She has two," McCoy explained, "one an 80-horse power and the other a 40-horse power machine."

Through the summer the legal proceedings involving McCoy and Indianola Arnold went forward slowly, so slowly that Broadway authorities on the matter decided that McCoy and Mrs. Ellis were not going to be able to marry. When a new performance of *The Other Girl* was announced in August the *Morning Telegraph* reported the speculation that McCoy was to play the fighter and Mrs. Ellis was studying the part of the heiress, and that the report of their engagement was merely a publicity build-up for the play.

In mid-October, however, the marriage of Indianola and McCoy was annulled in Providence, and on the evening of October 19, 1905, McCoy and Lillian were married in a suite at the Algonquin Hotel in New York.[17] The wedding party went to the Hotel Cumberland for dinner, after which McCoy and Lillian escaped the reporters who were following them. McCoy's name was again in headlines. Most of the headlines referred to Lillian's inheritance of $7 million. The *Morning Telegraph* said: "Along Broadway last night that same $7 million formed the chief topic of conversation." Norman Selby had just turned 32.

2

There was something about the title "the real McCoy" that made people want to knock McCoy down, take a poke at him, knock his hat off, or otherwise indicate their disbelief that he personally was the real thing. On one memorable occasion a group of college students spotted him standing at a bar in evening clothes, wearing a top hat and a dress cape.[18] They began loudly debating that he could not possibly be the *real* McCoy. To put it to the test, one of the students took a swing at McCoy. The test was a success. McCoy hit the student once and knocked him out. Some said he also knocked out the others, which was an exaggeration. The charges in the case were dropped. Usually McCoy went to great lengths to avoid trouble. He had an aversion to in any way getting involved with the police, as his name on a police blotter meant more newspaper stories.

He was determined to change his image, to become human again as Norman Selby. "I've taken to reading," he told a *Times* reporter. "I'm very fond of my books now. My Chaucer, Tennyson, Longfellow and Browning are great sources of delight to me. Poetry is fine."

It did not occur to him that these authors were not at the moment the latest thing in literature. Nor did he seem to be aware that the poetry he himself sometimes wrote was not taken seriously by the reporters who persuaded him to quote it to them. His best work candidly showed the influence of Longfellow, and his best lines had a certain endearing simplicity:

> Let dogs delight to growl and fight
> But let men rise above them.

But he was unable to sustain the tone for very long, and wound up his verse abruptly:

> 'Tis better to have a gal for a pal
> Who really knows she loves him.

The new Norman Selby he was trying to project was not a clear-cut personality; McCoy's reading and writing were interesting only as the expressions of a low-brow prizefighter. Yet there were hard interjections of knowingness or of a pride in his hard experiences in the midst of his assertions of his new respectability. McCoy said he was through with the ring, not only with prizefighting, but with the sporting world: "I've seen everything there is to see," he said.

His new image became clearer when shortly after his marriage he emerged as Norman Selby, the president, director, and principal stockholder of a firm of diamond dealers.[19] With H. A. Groen, an established diamond merchant, and Groen's brother, he operated two stores, one at 51 Maiden Lane, the traditional diamond center, and the other at 1503 Broadway near the Metropole, which catered to the theatre crowd. The Broadway store was an innovation; in an area of dingy pawn shops it was a large and handsome establishment modeled after the big Fifth Avenue stores of Tiffany and Cartier. There were really two companies involved in McCoy's jewelry business, for in addition to the retail stores he organized the Norman Selby Company, a corporation capitalized at $10,000 with Ben Marcus and G. R. Simpson, his associates in the business—"retailers and manufacturers of jewelry." What it amounted to was explained by the *Times*: "Selby introduced some innovations in his store which surprised his competitors. One of his ideas which he put into execution was to install in the back part of the (Broadway) store a diamond cutting factory on a small scale."

When the jewelry business was established, McCoy—or Norman Selby, as he now insisted on being called—organized the National

Detective Agency, with Frank Peabody as his partner.[20] Peabody was a husky New York police detective who became notorious for his testimony involving Mrs. Howard Gould in a sensational divorce case when Harold Gould, an heir to the $72 million Jay Gould fortune, divorced his actress wife.[21] Dismissed from the police force, Peabody went into business as a small private investigator. McCoy became his partner in the detective agency (president, Norman Selby) to make it a large business, with a four-room carpeted office in a building on Fifth Avenue, and with 25 operatives in cities throughout the country. The National Detective Agency announced that it would handle all kinds of investigations except divorce cases.

McCoy's third financial venture was an automobile agency that dealt in expensive imported cars.[22] He himself now drove a big, long, red, piratical-looking De Dietrich roadster, in which he was occasionally arrested for speeding. But on at least one occasion his automobile was responsible for a different kind of news story than those in which he usually figured. Shortly after his marriage to Lillian, they were driving near the Harlem River when a car ahead of them struck an iron trolley post, and a woman, later identified as the wife of a police sergeant, was thrown out and suffered a fractured skull. Selby saw the accident, helped the victims and got permission to drive the injured woman to Fordham Hospital. Her two small children were uninjured but frightened, and when Mrs. Selby discovered that preparations were being made to send them home by trolley, she took charge of them, took them home with her, and later drove them to their own home where arrangements were made to care for them there. This was one of the few accounts that did not refer to him as Kid McCoy; he was called merely Mr. Charles Selby.

A much more characteristic incident involved McCoy and his car in 1906; in the news story he was described only as Kid McCoy. He spent the afternoon of November 2nd at the Jamaica race track. After the last race he went roaring down the dirt road between the track and the town of Jamaica when there was a loud explosion under the hood. The car stopped as smoke came pouring out. As McCoy lifted the hood to investigate, there was a second explosion, which did not injure him, but started a fire that spread over the car. He ruined a new overcoat trying to put out the fire. At that point another motorist came along from the race track and stopped to ask what the matter was. "What was the ex-fighter's surprise," said the *Morning Tele-*

*graph,* "to recognize as the owner of the motor Ralph Thompson, who had married McCoy's first wife, Julia Woodruff." Thompson tried to help put out the fire, but the car was totally destroyed.

McCoy soon had another, for he and Estelle were now always on the move—to Hot Springs, New Orleans, the auto races at Ormund, Florida—and their automotive misadventures helped keep newspaper readers aware of their whereabouts. They also began traveling to Europe, usually together, but sometimes separately. For about three years after their wedding they were familiar figures in New York. They were seen together at the theatre or other places of fashionable entertainment, yet were not associated with the night life of the theatre or with the playboys and actresses who accompanied the playboys. They attended first nights, but they also went regularly to lectures and poetry readings. McCoy rode horses a good deal, and was frequently photographed on horseback at resorts such as Hot Springs, though Lillian never was. She kept her yacht, the *Kid McCoy,* moored in the yacht basin at 79th Street a few blocks from their West End Avenue home.[23]

The reasons for their trips abroad were always vague. Lillian had put on weight, for which she visited spas and hot springs. McCoy had various business projects under way that he mentioned without going into detail. Tod Sloan, the famous American jockey whose riding career was dogged with scandals of one kind or another, had settled in England (he was expelled from England as an undesireable alien about the beginning of World War I), and one of McCoy's projects was to form a partnership with him to build up a stable of racehorses in England. But the specific reason, whatever it might happen to be, for any trip was less important than the trip itself in the active and high-spirited life they were leading.

Some signs of disagreement showed up in McCoy's gradual scaling down of his business ventures. Lillian objected to the expense. Part of the diamond business went first, as McCoy sold some of his interest to the Groen brothers late in 1906.[24] The detective agency went next when McCoy decided to let Peabody carry on alone. "I am not a detective," McCoy said, "and I cannot be a detective."

Lillian was adamant that he should not go back into fighting, and he was equally determined to make Norman Selby a respectable businessman. In the summer of 1907, as the depression of that year was beginning, a prominent lawyer named Thomas Fenton Taylor offered his 18-room mansion in an exclusive residential section of South Orange, New Jersey, for sale. McCoy bought it for $42,000.[25] The property placed him in the midst of mansions owned by the Bambergers, owners of a large department store, Edgar Ward, a director of the Prudential Life Insurance Company, and Ira King, the head of the New York Stock Exchange. The reaction of the old residents at the thought of having the real McCoy for a neighbor was little short of horror. Taylor, who had gone to Los Angeles immediately after the sale, expressed astonishment. "Mr. Selby is a quiet, charming fellow," he said, "fit to enter any society. His younger brother has simply captured me. He is a very fine specimen of American manhood."

Personally McCoy was unconcerned about the uproar. Casually he said that his family was a good one and that his Uncle John Hume was related to Lord Hume of England. But Lillian was bitterly offended. She had gone through one period of hostile social scrutiny after her marriage to Edward Ellis; another was too much. In vain it was pointed out to her that other prizefighters had become socially acceptable. George Gully, a British fighter, had married a beautiful wife and was accepted in London society. Rube Goldberg, the cartoonist, picked up McCoy's remark about Lord Hume and prepared a series of sketches showing the fighter dreaming of his aristocratic lineage—in one he was King Selby of Staten Island, in another King Norman the Third, in another William the Conqueror. The sketches accompanied an essay entitled "From the Prize Ring to the Four Hundred." The New York *Evening World* reported that McCoy's fighting blood was up, and he was going to make the Four Hundred accept his wife socially: "His Wife Wants to Get In, and the Kid Says He'll Get Her In," ran the headline across the women's page.

As a more practical measure, McCoy capitalized on the nuisance value of his unpopularity with the New Jersey social world, and upped the price of the mansion for more "acceptable" people who wanted to buy it to keep him from moving in. He sold it in a short time to a man of good social standing named Cyrus Currie for $48,000, having cleared more than $5,000 solely on the strength of Kid McCoy's bad reputation. To assuage Lillian's hurt feelings he drove with her to Mardi Gras in New Orleans, where he was arrested for speeding as he ran through a polling booth in an outlying section, not knowing an election was being held.

Lillian was not greatly cheered. Their ceaseless travels began again, but now they traveled less frequently together. Lillian again went to Europe; McCoy drove via a roundabout route to Detroit, in connection with his automobile business, stopping on the way to hunt rabbits on the old farm in Moscow where he had hunted as a boy.[26] He stopped in Cleveland, where he genially recollected Billy Steffers' one-punch knockout. Treated as a distinguished visitor wherever he stopped, he gave an interview on the beauty of the Ohio River in Toledo—"It is beautiful. The scenery is magnificent"—and evoked wonder because, at the age of 34, with a career of prizefighting behind him, he still seemed young, and there wasn't a mark on his features.

Lillian's unwillingness to put any more money into his ventures led him to plan to fight again. She herself had financial troubles; the $7 million estate seemed to be melting away with each appraisal,[27] eventually being reduced to about $1 million. Various settlements she made—$75,000 on one occasion, $92,500 on another, and an agreement to accept $207,500 on a third—were made on the surrender of long-term rights for the sake of immediate cash. When McCoy signed to fight Peter Maher in the summer of 1908 Lillian was reminded that he had said he would leave the ring forever when they married. "I did not approve of his entering the ring again," she said, "but he was a winner in the ring, and he is a failure in business."[28]

McCoy knocked out Maher in two rounds. It was Maher's last fight. In the fall of 1908 McCoy fought a 10-round no-decision fight with Jim Stewart in New York.[29] *Vanity Fair* delivered a hard judgment on the event: "McCoy was thin to the point of ghostliness and instead of a cold sneer on his face there was a look of the liveliest apprehension. He was so nervous he could not sit still, and he fidgeted about like a novice. But for the ludicrous performance of lusty young Jim Stewart, McCoy would have been a pitiable figure. . . . McCoy said he did not train enough. He is mistaken. He is done as an athlete."

Lillian sailed for Europe again. She had now come to know a number of titled people in Paris and in Berlin. When she returned from a round of spas in the spring of 1909 she was accompanied by Baroness d'Heechereu, a statuesque German aristocrat of imposing dimensions and well-nigh regal bearing, whose lineage occupied a page of the *Almanach de Gotha*.[30] McCoy gave a welcoming dinner for Lillian and her guest at Rectors on the evening of their arrival. Midway through the meal a cable was handed to him. He gave an exclamation of dismay, saying he must leave for England at once; serious trouble had developed over Tod Sloan's purchase of a racing stable for him. The *Cedric* was sailing momentarily, which barely gave him time to pack and catch the ship. Lillian openly expressed her displeasure to reporters.

McCoy was in no hurry to return. Leaving England (nothing was ever heard of his racing stable, apart from that one cable) he went to France where he covered French boxing as a correspondent for the New York *Morning Telegraph*. He wrote breezy letters on such subjects as the McVey-Jenerette fight, which he said was a "classy affair," and the experience of American fighters in France: he advised them not to come over unless they had plenty of money to live on. He confided that he was traveling with the Prince of Monaco (the grandfather of Prince Rainier) who was a boxing enthusiast.[31] McCoy referred to the prince as his "old college chum."

When McCoy got back to New York[32] Ira Willard Hein, a mining engineer, met him in front of the Cafe Madrid and violently assaulted him.[33] McCoy was almost humbly pacific. He tried to hold Hein's arms to keep from being hit again; at last, when he had no alternative, he knocked Hein down and blacked his eye—as the *Times* reported, "McCoy had rather the better of the encounter." When the police arrived McCoy pleaded with them, saying both he and Hein had acted foolishly. "It was merely a childish spat," he said. His plea did no good; both were arrested and charged with disorderly conduct. So the name of Kid McCoy (Norman Selby) was again in the papers.

This time there was more to it. Hein had sued his wife for divorce, naming McCoy as co-respondent.[34] McCoy left New York on an eight-week hunting trip in Canada, though it was not the hunting season, and spent part of the winter in a cabin in the mountains near Posico, where the temperature dropped to 30 below zero. When Lillian started divorce proceedings he did not oppose her. Sometime later a reporter in Asheville, North Carolina noted the marriage of Norman Selby and Edna Valentine Hein.[35] It was McCoy's seventh marriage, three of them to the same woman.

Edna was the daughter of the head of Valentine Brothers, a large importing firm doing business in South America. Her father's property was largely in Honduras, where he lived much of the time. He was reportedly a millionaire, which seemed logical, since he was esteemed in Honduras as a national benefactor for his improvements of the commerce of the nation. Edna was beautiful—as McCoy's wives were invariably described as beautiful. She was dark-haired, with a very pale complexion, and, unlike McCoy's previous wives who tended to be robust, was very slight and somewhat shy—"a very fine little lady," McCoy said of her. In 1902 she married Hein, who had mining properties in Honduras, and bore him a daughter who was around seven years old at the time she married McCoy. Hein settled in New York, where he acted as consul for Honduras and an agent for the Valentine company interests. Edna was gracious and good-humored, if not actually self-effacing, tolerant and more mature than Julia or Indianola or Lillian, although, in Hein's opinion, in her case still waters ran deep, for in his suit for a divorce he enumerated 10 men, in addition to McCoy, with whom she had love affairs, to his great chagrin. It was conceivable that in her McCoy could possibly have found the domestic happiness that the ghost of Norman Selby wanted. Unfortunately, shortly after their marriage, the real McCoy was in jail, charged with jewel theft, and the six years of their marriage—she remained married to him longer than any of his other wives—were characterized by increasingly nightmarish episodes, disconnected and inexplicable, that led to his final tragedy.

# 5. McCoy in Europe

The Normandie Hotel at Broadway and 38th Street was a good hotel by the standards of the neighborhood. It was quiet, somewhat expensive and respectable, compared to nearby hotels. When McCoy opened a bar there, it was taken for granted on Broadway that Edna Hein had put up the money for it. But this may not have been the case, for the license was issued to Elsie Rush, who lived at the hotel.[1] The Normandie was favored by actresses whose rent was believed to be paid by their admirers, men of substance and position, and McCoy was generally popular with women. In his biography of Mack Sennett, *Father Goose,* Gene Fowler described McCoy's place as a smokey basement joint, but it was in fact a good restaurant and bar, not as glamorous as his place at the Casino Theatre, but still of high quality and definitely respectable, in keeping with McCoy's determination to live up to the good image of Norman Selby. What official name it had went unrecorded, though McCoy himself listed his address and occupation there—Norman Selby, president—it was usually referred to as McCoy's rathskeller.

Back of the Great White Way itself—back from the theatres, the Criterion, the Victoria, the Empire, the Casino (still the classical theatre in New York), the hotels, the Astor, the Cadillac, the Normandie, the Maryland, the Buckingham—was the maze of side street joints that made up the Tenderloin. Physically the area consisted of old brick townhouses and brownstones that had been converted to flats and apartments and into whorehouses and gambling parlors. Boxing had been outlawed in New York in 1900 and racetrack gambling in 1908. Therefore the sporting crowd concentrated its activities in the area that extended on both sides of Broadway from below 34th Street to well above Times Square—where isolated islands of respectable residences existed in the midst of illicit enterprises. Corbett lived on 34th Street, just off Broadway. In his playboy days Ed Ellis had a house on 38th Street. Odette Taylor, the actress who broke her engagement to the wealthiest playboy of the time, Howard Gould (heir to $72 million), lived in eminent respectability on West 47th Street in the home of her father, a retired general.

But increasingly the area was given over to dives. About 400 professional gamblers operated there. Some of the establishments, like Richard Canfield's famous gambling house, making a profit of $2 million a year, were well run, handsomely appointed, and expensive. More often, though, the joints were ramshackle affairs—temporary, sleazy, dark, and crooked. They were "raided" by Lieutenant Charles Becker's 47th Street precinct antigambling squad, allowed to remain open if they paid protection; or they were bombed, broken up, or smashed in assaults by hoodlum gangs working for rival gamblers. Most often they were poker houses consisting of a few tables and chairs, like Bridgie Webber's place on 6th Avenue at 42nd Street, two blocks from the Metropole. Sometimes they offered both cards and roulette, like the house Herman Rosenthal ran with Lieutenant Becker as his silent partner, with profits up to $5,000 a night, and which paid protection of about $500 a week.

William Surrey Hart, the future star of Westerns, who grew up in the area, left the best account of what it was like to live in the Tenderloin if one was not a part of its night life.[2] Hart's father was the superintendent (janitor) of an apartment building where the Hart family lived in the basement. Once Hart saw his sister walking home after school with a group of her girl friends, laughing and talking as she passed her own door so they would not know she lived there. "It hurt, it hurt!" Hart wrote.

He used to watch the gamblers who had a second-floor room in a house across the street, where supposedly there was a tailor shop. They would bring in one or two visiting strangers, or a small party of them and, sometimes not bothering to go through the trouble of a crooked game, rob them. As soon as the suckers left, the gamblers took down the sign for the tailor shop, put up other signs for other businesses, rearranged the furnishings, changed the external appearance of the corner, and waited. Invariably their victims returned with the police to point out where they had been robbed, and they could never find it; they knew there was a tailor shop on the corner with a big yellow sign, but nothing of the sort could be found anywhere. They hurried to another corner and then another, until the police dismissed their complaint as imaginary.

Some of the patrons of McCoy's former bar in the Casino Theatre building came to his new place, but after *The Other Girl* and the break up of his marriages to Julia Woodruff and Indianola Arnold he was no longer even a part-time member of the theatrical crowd. Gus Thomas and Lionel Barrymore had effectively put him in his place, and his place, wherever it was, was certainly outside their group. DeWolf Hopper, however, remained a faithful patron, but Hopper, as he related in *Once a Clown, Aways a Clown,* was a faithful patron of many bars. Still he was a valuable ally of McCoy's when McCoy needed friends. William S. Hart, starring in *The Trail of the Lonesome Pine* on Broadway, was likewise a friend and supporter, though Hart did not drink much and preferred the Hoffman House, once the favorite bar of Walt Whitman, where the intellectuals of the theatrical world met. Barney Oldfield was another celebrity often present—too often, in fact, for he began to drink heavily and later, after opening his own saloon in Los Angeles, drank himself into bankruptcy.

The two customers who gave McCoy's bar in the Normandie a claim to historical importance were Mack Sennett and David Wark Griffith. Ejected from theatrical circles, McCoy now took up with movie people. His bar became a center for the film crowd, insofar as such a thing then existed in New York. Griffith in 1908 still listed his occupation as a journalist, though he directed eight films that year. To him, film-making was nothing to be proud of. Griffith was born in Kentucky, the son of a Confederate colonel.[3] His father died in 1885 when he was 10, and the family a few years later moved from their farm near Louisville into the city. There Griffith worked at a number of jobs as a boy. McCoy and Griffith probably did not know each other in Louisville, though they were there at the same time and both worked in a department store.

But Griffith went on the stage and toured with the road companies of Walker Whiteside and Nance O'Neil, both prominent theatrical figures, while McCoy was fighting Pete Jenkins in Minneapolis or being beaten up as Tommy Ryan's sparring partner or traveling through the night to an illegal fight with Jack Welch in an abandoned amusement park on the banks of the Ohio River. When Griffith was not appearing in stock, he worked as a laborer all over the country—in a steel mill, on a West Coast freighter, and in the hop fields of northern California. In 1906 Griffith married Linda Johnson, who had been a member of the company with which he appeared in San Francisco. They lived in New York where Griffith played the lead in *The One Woman,* a play by the Reverend Thomas Dixon who at the time was a controversial figure. His melodrama, *The Clansman,* the Civil War story Griffith later adapted as *The Birth of a Nation,* had recently toured the Southern states, where it aroused intense antagonism among Negroes and white liberals for its version of racial conflict; its progress from city to city caused riots and the threat of riots.

Griffith wrote a play, *A Fool and a Girl,* which opened in Washington early in 1907, with Fanny Ward as its star. It ran for a week there and a week in Baltimore, but closed before it reached New York. He also wrote poetry, in Whitmanesque free verse; one of his poems, "The Wild Duck," appeared in *Leslie's Magazine.* His poetry was diffuse and misty; in it, as in the subtitles of his movies, Griffith strung words together with a wild rapturous intoxication with their sound and with the images they were intended to summon up—ivory, alabaster, lyric moonbeams, and other conventional poetic terms. Griffith's poetry, and the view of life embodied in his films, were derived from Walt Whitman, but a Whitman diluted by softness and vague allusions.

Griffith's debt to Whitman was great. It was embodied in his concept of a harmony of nature, or of a broken allegiance of man to natural law. In *Intolerance,* the spectacle he produced before *Broken Blossoms,* he used the theme of a mother and a child to unite the separate sections of the film that ranged from Babylon to modern times, borrowing from Whitman's "Out of the Cradle Endlessly Rocking."

McCoy's bar was an exceptional hangout for Griffith, who was a reserved, self-contained individual. But Griffith had a reason for being there—he wanted McCoy to give him boxing lessons.

Griffith first approached the movies with a scenario called *La Tosca.* He took it to Edwin Porter, the director of the Edison Company, who turned it down. Porter, however, gave Griffith a part in a film he was making, *Rescued from an Eagle's Nest.* Griffith subsequently sold a number of scripts to the Biograph Company, where he was hired as a director and given a contract at $50 a week. Around

1909, when he directed 25 one-real films, he moved to Los Angeles, the third producer to settle there; but he continued to shuttle back and forth between California and New York. Now separated from his wife, Griffith lived at the Astor. McCoy had a gymnasium on 35th Street, just off Fifth Avenue. Each evening after the day's filming, Griffith and McCoy walked from the bar and put on the gloves. According to Homer Croy, who was Griffith's first biographer, Griffith had seen at close range the strong-arm attacks on the studios in Los Angeles. "He kept up his Indian-club swinging," Croy said, "and to this he added sparring with a boxing partner. He engaged Kid McCoy, and nearly every evening the two went to the gymnasium, and thus Griffith found a new kind of exercise. He was immensely proud of his athletic ability and said that if some ruffian attacked him he would be able to take care of him."

The possibility was by no means remote, in view of conditions in the movie industry. American film history began with fight films, and for the first decade prizefighter movies were the filmmakers' largest source of revenue, much as sports features provided television with some of its biggest money-makers a half-century later.[4] The first hall for viewing motion pictures opened in New York in April 1894, but the popularity of the movies began with the first fight film, shown in August of that year. The fighters, Michael Leonard and Jack Cushing, were lightweights of some standing, though neither would be remembered if they had not been in this first fight movie. The fight was to last 10 rounds, but in the sixth Leonard caught Cushing with a right to the jaw, and that was the end of the picture. In September 1894 Corbett met Peter Courtney, a lumbering heavyweight, in a six-round staged battle in Thomas Edison's studio. The shadowy background, the tense figures at the ringside, Courtney's awkwardness, the poise and stage presence of the champion, and the serious, unadorned, improvised atmosphere over the whole affair made it appear almost a part of some larger story whose opening scenes had been lost; one could catch a glimpse of the appeal Corbett had in the ring, and sense something of the art and intelligence he brought to the world of professional fighting.

There was an odd intensity in those primitive fight films. They were entirely unlike anything in the theatre. Their quality was almost perfectly captured in the great prizefight sequence in Griffith's *Broken Blossoms*. The fight of Kid McCoy and Donald Crisp was, in a sense, a deliberate attempt to recapture the spirit of the first movies, which one saw through a peep-show apparatus, and fuse them with a human drama. Here Griffith was making a sophisticated reenactment of the form in which the movies began.

Griffith was alone in his esthetic appreciation of fight films. Movie-makers produced them because they made money. The third fight film—*Young Griffo and Battling Barnett*—was the first to be projected on a screen rather than viewed through a peep-show apparatus. The fourth (February 22, 1896) was a brief, savage fight between Fitzsimmons and Peter Maher in Mexico, across the Rio Grande from Langtry, Texas, with a purse of $10,000 put up by the Kinetoscope Company. It was a commercial failure because rain obscured the action. The fifth, the fight of Corbett and Fitzsimmons for the heavyweight title in Carson City, Nevada on March 17, 1897, cleared $750,000. "The day was warm and beautiful," said the New York *Herald,* "and just right for the kinetoscope."

Thereafter film rights became the major source of money in fight promotions. The cost cut out small filmmakers. Siegmund Lubin, in his Philadelphia studio, came up with an ingenious answer. He hired actors to impersonate Corbett and Fitzsimmons. They went through the motions of the fight as newspaper accounts reported them, and the staged fight film was copyrighted as an "impersonation," though exhibitors generally advertised it as the real thing. Jeffries' fight with Fitzsimmons for the heavyweight title at Coney Island in June 1899 was the most elaborate movie production attempted up to that time, with arc lights along the ring and overhead. It was dwarfed by the battle of Jeffries and Tom Sharkey in November of that year: 400 lights were used to illuminate the ring. The official opening of the movie (pirated copies were shown earlier) at the New York Theatre on the night of November 21, 1899, was the first full-length movie presentation in a theatre—the full 25 rounds of the fight, with an intermission filled with vaudeville acts.

Innumerable filaments connected the sporting crowd and the film-makers.[5] William Rock, a partner in the pioneering Vitagraph Company, owned a Harlem pool hall which was an uptown center for the sports crowd. Max Aaronson, who became the first star of movie Westerns under the screen name of Bronco Billy Anderson, promoted fights in his spare time. Big Tim Sullivan, the boss of Tammany Hall, whose presence was reported at every major fight, was a partner of

William Fox in building one of Fox's first movie theatres in New York. William S. Hart, after making money in the movies, bought the Western Athletic Club in Los Angeles, a fight arena. Jim Jeffries who, like Mack Sennett, was a former boilermaker, ran a Los Angeles bar that became headquarters for the emerging movie colony. Victor McLaglen was a prizefighter before he became a movie star; he fought a six-round bout with Jack Johnson before Johnson became the heavyweight champion. Leo and Roy McCarey, both later famous directors, were the sons of Tom McCarey, the leading fight promoter of the West Coast.

Adam Kessel and Charles Bauman were two minor figures in the New York sporting crowd. Originally printers, they printed a daily handout of race results and baseball scores which they distributed in barber shops and pool rooms. This brought them into contact with the sporting crowd, and they began making book. There were then 60 professional bookmakers in New York who paid the track $100 a day for the right to make bets at the races. One of Kessel and Bauman's customers, Charles Streimer, owned a small film exchange. He was unable to pay Kessell and Bauman $2,500 in racetrack losses, so they took a half interest in his business to cancel the debt. There were by that time so many film-renting exchanges on 14th Street in New York that it was known as "Film Row." Kessel and Bauman moved to a building next door to Tom Sharkey's saloon. The business became profitable—there were 180 places in New York where films were shown—and Kessel and Bauman soon moved uptown to the Longacre Building in the theatrical district. They were close to McCoy's saloon in the Hotel Normandie, just as they had once been next door to Sharkey's place.

In their new offices Kessel and Bauman made two decisive moves in movie history. They signed Mack Sennett, and in so doing began the corporation that originated movie humor; and they persuaded Charles Chaplin to leave music halls for films. (They failed in their attempt to get Griffith away from Biograph, though they offered him more money.)

Sennett was at McCoy's bar every day. It was there that he met DeWolf Hopper, who got him his first parts on the stage. There also, he got to know Kessel and Bauman whom he owed substantial sums from his losses at the track. (Racetrack betting was illegal, but bets between friends were not prohibited.) Sennett had some film experience. One of Griffith's one-reelers in 1909 was *The Lonely Villa,* written by Mack Sennett and starring Mary Pickford. Sennett got a better bargain than had the unfortunate Charles Streimer. Kessel, Bauman, and their cameraman-manager, Fred Balshofer, organized the Keystone Company with a trial budget of $1,500; as director and leading man, Sennett got $125 a week and one quarter of the profits.

Adam Kessel, born in 1866, was tall, thin, and wiry. A bachelor, he was deliberately inconspicuous, neatly dressed, with a quiet and agreeable manner and a gambler's small, trimmed moustache. He lived in some style at the Hotel Savoy. As his film operations expanded, he bought a house in a quiet residential area of Brooklyn where he lived with his family. His partner, Bauman, was four years younger, short, dark, and heavyset. Bauman had originally been a streetcar conductor and acquired his capital by pocketing fares—or so his enemies said. Both men were shrewd and imaginative pioneers in a mystifying business.

In 1908 the major film companies—Vitgraph, Selig, Essanay, and Kalem—agreed to be licensed and pay royalties for the use of Edison's patents. These companies controlled almost 85 percent of the industry. (Biograph was not involved, at first, since its cameras did not infringe on Edison's patents.) The Motion Picture Patents Company, the name of the company after the merger, took up the entire film output of the Eastman Company, the only manufacturer of film in the United States. Under the agreement Edison received one-half cent a foot for every foot of film ordered from Eastman by anyone, which amounted to about $500,000 a year for the Edison Company. In addition, the trust levied a license fee of $2 a week on each movie projector—estimated at 17,000 machines. Finally, most of the 58 film exchanges were combined into the trust-operated General Film Exchange.

There were gaps in the wall the trust built around film production. Detectives hired by the trust had to look inside a camera to see if the sprockets and film perforations infringed on Edison's patents. Foreign filmmaking equipment, including Pathé cameras, was still legal. When Balshofer was making Westerns in a dance hall in south Brooklyn, a detective appeared and demanded to see the cameras. Balshofer refused to show them; through Kessel's bookmaking friends he secured a bodyguard six feet tall, 225 pounds, who looked like a prizefighter. Balshofer had a gate at the back of a garden behind the dance hall, with a warning bell operated by a lookout. When a detective was spotted Balshofer would pick up the camera and tripod and dash for the gate.

By the time the detective got in, there was no camera for him to investigate. But the detectives sent to investigate Balshofer's cameras knew something was going on. One did not ordinarily find men in cowboy attire drinking beer at mid-morning in a Brooklyn beer garden. The trust company's security force was certain someone was making motion pictures there. They spied on the premises so constantly that the filmmakers left. Each morning Balshofer sent out dummy crews to mislead the detectives, while he sneaked the real crews and cameramen across the 125th Street ferry to Fort Lee, New Jersey. But there too they soon spotted detectives in the underbrush.

The world of the early moviemakers became one of constant flight and pursuit. They were always picking up their cameras, packing up their costumes, and hurrying away with more stuff than they could carry. They hid out in Neversink in the Catskills to avoid the trust company's surveillance. Near where they acted in Western and Indian garb, Theodore Gordon, the pioneer American fly fisherman, was living alone in a cabin, writing his classics on trout fishing for English sporting journals. The filmmakers used the side of a barn for interiors and the Neversink River for outdoor locations. But the weather was often stormy, and they joined the migration of filmmakers to California. They had no sense of wrongdoing or guilt; they were merely trying to get on with their work.

This was the state of the independents in the film industry when Mack Sennett tore himself away from the pleasant company of Kid McCoy's saloon and began producing comedies. The first original invention of the movies was his Keystone Cops, who came right out of the daily conditions of the business. Film comedy emerged in scenes of startled innocents, generally of dubious financial standing, running rapidly down streets, pursued by increasing crowds of bluecoats. The details varied; sometimes the police were in automobiles or in locomotives or handcars, but most of the time they were on foot, coming out of garden shrubbery or surrounding a house in which the unfortunate hero was hiding and around which, as they raced to head off the fugitive, they often bumped into each other. They were easily deceived; it was only necessary for the fugitive to put on a false moustache or pretend to be painting a room or to submerge himself in a tub of water, to evade them. But in their ineptitude they were dangerous, because of their tendency to pinch a maid if the fugitive had disguised himself as one, or to start eating from a barrel of apples if he had hidden in it. They were always unnaturally shocked at what were really very minor transgressions or lawbreaking, listening on the phone with expressions of horror—exaggerated in any case by the limitations of silent films—and racing from the station house by the dozens, piling into cars and falling off in their haste to capture the offender who, most often, did not know he had done anything wrong, or who experienced some general feeling of guilt at being pursued for he knew not what transgression. The comedy chase was not an accidental invention of Mack Sennett and the comedians: it was a slapstick reproduction of the actual conditions under which they worked.

2

While McCoy was teaching Griffith to protect himself against physical assault he was in more serious trouble himself from persistent assaults on the reputation of Kid McCoy. He was totally unable to understand why. There was now a real division in McCoy's life, two separate existences, a public image and a private identity. While McCoy was more than willing to admit to shortcomings in his private life, the image of Kid McCoy remained unchanged in his mind—Kid McCoy was still popular, still young, still the casually expert, unbeaten fighter willing to fight anyone. Even the caricature of himself in *The Other Girl,* acid as it had been, was partially redeemed by the reviews that called the role a picture of an engaging young fighter. As he grew older and his troubles deepened, that was how he came to think of himself.

But McCoy found he needed the help of people far less famous. His bar was considered disorderly, if not disreputable, and such friends as Griffith and Hart were more than customers; they were supporters. Even more disturbing than the reports of wild hilarious evenings at the Normandie bar that occasionally reached the newspapers were rumors that McCoy's bar had become a meeting place, not only for the film crowd, but for jewel smugglers. The private life of Norman Selby, his frequent trips to Europe, the diamond stores he had previously owned, the diamond-cutting factory he had operated, perhaps generated the rumors. He either ignored them or met them by becoming more exaggeratedly the real McCoy, the soft-spoken ex-hobo and well-groomed man about town, on whom the spotlight played and whose doings distracted attention from anything that happened in the shadows.

A curious story, found among McCoy's clippings, from an unidentified newspaper, appears libelous in its insinuation that his bar was a cover for jewel smugglers. The account said that on the night of April 10, 1910, McCoy gave a party for friends newly arrived from Paris. The visitors were unused to American ways, "and had been terrified at passing through customs." They got through all right, but the mood of the dinner was apprehensive until the entree was served. "When that course was safely passed," said the reporter, "the guests gave thanks."

But at that moment the police arrived, arrested McCoy, and took him to the Jefferson Market Court.[6] His arrest had nothing to do with suspected smuggling, at least not on the surface. He was charged with having ignored a summons for keeping his restaurant open after the legal closing hour of one a.m. It was a trivial matter, but it subjected McCoy to the charge of operating a disorderly business.

Shaken and ill at ease, McCoy defended himself in court, but without the fire people expected of him. "I run a respectable place," he said, "and cater to the right sort of people." He seemed far from confident, and the question was asked why he had not demanded to know wherein he had offended the morals of Broadway, or the lack of morals, everywhere evident in far more serious transgressions.

McCoy became almost desperate, as one charge followed another, in his effort to prevent incidents. He kept $1,000 posted for the appearance of his manager, Charles Hall, in court. Since the court convened at nine in the morning, and Hall worked late, there were repeated periods of anxiety after each summons, caused by fear that Hall would not make it in time and the $1,000 would be forfeited. And as McCoy had an accumulation of violations he was increasingly afraid of some trouble in the restaurant that would give the authorities an excuse to close it. One night early in 1911 he threw out two hoodlums, or beat them unmercifully according to one account. McCoy said he didn't know who they were, which was doubtless true. One was Louis Rosenberg, known as Lefty Louis, the son of a respectable family, slight and almost boyish in appearance, but an underworld figure renowned as a knife and gun man. The other was Harry Horowitz, known as Gyp the Blood; Horowitz was an almost illiterate hired assassin and a brutal terrorist.[7] These were two of the four gunmen who the next year killed Herman Rosenthal on Lieutenant Becker's order.

Each time McCoy or his manager appeared in court and paid a fine for keeping the bar open after one a.m. he received another summons on a fresh charge. There were five summonses, one right after the other, until, on April 9, 1911, his license to operate the bar was cancelled because he had permitted the place "to become and remain disorderly."[8]

With his bar closed, McCoy went back to the ring.[9] It appeared to be a suicidal venture—he was now 39—but he wanted to keep the image of Kid McCoy the fighter alive, not for its usefulness in the United States, but in Europe. He calculated, correctly, that the foreign fight crowd might be less aware of the low calibre of the fighters he had fought. He got through a six-round, no-decision fight with a youngster, Jack Fitzgerald, in Philadelphia. In September he met another aspirant, Bob Day, in Toronto, and knocked him out in one round. That same month he scored a one-round knockout of one Kid Ely in New York, followed in October by a four-round knockout of Jim Savage. With four victories in a row behind him he looked good enough to be matched in Paris for a 10-round fight with Hubert Roe in December.

He got away just in time. On November 27, 1911, shortly after he sailed, he was declared bankrupt.[10] Among his many debts was $45 owed a press clipping service. The *Morning Telegraph* commented: "It seems he was deeply engrossed reading about how he went to the wall." So he was, but there was a kind of stock-taking in the process, as though the shadowy figure of Norman Selby now studied the figure of Kid McCoy to see what use might still be made of him.

McCoy could still fight. He was still in good condition, still young-looking except for his receding hair. He won an easy decision over Roe and looked good enough to be matched with an English fighter, P. O. Curran, for a 20-round fight at Nice in February 1912. There was still some lingering magic in the name Kid McCoy. After McCoy forced the fight all the way and won after the full 20 rounds—Curran, who covered up, had expected him to tire—even the London *Times* reported the event as major international sport news.[11]

It so happened that Maurice Maeterlinck, one of the most cele-

brated figures on the Riviera and the 1911 winner of the Nobel Prize
for literature, was a passionate follower of prizefighting. Maeterlinck's princely position in pre-World War I European intellectual
aristocracy was on a scale so great that postwar intellectuals could
scarcely envision it. He had a grand villa in Nice, a chalet in Switzer-
land, a luxurious apartment in Paris, and at the Abbey the St. Wandrille in Normandy he had one of the most sumptuous private estates
in Europe. The estate had formerly been a Benedictine monastery
with living quarters for 300 monks. When the religious orders were
expelled from France the abbey fell vacant and Maeterlinck got it in
1907 on a 99-year lease to prevent it from being sold to a chemical
company making war supplies. There were old ruins on the beautiful
grounds, wide lawns, and miles of river frontage on the Fontenelle,
which was a superb trout stream.

The estate could accommodate 400 guests. The bedrooms were
as big as churches; the ceilings were as high as church ceilings. The
long stone halls led endlessly from one section to another. Maeterlinck roller skated down them to keep warm, sending echoes rever-
berating through the dark chambers. The buildings and grounds of
St. Wandrille were an ideal backdrop for outdoor theatrical presen-
tations of Maeterlinck's work and of others. Sometimes as many as
50 actors and actresses lived at the abbey while they rehearsed a private performance of one of Maeterlinck's poetic dramas. The first
drama to be presented there was Shakespeare's *Macbeth,* done with
a professional cast, for 85 guests headed by Princess Marat.

Maeterlinck was born in Ghent in 1862, the son of a prosperous
Flemish family.[12] He was educated by the Jesuits, but broke with
them, studied law, and was admitted to the bar at the age of 24; he
never won a case, however. He was short, stocky, scarred from football games, a hearty eater and drinker, a physical fitness enthusiast,
and, as a biographer observed, "there were grounds for believing he
was over-sexed." He skated, climbed mountains, canoed, and loved
boxing. When he took up poetry under the influence of his friend, the
French symbolist poet, Villiers de L'Isle-Adam, he poured into writing the tremendous energy he had previously devoted to sports. He
was also greatly influenced by Emerson's essays, and developed an
affirmative, somewhat mystical sense of the unity of all life forms—
a popularizer, in a sense, but one of high quality and independence of
expression. The poems and essays in which he expressed his philos-

ophy made him known, and *The Life of the Bee,* which propounded his conviction that insects, as well as man, possessed intelligence, was ranked in his own time with the world masterpieces of natural history and philosophy. In 1889, when he was 27, his play *Le Princess Moleine* received praise which was outrageously undeserved. The normally skeptical *Le Figaro,* in a front-page article, called it "superior to what is most beautiful in Shakespeare." Maeterlinck's *The Blue Bird,* originally dashed off as a children's Christmas story and then made into a theatrical production, was first presented by Stanislavsky at the Moscow Art Theatre. It ran a year there before moving to London, where Mrs. Patrick Campbell played the leading role of Light, then to Paris, where Sarah Bernhardt was Light, and on to New York, where Light was made to look like the Statue of Liberty.

Maeterlinck had a short, powerful, athletic build and was in fact a good soccer player. He was a tireless hiker and trout fisherman, a follower of bicycle racing, a lover of fast motor cars, and one of the first persons in France to ride a motorcycle. His mistress, Georgette Leblanc, came from a family that owned property all over France, property that was involved in savage family battles over their upkeep. She was an opera star with the Opera Comique. Her brother, Maurice Leblanc, was a novelist, the creator of Arsené Lupin, the French answer to Sherlock Holmes, and the author of many enormously popular mystery stories. Unlike Sherlock Holmes, who was on the side of the law, Arsené was a jewel thief. His triumphs consisted of outwitting the police, though in later volumes he turned around and aided them, not from any moral reformation, but to demonstrate in a fresh field the superiority of his intelligence.

Such was the heady society McCoy now found himself in. In the spring of 1912 the *Morning Telegraph* reported that McCoy was Maeterlinck's constant companion in Nice, and Maeterlinck himself proudly revealed that McCoy was giving him boxing lessons. Early in the summer he moved with Maeterlinck's party to St. Wandrille. It was a great change from his failure in the Normandie Hotel in New York to an honored guest at a showplace in Normandy. As a rule McCoy was not a name-dropper, but he recognized that it helped the image of Kid McCoy to be associating with the most eminent literary man in the world. A photograph widely distributed in the United States showed him boxing with Maeterlinck before one of the abbey's ancient buildings.

It would be more accurate to say that McCoy was a partially honored guest. Georgette did not like him and did not mention him in her writings on her life with Maeterlinck. But then, she did not mention Raymond Bon, a French fighter who was Maeterlinck's regular boxing instructor, or Georges Carpentier, with whom Maeterlinck fought a charity bout in 1912. In the 20 years of Georgette's relationship with Maeterlinck she had progressed from the role of mistress to a kind of general manager, housekeeper, nurse, critic, fixer, and occasional go-between in his love affairs. Maeterlinck was, however, now on a more or less permanent basis with a much younger woman, Renée Dohan, who had attracted him when as a young girl she played the part of Cold-in-the-Head in the original Moscow production of *The Blue Bird*.

Life at the abbey was not altogether easy. Maeterlinck was a gourmet, and meals were intense rituals as he bowed his head over his plate and relished each bite with fine discrimination and visible annoyance at any conversational interruption. He rose early, and walked. Tramping through the fields in his heavy boots he looked like a farmer; when he sprawled in a chair with a glass of beer in his hand and talked, he looked even more like one. He was interested in psychic phenomena, and was something of a hypochondriac.

In his boxing costume, with his short thick body and powerful arms, he looked like Jim Scully, the Woonsocket fighter McCoy had knocked out in New Bedford 15 years earlier. Maeterlinck earnestly pursued his training and boxing lessons. It was possible that he really hoped to defeat Carpentier, a handsome, gallant, and overwhelmingly popular young fighter, in their charity bout. McCoy thought that for a man of 50, Maeterlinck was a fairly good boxer and a good sport.

McCoy learned French, and, in keeping with the requirement that guests at the abbey admire Maeterlinck's writing, he steeped himself in the poet's essays, though the meaning of some parts, dealing with Maeterlinck's belief that intelligence and emotions were not solely human characteristics but were shared by insects and even by plants and flowers, eluded him. McCoy's belief was rather the reverse of this; he did not believe that human beings had intelligence. Still he stuck with it, and even memorized some of Maeterlinck's poems.[13]

Another source of disquiet in St. Wandrille was Georgette's tenseness. The summer of 1912 marked the crisis in her life with Maeterlinck. She was rehearsing the part of Melisandé in Debussy's opera,

*Pelleas and Melisandé,* which was based on Maeterlinck's drama. Many years earlier, Debussy had refused to allow her to sing the leading role, with the result that Maeterlinck sued him, challenged him to a duel, and tried to beat him up, all without success—Debussy would not fight. Now Henry Russell and the Boston Opera Company offered Georgette a chance to sing the role; she could not refuse it, though she was terrified at the thought of a long absence from Maeterlinck if she went to America.

Lately, she felt, Maeterlinck had changed. The poet, as she wrote in her autobiography, *Souvenirs,* "was now surrounded by new faces which gradually replaced those of our familiar friends." She remembered the faces of people she admired who had been guests in the old days—Anatole France, Saint-Saëns, Mallarmé, Maurice Barrès, Rodin. She liked them better than prizefighters.[14] There were still many ballet dancers, avant-garde artists, modern composers, poets, sculptors, critics, scientists, and opera stars visiting at the abbey, but the atmosphere had changed. One of Maeterlinck's many delusions was that everyone liked to box as much as he did. He greeted visiting artists, musicians, and producers with a cordial invitation to put on the gloves and spar a few rounds with him. He had a splendid black eye on one famous occasion when he greeted Albert Wolff, the composer of *L'Oiseau bleu;* Maeterlinck insisted they box before enjoying their visit.

Georgette's foreboding was justified. During her successful appearance in Boston and private recitals at the homes of the Belmonts, Vanderbilts, and other wealthy people in New York, Maeterlinck never wrote. Not long after her return to France, Maeterlinck married the former Cold-in-the-Head; soon Georgette found the girl's parents installed as caretakers of the abbey. She emigrated to the United States, where she became a fairly important literary figure. She became an intimate friend and the lifelong companion of Margaret Anderson, the founder of *The Little Review,* which first published James Joyce's *Ulysses* and which exercised a powerful influence on avant-garde writing. (Margaret Anderson grew up in Columbus, Indiana, not far from Norman Selby's home town.)

The year 1912 was also the high point of Maeterlinck's career. McCoy saw him at the peak of his fame. His reputation as a great poet and philosopher quickly declined, although after World War I Samuel Goldwyn momentarily made him popular with the public when he brought Maeterlinck to Hollywood for the filming of *The Blue Bird*.[15] On that glittering occasion Goldwyn provided Maeterlinck with a private railroad car formerly used by the president of the United States, with two Goldwyn aides, a stenographer, a press agent, a Chinese chef, a Japanese butler, a Negro houseboy, and a quadroon chambermaid. At innumerable small town stops Maeterlinck was pleased to see crowds of young girls gathered to cheer him. He did not know that Goldwyn had also managed to have Maeterlinck made honorary president of the Campfire Girls.

### 3

With the heightened confidence his social lionizing had given him, McCoy brought his wife and stepdaughter to London and prepared to enter British social and sporting circles as he had done in France. His plan was to start an exclusive health club and boxing salon.[16] He set up headquarters in the Hotel Cecil, operating very quietly with no open publicity or promotion.

He had reason to believe that it was good he was out of New York. The murder of Herman Rosenthal in the summer of 1912 was a sensation that not only involved gamblers but half the sporting crowd of New York. Sportswriters, saloon-keepers, and promoters provided almost as many witnesses as did the underworld.[17]

Rosenthal was killed as a result of a fight over the spoils of illegal gambling. The reform administration had gained political control of New York, and Lieutenant Charles Becker of the 47th Street Station had been appointed head of a special antigambling squad. Becker, a friend of Tammany boss Sullivan, was a powerful, heavily built figure who dominated the Tenderloin. He collected large sums from gamblers and others for police protection, banking as much as $60,-000 a year in one of his accounts (with a salary of about $3,000). He forced gamblers to collect the protection money from other gamblers for him, under threat of closing their establishments.

Becker and Rosenthal were co-owners of a gambling hall in the Broadway area. They quarreled when Rosenthal refused to come across with an additional $500 for a defense fund—Becker's press agent, Charles Plitt, had killed a Negro dice player in a raid and was charged with murder. Rosenthal, believing his life was in danger, went to see District Attorney Whitman and to the newspapers.

At 2 a.m. on July 15, 1912, Rosenthal entered the Hotel Metropole bar and sat at his usual table reading a newspaper. The Metropole, at Broadway and 43rd Street, had succeeded Corbett's and McCoy's bars as the meeting place for the sporting crowd. It was open all night. Race results and other sports results were posted in the front of the building, where there was always a crowd of horseplayers and other gamblers. While Rosenthal was reading newspaper accounts of his charges—he was to testify before a grand jury later that day—a touring car stopped at the 43rd Street entrance of the hotel and four young men got out. Besides Lefty Louis and Gyp the Blood they included Frank Cirofici, known as "Dago Frank," and Jacob Seidenschmer, known as "Whitey Lewis." They scattered the spectators, telling them to keep moving, a maneuver that later aided in identifying them. Bridgie Webber, a wealthy gambler and former associate of Rosenthal went into the bar, said hello to Rosenthal, and patted him on the shoulder to identify him. One of the gunmen then approached Rosenthal and ordered him to walk to the door. There the gunman put his hand to his hat as a signal. His companions stuck their revolvers in Rosenthal's face and fired. They returned to their car and drove off without interference.

But the waiters had recognized them, as had passersby on Broadway, and they were quickly caught. The automobile was traced to Jack Rosenzweig, known as Jack Rose, a former fight promoter, partner of Tom O'Rourke, a big-shot gambler and close associate of Lieutenant Becker. Rose, Bridgie Webber, and a number of other gamblers were charged with hiring the gunmen to kill Rosenthal. They turned state's evidence and testified they paid the killers $1,000 on Becker's orders. Their actions were never entirely clear, but their story was confirmed by Sam Schepps, a gambler not directly connected with the murder, a dapper, shrewd, and unscrupulous hanger-on and diamond merchant who lived at the Lafayette Baths and Hotel where Rose and Becker met to work out the murder plot.

Jack Rose, Bridgie Webber, and the other gamblers involved made their contact with the killers through a gangland boss, Frank Zelig, who happened to be in jail at the moment on a gun-possession charge. The gamblers tried to cut expenses by dealing with the gunmen directly, but the gunmen refused to act unless Zelig was first gotten out of jail, which cost the gamblers another thousand. Zelig himself was shot and killed the day before Lieutenant Becker was tried for murder. The four gunmen were convicted and died in the electric chair. A new trial was ordered for Becker. Some of his accusers had vanished. Sam Schepps was now a prosperous jeweler in Vancouver, British Columbia. Adding to the mystery was the strange fate of Big Tim Sullivan, the Tammany boss, former king of the sporting crowd, and the partner of William Fox in his movie theatre building, who tried to fleece Fox of his share of the structure. Convinced that Becker would be freed, Sullivan took no action to help him, and was reported to have suffered a mental collapse. After resting in a sanitarium, he went to Europe to recover. But Becker was found guilty and sentenced to death. Returning to New York, the political boss appeared at the office of his lawyer, who said he was in good physical and mental health. Sullivan left the office and disappeared. Two weeks later his body was found beside the New Haven railroad tracks on the outskirts of the city. A coroner's jury found that he had been struck by a train, though why he should have been wandering along the tracks and why his body should have been rigid and cold, if he had just been struck, were questions that were never answered.

4

McCoy made little progress in interesting British social figures with his project; London in the summer was not the place to locate them. The next international celebrity to figure in his life after Maeterlinck was the Princess of Thurn und Taxis in Ostend in July 1912.[18]

The princess was Lida Eleanor Nicolls, the heiress and niece of Josiah Thompson, a wealthy coke operator of Pittsburgh.[19] She was a bright young American girl when she happened to meet on a train a handsome visiting British Army officer. When their romance began, it looked like the typical episode of the time—the pursuit of an American heiress by a foreign fortune-hunter. But the usual pattern was reversed this time: the British officer was richer than she was. He was Gerald Purcell Fitzgerald (later General Fitzgerald) with large landholdings in Ireland.

After seven years of marriage and two children, she divorced him in 1906, receiving $20,000 a year alimony and a trust fund of $300,-000 for the children. Five years later, in what was the major social event of the year in Uniontown, Pennsylvania, she married Victor

Theodore Lamoral, the Prince of Thurn und Taxis, a small principality in the Austrian empire.

The aristocratic lineage of the princes of the tiny country stemmed from the heroic part played by Count Heinrich Matthias von Thurn in the Thirty Years' War, but its once great financial power was the result of a monopoly on carrying the mail throughout the German empire, which the family enjoyed from 1560 to 1863. When Bismarck took over the mail service he compensated the family with money and enormous estates in Württemberg, Bavaria, Bohemia, and Croatia. The former Mrs. Fitzgerald's husband, Prince Victor, then 35, was not the reigning prince in the sense that, if things so happened, he could become the emperor of Austria. That distinction fell to his cousin, Albert Marie Joseph Maximilian Lamoral, 10 years older, who in 1890 married Margarete, Archduchess of Austria and Princess of Hungary. Still, Lida was a genuine princess, and when she visited Ostend, Belgium with Margarete in the summer after her wedding she wanted to make the occasion one that would be suitable for her rank and that of her husband's cousin.

She took a suite of 20 rooms in the Palace Hotel, overlooking the sea, for her retinue and that of the archduchess. The racing season at Ostend was fashionable, and both women had a good deal of jewelry with them. Princess Lida's jewels were relatively modest, valued at best at $80,000, but Margarete was really loaded with diamonds, reportedly valued at nearly $1 million. The rooms adjoining the two ladies' suite was accupied by a Mr. Arthur Kemp, who said he was a London industrialist, and Mr. Kemp's lady friend, Miss Dolly Bloom, from New York, and two Russian gentlemen named Lavine. There was in London a wealthy American also named Arthur Kemp, whose father owned a large drug company and much real estate, including the Hotel Buckingham in New York. The resulting mistake in Kemp's identification was understandable.

The Arthur Kemp in Ostend was really "Squealer" Kemp, a well-known New York gambler who had found it wise to leave that city and live in England.[20] On July 20, 1912, Squealer, Dolly, and the two Russians were joined in Ostend by Norman Selby who, it was said, had come over from London for the racing. Selby stayed two days. Evidently his luck was bad, for when he left the hotel there was some trouble about his paying by check; Squealer Kemp paid his bill.

Shortly after his departure by steamer on the morning of July 22,

1912, Princess Lida returned from a horseback ride and discovered that her jewelry was gone. Just how the thief, or thieves, gained access to her suite, and what Selby had to do with it (or whether she had met him during his visit) was not recorded. Squealer, Dolly, and the two Russians were arrested, and the theft was attributed to a gang of Russian and English jewel thieves. Assistant Police Commissioner Godefray, a fingerprint expert with the Ostend police, refused to comment beyond saying, "I know who has the jewels. An arrest will be made in a few days."[21]

An arrest was made four days later, on July 26, 1912. McCoy left the Hotel Cecil, where he was living with Edna and his stepdaughter, and was crossing the Strand on his way to his office when Detective-Sergeant Burton of Scotland Yard informed him that he was under arrest. "I was the most surprised man you ever saw," McCoy said. He asked why he was arrested.[22]

"It is in connection with an offense committed in Ostend," Burton replied.

At the Bow Street station McCoy was told he was being held at the request of the Belgian authorities.

"I know absolutely nothing about that offense in Ostend," McCoy said. "I am a man of family and am in business in the city. I know nothing whatever about it."

When he heard that the offense had to do with the theft of jewels from the Princess of Thurn und Taxis, he said, "I didn't even know there was a Princess of Thurn und Taxis!"

Bail was denied, and he was locked up in Buxton Prison. In spite of all the reputed hobo years of Kid McCoy, this was the first time Norman Selby had ever been behind bars. He spent a sleepless night. The following day Edna was permitted to visit him. McCoy, who had not decided what he wanted to do about getting a lawyer, expected her to return during the day after she had consulted the American embassy. But Edna was allowed only one visit a day, and when she did not return he became increasingly anxious. He was afraid she would leave him.

Her appearance on the morning of the third day revived his spirits, and when he spoke of Edna in his later life he always said, "A fine little woman." The American embassy promised to look into his case, but a week passed before it got around to sending a functionary to Buxton to ask McCoy why he was in jail. Meanwhile the Belgian authorities were convinced that the theft was a well-planned operation by a large gang of thieves. Since they did not find the missing jewels after they arrested Squealer Kemp and his associates, they thought McCoy had taken them to England with him. They also reported that he had traveled "with a male accomplice."

Until this point nothing had appeared in the newspapers about the case, but a correspondent of the New York *Times* got word of it and interviewed Edna at the Cecil. The correspondent got things a little wrong. He wrote that McCoy went to Ostend for the racing, and was seen there with Squealer Kemp who was a well-known operator at the track, and that McCoy was suspected because the Palace Hotel refused to cash his check and Kemp had paid McCoy's hotel bill.

"It is all a horrible mistake," Edna said. She was more than ever convinced of her husband's innocence. He was a victim of a conspiracy to shield the real criminals. Then she left for Paris.

McCoy's story was that he went to Ostend because Kemp said he had lined up a fight for him. That was why Kemp paid his hotel bill. When McCoy discovered that no fight had been arranged, he returned to London. About his wife's flight to Paris, he said: "She left to avoid the scandal caused by my arrest."

McCoy exaggerated the extent of the scandal in London. Nothing had been published in the newspapers there. The news that he was in jail in London was certainly sensational when it reached New York; it was headlined on the front pages and temporarily surpassed the murder of Rosenthal. American newspapers displayed a surprising unanimity in disparaging the charge that McCoy was part of a ring of jewel thieves; even the New York *Times,* which was usually critical of McCoy, called the charges bewildering, absurd, ridiculous, and unfounded.

The Paris edition of the New York *Herald* had it that Dolly Bloom told the police McCoy had taken the jewels to London (though it did not mention her by name, calling her "a woman confederate" of Squealer Kemp), and implied that McCoy had traveled, not with a male accomplice, as the Belgian police asserted, but with a girl. That seemed to be the only possible interpretation of the *Herald's* remark that the jewels "were really taken to London by a woman who is a friend of the robbers. So confident are the English and Belgian police that McCoy was the victim of a plot," the *Herald* concluded, "that it is possible the Belgian government will withdraw its charges and ask for his release tomorrow."

But the Belgians did not. Shortly after Edna went to Paris the

THE REAL MCCOY

Princess of Thurn und Taxis reported that many of the missing jewels had been found and her losses amounted to only about $8,000, instead of the $80,000 she had previously claimed. The police, however, believed the main target of the thieves was the million-dollar horde of diamonds of the Archduchess Margarete, which they could have stolen but had overlooked, and the police were not disposed to let anyone connected with the whole affair off lightly. McCoy remained in jail 10 days, then was released on bail of £3,000. He put up two-thirds of the amount himself—$10,000, which in itself indicated a rather sudden affluence—and an unidentified friend put up $5,000. McCoy was brought before Sir Albert de Rutzen, the chief magistrate of the Bow Street Police Centre, who expressed surprise that a warrant for his arrest had been issued in the absence of evidence. McCoy was held, not under charges brought in England, but in response to the request of the Belgian police only. (Subsequently three Frenchmen were arrested in connection with the theft, but it appeared that, as the Princess of Thurn und Taxis got most of her jewelry back, there were no prosecutions in the case.)

McCoy eventually received the help of an eminent solicitor, Sir Charles Russell, and on August 23, 1912, the charges against him were finally dropped. Saying that Sir Charles was going to sue the Belgian government for $250,000 for his false arrest (he did not), McCoy caught the *St. Louis* for New York, leaving Edna and his stepdaughter in Paris. He tried to laugh off the jewel theft charges when reporters met him at the boat in New York, saying that while in prison he had been influenced by Wilde's *The Ballad of Reading Gaol* to write his own poem, which he called *The Ballad of Buxton Jail*. It was not a very good poem, even by the standards of Wilde, with such lines as "Kindness seeds are sown by deeds/Cultured by Love's protection," and it affirmed that nature's arm protected from harm all those who needed protection. The final lines were:

> Let reason's bright light
> Guide desire and appetite
> Should happiness be your goal.
> Don't scatter to the wind
> The thoughts of your mind,
> Those that come from the soul.[23]

McCoy was wrought up emotionally. On September 14, 1912, two weeks after his return to New York, he wrote an eloquent letter to the *Morning Telegraph*. Mrs. Jack Johnson, the white wife of the Negro heavyweight champion, had committed suicide; McCoy's letter was in defense of her and a plea for tolerance and understanding between the races.[24] The dead woman, he wrote, was "another victim of society's fashions and conventions." He concluded that it was each man's duty "to treat his fellow man as a brother, and each woman as you would have your own mother and sister treated." McCoy's letter shocked the staff of the paper. It hardly seemed the statement of the debonair Kid McCoy; it was certainly unlike anything said by Kid Garvey in *The Other Girl* or the usual comment of a man just released from jail on a charge of jewel theft. The *Telegraph* printed the letter with an apologetic disclaimer: "The *Telegraph* can scarcely agree with Kid McCoy, but the comment is printed as one view of a painful incident."

It was, at the time, a very unpopular view. Whatever else it indicated it was obvious that McCoy was not going to be invited into the homes of people who held more conventional views, or, for that matter, into the homes of people who owned a lot of jewelry.

# 6. McCoy and the Movies

How McCoy lived during the three years following the Thurn und Texis scandal is not clear. Socially he was ostracized, and he had no tangible sports connection on which he would depend. Damon Runyon wrote that he fought as "The Masked Marvel," meeting and beating fourth-raters in obscure fight clubs, until the reputation of The Masked Marvel reached the point where no self-respecting fourth-rater would get in the ring with him.[1] The end of that livelihood came at the Manhattan Casino in Harlem when The Masked Marvel got in the ring alone; his victim never showed up.

McCoy may well have been The Masked Marvel, or he may have fought in outlying towns under different names, but he was, if not in hiding, leaving no trail that could be followed. Yet from time to time he emerged briefly, always in circumstances that suggested financial well-being. He reportedly went to Paris to join Edna and her daughter. In 1913 the New York *American* discovered him in southern France, shortly after his 41st birthday, in good health and spirits.[2] Maeterlinck was then at his villa in Nice; according to one published news story, Maeterlinck said that McCoy was "the handsomest human being in the universe." The *American* said McCoy was spending every afternoon with Carpentier.

"I never met McCoy," Carpentier said later.[3] "I never saw him fight. My recollections are indeed very vague, but I seem to recall people saying he was on the decline when he came to France—like most American fighters when they come to France. I was very young. It was about the time I knew Maeterlinck, but I did not know Maeterlinck knew McCoy."

In 1914 McCoy was in Los Angeles, where his family had moved

118

from Indiana. His widowed mother lived on Van Ness Drive; his sister
Jennie was now Mrs. Fred Thomas; Georgia was the wife of Roy
Davis, who became vice-president of the Citizens Trust and Savings
Bank; Mabel was now Mrs. Judd. But it was the movie colony that
attracted McCoy.[4] The period of huge salaries for movie stars was
just beginning, starting with Chaplin, whose salary jumped from $200
a week to $1,000 a week in one year. In their effort to help Chaplin
(who nevertheless soon went to Bronco Billy Anderson and got
$10,000 a week), Kessel and Bauman got his brother Syd Chaplin
out of war-locked Britain and brought him to Los Angeles through
Canada—"a difficult time," Kessel said, "because he was an alien.
Cost us something like a thousand dollars in attorney's fees." As the
rivalry for stars continued, Kessel and Bauman sent one Broadway
actor after another to Los Angeles, paying Weber and Fields $3,500
a week, Raymond Hitchcock $2,000 a week, Eddie Foy $1,200. Even
DeWolf Hopper was hired at $1,500 a week.

Sennett, who had already made a fortune, lived at the Los Angeles
Athletic Club and never missed a fight at Tom McCarey's arena or at
the fight club that Jack Doyle, a former locomotive engineer, opened
in Vernon outside the city limits. They were all fight fans. Chaplin
went to every Tuesday night fight, pondering the fight stances and the
ringside antics that he used to perfection in two of his greatest comedies, *The Champion* and *City Lights*. Charlie Murray, Fatty Arbuckle, Mabel Normand, Slim Somerville, and Bobby Dunn, along
with Sennett, were regulars at the fights at the Western Athletic Club,
held upstairs above the saloon run by Jack Root, who had beaten
McCoy for the light heavyweight title. Al McNeil, the West Coast
bantamweight champion, worked for Sennett, as did Kid Blue, a
former Negro fighter, and Frankie Dolan, a featherweight. Half the
sports staff of the Los Angeles newspapers went into the movies.
Franklin Starr left the *Record*'s sports department to become Sennett's
publicity man; Malcolm St. Clair, the cartoonist of the *Times*' sports
section became a director; Henry Carr, the *Times*' sports editor,
joined Sennett's publicity staff; Leo McCarey left the *Times,* where
he was a sports reporter, to become a director and eventually a director of the Marx Brothers.

McCoy's project was ambitious. He wanted to start a California
health farm comparable to William Muldoon's establishment outside
New York.[5] A former champion wrestler, Muldoon operated an ex-

pensive sanitarium that was more than a drying out place for wealthy alcoholics and a little less than a rigorous training camp for fighters, though many fighters, including McCoy trained there. Muldoon's property adjoined the estate of the theatrical producer Charles Frohman, and was favored by actors as well. But bankers, clergymen, and lawyers, if they had enough money, went to Muldoon's place for rest and recreation. His clients included such people as Grover Cleveland and Secretary of State Elihu Root.

Unfortunately, the movie people did not want to be put in better physical condition; they liked things the way they were, and McCoy's project never got started. (Coincidentally, Lloyd Hamilton, who was Sennett's favorite comedian, soon afterward produced a comedy, *Ham and the Masked Marvel,* in which Ham was supposed to be slipped a brick with which to knock out the unknown fighter, but the brick was accidentally handed to the Masked Marvel instead.) The name Kid McCoy no longer inspired the confidence of backers. Such luster as it may have once possessed was perhaps tarnished in 1915 during a fairly sensational lawsuit that revived the old Ed Ellis-Ralph Thompson-Estelle Earle-Julia McCoy scandal. Julia, now Mrs. George Wheelock, the wife of a bookmaker, wrote children's stories. A suit brought against her husband for legal fees required her testimony about the circumstances of her marriage to Ralph Thompson after she left McCoy and her subsequent divorce from Thompson.[6]

Julia pictured McCoy as a cold and malignant plotter. She was afraid of him when she ran away with Thompson and more afraid afterward, not only for herself but for Thompson. She pictured herself as a crusader who had exposed the corruption of prizefighting, and believed that McCoy planned to ruin her and Thompson by his suit for alienation of affection. Among the worldly men of the ring, Thompson was only "an innocent banker," she said. To save him from such an attack she agreed to let him sue her for divorce—"I did it to protect him."

By 1916 McCoy was living obscurely on 92nd Street in New York, in quarters far less elegant than those he had known since his first success in the ring. For perhaps the first time since 1899, his address was not listed in the city directory. He had always been there one way or another: Selby, Norman, residence 249 West 44th, business, liquor, 1432 Broadway (the Casino Theatre) 1900 to 1904; Selby, Norman, living at 230 West 50th Street; Selby, Norman, jeweler, 1503 Broadway and 51 Maiden Lane; and so on.

McCoy may have lived at the 92nd Street address under another name, a practice he followed in later years. He kept out of sight, only once having trouble with the law—because he wouldn't answer his doorbell. A messenger boy with a telegram rang his bell repeatedly. When McCoy did not answer, he held his thumb on the bell. The tactic finally worked to the extent of proving that McCoy lived there. An angry McCoy opened the door and—so the boy charged in court—punched him in the nose. McCoy denied the charge, but paid a $25 fine and moved out of the apartment.[7] He enlisted in the New York State National Guard on June 27, 1916. As a private in Company K, 71st Infantry, was ordered to duty on the Mexican border during the Mexican revolution.

He knocked two years off his age, beginning a practice which left him hovering around 40 or 41 for the next seven years. Little active training for combat was required of him. The New York National Guard was commanded by Major Gen. John O'Ryan, a fight enthusiast who, when not engaged in hunting Mexican revolutionists, was continually trying to get New York's antiboxing law repealed. McCoy served as O'Ryan's aide (or orderly, in adverse reports) while he gave boxing lessons and staged fights to entertain the troops. The last fight officially credited to him in the Boxing Hall of Fame was with Artie Sheridan in Mission, Texas in the summer of 1916. McCoy won in four rounds.[8]

Army records indicate that he served only until "approximately" September 27, 1916. The New York National Guard became part of the United States Army as the 27th Division, and when the United States entered World War I in the spring of 1917, the draft called up men between the ages of 20 and 30. McCoy aged 44, became a recruiting sergeant. Damon Runyon, who heard him speak to a crowd at a fight in Chicago, said he was a very effective recruiter. The legend of the real McCoy still held some magic. Fervent oratory and emotional patriotic appeals were then customary, but McCoy dispensed with them and spoke in a forthright, down to earth fashion. He talked the language of the men he was appealing to; he shared their distrust of lofty sentiments. The most eloquent appeal he made to their patriotism was that they would probably be drafted anyway.

While he was carrying on this work, plus occasionally working as a boxing instructor at training camps, Edna divorced him.[9] "McCoy is a good fellow," Edna said wearily, "but he's the kind of a man who ought not to be married. He belongs to the public." There were varying reports of this statement. The New York *Times* man heard her say that McCoy was a likeable person, but should not be married to any one woman—"He belongs to the public." Everyone agreed that Edna said "He belongs to the public." It was true in the sense that McCoy had become a kind of public creation, not so much a human being as a composite of ideas and impressions compounded of a newspaper headlines and barroom gossip. He spoke of himself with detachment, almost as though he were discussing a historical person, and met each event in this troubled period of his life with a grave and unusual seriousness, no matter how important or how inconsequential the event.

Edna's suit for divorce was typical. He allowed her to divorce him for adultery, it having been arranged between them that he should be caught in compromising circumstances in a hotel room raid. McCoy offered no defense, but he asked the judge that the girl he was caught with not be called to testify, not, as might be supposed, to protect her reputation, but because the Hotel Seville, where the raid had taken place, was, he said, a respectable hotel and he didn't want to injure its reputation for dignity and decorum.

## 2

McCoy interested Clara Kimball Young who was making a film dealing with a jewel theft, and she assigned him a part in it.[10] Miss Young had been a prominent stage figure. In her movies she became almost a type, with an air of domesticated passion or sophisticated worldliness that was somehow combined with a housewifely common sense. She moved effortlessly from a position of respected actress on Broadway to a better-paid eminence as a vampire on the screen, an odd and disquieting sort of vampire, with a moon-faced expressionless indifference to the raptures of her lovers. But she wanted other roles. She had been interested in prizefighters ever since her girlhood in Goldfield, Nevada, the scene of the 42-round battle of Joe Gans and Battling Nelson for the lightweight championship. Schoolgirls used to go to the training quarters and spy on the fighters as they worked out. Her early starring roles were unconventional, and the casts of her pictures were sometimes also unconventional. In *My Official Wife,* made in 1914, one of the extras was Leon Trotsky, then in exile in New York. Trotsky appeared in the film between his teaching duties at the Labor Temple on 14th Street.

Miss Young's husband was James Young, a director, the former husband of Rida Johnson Young, a clever and unjustly neglected playwright who wrote the book for the Victor Herbert operetta, *Naughty Marietta,* and *The Boys of Company B,* in which John Barrymore starred and in which Mack Sennett got one of his early roles, She was the author of the durable *Brown of Harvard,* which was made often as a movie—the story of admiration of a sickly intellectual for a breezy football hero who is matured by his worshiper's death which he inadvertently caused. Sports and sportsmen figured in the theatrical works of Rida Johnson Young and James Young. She was also the author, with Christy Mathewson, of *The Girl and the Pennant,* one of the first attempts to put baseball on the stage, a funny play about an heiress who inherited a hopelessly inept, last-place major league ball club.

As Young's second wife, Clara Kimball Young was also part of the theatrical and movie world that interacted with sports. It was a sensation in all three spheres when Young in 1917 sued producer Lewis Selznick for half a million dollars, alleging that Selznick had given Clara Kimball Young a lucrative film contract on that condition that she divorce Young. She formed her own producing company in New York (thereby setting a pattern for stars producing their own pictures, soon followed by Mary Pickford, Anita Stewart, Chaplin, and Harold Lloyd). In one of the first of these, *The House of Glass,* she picked Kid McCoy for one of the main supporting roles, though he had no previous stage or screen experience.[11]

McCoy was cast as a detective investigating a jewel robbery. The New York *Herald* dryly observed, "it was a role for which McCoy is said to be singularly adapted." *The House of Glass* was a melodrama by Max Marcin that had a long run on Broadway and in London; it was good, standard, often revived, mystery drama fare. The director was Emile Chautard, a French film pioneer and formerly the leading director of Campagnie Eclaire, a major French movie-producing company. Associated with Chautard was Maurice Tourneur, one of the most brilliant of the silent screen directors and an innovator ranked second only to Griffith.

Tourneur's background was obscure. His real name was Maurice Thomas. According to a movie history published in the 1960s he fled to the United States as a conscientious objector at the outbreak of World War I. This was not suggested by the extensive writing about him during his lifetime. Tourneur was an artist, a student of Rodin, and a workman in the studio of Puvis de Chavannes, the French painter and muralist. He was a large, hearty, athletic individual, with a deep, strong voice. His stage career was brief, involving a foreign tour with Rejane in her declining years. When it ended he worked with Emile Chautard in the Campagnie Eclaire, especially in England, where Eclaire maintained a company turning out Sherlock Holmes mysteries. During his own service with the French Army, Tourneur was sent to North Africa to produce war films and training films, an experience he said he enjoyed because he could direct huge crowds of men without having to pay them wages as extras. Early in 1914 he came to the United States as the producer for the American branch of Campagnie Eclaire. First the duplication of films and later import restrictions made it essential for foreign companies to form their own American subsidiaries. The director Clarence Brown, who got his first experience in films working with Tourneur, said that the films of Emile Chautard and Tourneur, made in the Peerless Studio in Fort Lee, New Jersey, were recognizable by their quality when the directors were still unknown in the United States.

Tourneur was a friend and admirer of Maeterlinck, Gordon Craig, Max Reinhardt, and Stanislavsky. He wanted to bring to the screen the experimental dramas they produced in the theatre. The best known of his 56 American films were *The Doll House, Treasure Island, The Last of the Mohicans, Trilby, Sporting Life,* and above all, *The Blue Bird.* Tourneur was a crusader against the cliches of American film-making that even then were hardening into formulas: the compulsory happy ending; the black-and-white division of heroes and villains; the concentration of stories and settings on glamorized society and romantic backgrounds. Tourneur believed that the true purpose of movies as a great mass entertainment medium was to deal with everyday life and ordinary people—"to diffuse thought and imagination through the opaque substance of today," as Hawthorne phrased it—and to find the value hidden in the routine of the everyday life. "We must learn to find romance and beauty in everyday life, among everyday people," Tourneur said. Another of his messages was: "Think of the relief it would be to show the bad man doing a good turn for once; to allow the hero to slip occasionally."

*The House of Glass* exemplified in many ways Tourneur's theories of movie-making, for Chautard followed them more faithfully than did Tourneur himself. It was an expensive production. Clara Kimball Young paid $25,000 for the movie rights of the play, a very large sum at that time. But she got her money's worth; the starring role might have been written for her.

She played the part of Margaret Case, a stenographer in love with an engaging young chauffeur, James Burke. A good-looking young-ster, Pell Trentor, was well cast as Burke. As Margaret is happily preparing to marry him and leave for the West, he is arrested as a jewel thief, building up to the first climax when he hands over the stolen jewels and Margaret, who had defended him, faints from shock.

McCoy is the detective, unemotional but persistent. Burke testifies that Margaret had nothing to do with the theft, but she is sentenced to prison as an accomplice. Paroled, she has to report every Wednesday night to the parole officer and detective (McCoy). The time comes when, after losing one job after another because she has to report to the authorities when her employers want her to work, she runs away, boarding a train for the West and freedom.

In a Western railroad town she becomes the secretary of a rising young railroad executive who falls in love with her and marries her. Then she meets Burke, released from prison and deeply regretting the way he had involved her. Burke warns her not to return to the city, where McCoy is still searching for her. But her husband is made manager of the railroad and her home thereafter is a luxurious man-sion in the city, where she keeps the shades drawn by day and from which she ventures only at night.

McCoy plays Detective Carroll, a professional cop doing the job he is supposed to do. He had an unsympathetic part in *The House of Glass,* and played it well.

A theft in the railroad executive's office brings him to the execu-tive's home. The thief is young, a first offender. His family makes restitution. The governor of the state—a friend of the family and of the railroad executive—urges compassion. But the magnate is de-termined to prosecute. Detective Carroll has long known that Mar-garet is innocent of the jewel theft. But his job is to find a parole violator, and when he discovers that Margaret is the wife of the rail-road executive, he must make a choice between arresting her and keeping quiet. He arrests her. In a somewhat implausible happy end-ing she tells her story to her husband who believes her and drops the charges against the thief in return for the governor's pardon of his wife.

*The House of Glass* was a thriller, and a good one. The notices

Kid McCoy as Detective Carroll in the movie, *House of Glass,* kneels over the heroine, who has fainted. Courtesy United Press International.

In a scene from the movie *Broken Blossoms* McCoy knocks down his opponent, "Battling Burrows." Film Archives, Museum of Modern Art.

singled out McCoy's good support of Miss Young's fine acting. Tense situation, fine continuity, splendid direction, a good cast, should be a box office winner—so ran the critical comments. One minor objection was raised about a subtitle (this was a silent film.) The actor playing Detective Carroll was identified as Norman Selby. An accompanying note explained that Norman Selby was the real name of the fighter Kid McCoy, an unnecessary comment "that distracts and temporarily hurts the situation," said a trade paper.[12]

It may have been McCoy's acting that inspired David Ward Griffith to give him a part in *Broken Blossoms*. Or Griffith may have remembered the treatment McCoy received on the stage in Lionel Barrymore's portrayal of Kid Garvey in *The Other Girl*. Shortly after *The House of Glass* was released, Griffith got something of the same treatment, less cleverly done, when Lowell Sherman parodied him in a satire on Hollywood called *The Squab Farm*. The play was far less successful than *The Other Girl;* it ran for only a month and is remembered mainly because Tallulah Bankhead had her first stage role in it. Griffith, as the posturing poetic Hollywood director surrounded by aspiring actresses, was not so photographically copied as McCoy had been, but he was nevertheless stung by the satire, which came at a time when he was almost bankrupt. *Intolerance,* which cost millions, was a financial failure in 1917, and *Hearts of the World,* which followed it, was an artistic failure as well.

Griffith wanted to make a film without the huge crowd scenes, huge sets, and huge expense of *Intolerance.* In the fall of 1918 he signed McCoy for a supporting role in *Broken Blossoms.* The film was based on a chapter of Thomas Burke's *Limehouse Nights.* The story revolved around a sadistic prizefighter, "a gorilla of the jungles of East London," according to the subtitle, and his horrible mistreatment of his 12-year-old daughter, played with pathos and delicacy by Lillian Gish.

*Broken Blossoms* was received with a sense of stunned admiration never before given a motion picture. Fifty years after it opened it still seems one of the most remarkable films ever made. The excessive ambition that weakened Griffith's great spectacles was absent from *Broken Blossoms,* and the preaching that had distorted his narrative sense was nearly so. The tight, compact, unrelenting story was so concentrated as to be painfully tense, and the range of Griffith's genius in moving from his enormous panoramas to this direct and simple

story was a revelation of the intensity of his determination to be the
Shakespeare of a new art form. The original story scarcely suggests
the power of the tragedy that Griffith made of it. The Chinatown
section of London, known as the Limehouse, was remote from anything in the normal experience of an American audience, and the
story was deliberately overdrawn. The prizefighter father is too monstrous to be credible; the daughter is too winsome and lovely, even
amid the beatings and the squalor, to be believed. Her Chinese friend
is too sensitive and gentle to be real, and the climax, in which the
child is beaten to death by the father, who in turn is killed by her
Chinese benefactor, is almost too harrowing to be endured.

McCoy had a strange role in *Broken Blossoms*. He was the only
"normal" person in it, the only character with whom the audience
could identify as an ordinary man who has natural, human impulses
in a world of grotesques. A brief introduction evokes a dreamy Orient
with a young Chinese saint, played by Richard Barthelmess (with
rubber bands under his skullcap to make his eyes slanted), setting
out on a mission of peace to the warring Western world. After an
indefinite amount of time he becomes a marionette-like shopkeeper
in London's Chinatown, living on opium dreams. The girl, shuffling
through the streets as though it pained her to walk, hoarding scraps
of tinfoil, enduring the beatings—or, it is suggested, the incestuous
assaults of the fighter—is idolized by the Chinese; he is, a subtitle
gravely informs the audience, the only person who sees her beauty
which is hidden by the drab world.

The prizefight divides the film from its episodic opening sequences
to the convulsive violence of its end. Battling Burrows was overplayed
with horrible grimaces and exaggerated tough-guy swagger by Donald
Crisp. A distinguished English actor and an amateur athlete, he had
taken on another job as a director and could only appear for the
shooting of scenes in *Broken Blossoms* at night and on Sundays.
Battling Burrows, as Crisp saw him, was demented. With what was
for the time explicit sexuality—the handle of his whip as a phallic
symbol, the beatings of his daughter ending as he throws her on the
bed and falls across her—he emerges as a sadist who attacks with
his whip in blind explosions of brutality to work himself up to his
sexual assault. Then with the whip lax in his hand and the girl's body
crumpled before him, he is momentarily dazed and frightened, until
he could swagger out and reassert his position of power with the
shabby crowd of Cockney street figures around him.

One hanger-on discovers the daughter in the room of the Chinese shopkeeper. (A subtitle, violently out of key, and perhaps ordered by a censor, stated primly that the Chinese's love for the girl was pure —"Even his worst enemies admitted that.") The hanger-on, called only The Spying One, tells Battling Burrows on the eve of the fight. Made up to resemble Charlie Chaplin, though not in tramp costume, The Spying One lifts his shoulders, spreads his hands, grins slyly, and moves with characteristic Chaplinesque motions and gestures in a remarkable portrayal of a slum-bred Cockney crook and comedian whose news rouses Battling Burrows to lethal fury.

In the film the fight lasts three rounds. McCoy is merely the opponent, tall, composed, good-natured, and completely at ease as he sits in his corner and watches Crisp glowering from across the ring. There is no elaborate setting. The fight is merely an after-hours entertainment for munitions workers. The crude background and small crowd enabled Griffith to duplicate with fidelity the atmosphere of the first fight films. He did so with a touch of genius: the jerky, interrupted action and the deliberately bad lighting harked back to the first days of the movies, the crude fights of Corbett and Courtney, seen through a peep-show 24 years earlier, or the shuttling figures of Fitzsimmons and Sharkey as they appeared in alternate clarity and shadow moving about the ring under the hot arc lights of the Coney Island Arena. Even the casting of McCoy contributed to the effect. In the picture he is fast and fights expertly, with enough skill to suggest what he might have been like at his best. But his age was evident in his receding hairline. Authenticity was served by Griffith's casting of McCoy for the part. A good young fighter in his prime would not be fighting in such surroundings; an aging one might be.

Even the action seems speeded up, as it often was in the early movies—arms flying, fighters knocked down and rising in an instant. As a fighter, Burrows is a slugger on the model of Sharkey. In the first round McCoy has things his own way, landing one long overhand jab after another, and knocking Burrows down. At the start of the second round Burrows jumps across the ring before the bell and knocks McCoy down as he is getting off the stool in his corner. The foul was very obvious; it is intended to indicate that there was no limit to the moral degradation of a man who would assault his daughter. Such a prizefighter could not be trusted to observe Queensbury rules in the ring. But as was often the case in the early fight films, the subsequent action is blocked by yelling spectators and it is hard to see what is going on. The fighters disappear in the melee. McCoy knocks Burrows down. Burrows knocks McCoy down. The action gathers momentum, the fighters almost whirling around, now in one corner, against the ropes, now trading punches in the middle of the ring, but always moving, jumpily, as though the camera had been slowed down and made them move more rapidly and erratically than people do in real life. The end comes suddenly, as it did in the early fight films, with one clear punch that catapaults McCoy and leaves him lying on the canvas as though he had been shot.

There follows the triumphant swelling of Burrows, the frenzy of the workmen at the ringside, the wrecking of the Chinese's quarters by Burrows and his gang, the dragging of the girl to Burrow's home for the final assault. *Broken Blossoms* opened on Broadway on May 13, 1919. The crowd, largely made up of international celebrities, filed silently from the theatre. The reviews said little about the subject matter of the movie, limiting themselves to dazed superlatives about "this masterpiece of motion pictures," and references to the promise of a new form of art.[13]

3

McCoy at the age of 47—or 41 by his count—had begun a new career. In March 1920 he was signed to appear in an important supporting role with Bebe Daniels, in a movie to be made from another stage favorite, *The Man from Blankley's*. In April 1920 a 19-year-old Chicago dancer named Carmen Browder announced that she and McCoy would soon be married (they did not marry). In May 1920 McCoy was locked up overnight in the 47th Street station, charged with disorderly conduct.[14] He had been celebrating the repeal of the anti-boxing law at the Paradise Room of Reisenweber's, where the Original Dixieland Jazz Band introduced New Orleans jazz to New York. He celebrated so noisily that the manager asked him to leave, which he refused to do.

McCoy was again prosperous; he was single and again at his favorite hotel, the Cumberland, when he was not in Los Angeles. At some point he came to know Albert Moers, an art dealer who dealt in smuggled gems as a sideline and who found his customers in the theatrical and sporting crowd. Moers was in his late thirties in 1920.

He was a member of a family engaged in the metal-importing business, with headquarters at Jones Slip on the New York waterfront. It was possible that McCoy had met Moers much earlier, for one member of the family had lived at the Hotel Ansonia when McCoy lived there, and McCoy's own diamond stores and jewelry business had brought him into contact with many jewelers and their suppliers.

During World War I Moers prospered as a wholesale metal dealer. He had offices on Front Street and on Peck Slip on the waterfront. His stenographer there was Theresa Weinstein, who was born and raised in the Bronx. She was a rather short, dark-haired, buxom girl. Moers had known her since she was 22. In 1919 Moers and Theresa went to Vienna with a substantial sum of money—more than $100,000—with which to buy jewelry that had been taken out of Russia and Germany by refugees. There Moers came in contact with an Arthur Mediansky, subsequently indicted by the United States Customs Service as the head of a large jewel smuggling ring.[15] Mediansky was a former New York jeweler whose store was a few doors down Broadway from McCoy's old bar in the Normandie Hotel.

According to Mediansky, the former metal importer gave him a letter of credit for $100,000 with which to purchase jewelry, and also consulted with him about the value of stones which Moers himself bought. Returning to New York, Moers started an art store, the Ritz Art Company, near the Ritz Carlton Hotel on Fifth Avenue. Testimony indicated that Moers' connection with McCoy, whenever it began, started with McCoy suggesting possible purchasers in theatrical and sports circles, and receiving a commission whenever Moers completed a sale.

More and more potential customers from the theatre were leaving New York for Los Angeles, where McCoy himself located after 1920. Moers and Theresa, after about two years at the Ritz Carlton, moved to Los Angeles also. Moers changed the spelling of his name from Moers to Mors. He opened an "art and antiques" shop on West 7th Street next door to a millinery shop owned by Sam and Anna Schapps. Anna had known Theresa since childhood. Sam's background was a mystery. (At McCoy's trial for murder it was charged that he was none other than Sam Schepps, the witness in the Rosenthal murder trial whose testimony helped send the four killers and Lieutenant Becker to the electric chair and who had changed the spelling of his name from Schepps to Schapps when he left New York for Los Angeles.[16])

However their names were spelled, Mors and Schapps were dangerous acquaintances for McCoy when his fortunes were high (as they were in 1920) and still more dangerous when they declined, as they did soon after. Conversely, the real McCoy, or the real Norman Selby, was an even more dangerous acquaintance for Mors and Schapps. A new career in the movies was an intoxicating experience for a middle-aged fighter; the New York *Times* described McCoy as enjoying "an enormous income, which he spent fast." Success or the prospect of success in the movies put the final touches to the image of the real McCoy that had taken possession of him—a myth, a legend he would do anything to protect, and without which he could not live.

The myth of Kid McCoy was ready-made for Hollywood publicity. He was photographed wearing a trim Douglas Fairbanks moustache for his next role, together with his bride-to-be, a 19-year-old dancer, Dagmar Dahlgren. Pauline Stark, returning from the South Seas (where, as the picture captions revealed, she had been filming the soon-to-be released *Captain Blackbird*) learned that in his nine marriages McCoy had never received a wedding present. Touched, the actress ordered a fine bronze of a gladiator to be made, which she presented to him on the Goldwyn lot, with plenty of photographers there. Unfortunately Miss Dahlgren decided she did not want to marry a man so much older, which stimulated further publicity that was intensified later when she did marry him and additionally stimulated when she divorced him after a year of married life.[17]

Meanwhile McCoy's acting ability, after his genuinely promising beginning under Chautard and Griffith, went through temperamental changes that would have done credit to a ranking star. He was still, after all, only a minor supporting character, but the pictures he was in often loomed in his mind as being dependent for their success on his performances. It was odd that all of his movies except *Broken Blossoms* dealt with jewel thieves. (The Motion Picture Academy credited McCoy with parts in seven films, but since three of these were made while he was in prison, there was evidently another Kid McCoy—an unreal McCoy—working on the sets.)

McCoy was cast for an important part in *The Fourteenth Man,* a Paramount picture starring Bebe Daniels.[18] His part remained important; unfortunately the movie did not. It was originally an adaptation of *The Man from Blankley's,* which had survived many Broadway revivals. One revival, in fact, was staged during the first run of *The Other Girl,* but in the process of being transferred to the screen, much of the comedy and most of the mystery disappeared. The story concerned a Captain Douglas Gordon of the Highland Guards, whose troubles stemmed from his irresistible impulse to come to the aid of the underdog. Intervening in a quarrel between a husband and wife, Captain Gordon high-mindedly knocks out the bounder who was mistreating the wife only to learn that he had knocked out his commanding officer. He flees, pursued everywhere by a mysterious stranger he assumes to be a man from Scotland Yard, but who in fact is a representative of a law office trying to tell him in private that he has inherited a title.

In the United States, in disguise, Captain Gordon meets the vivacious heiress, Margery, played by Bebe Daniels, who "had a peculiar friendship with a prizefighter" (McCoy). To frustrate the prizefighter her family stages a dinner on short notice to announce her engagement to a man she dislikes, not knowing that a gang of thieves headed by a crook Gordon had come to know, planned to blow open the family safe and steal her jewels that same night. In the meantime, Captain Gordon, pretending to be a professional fighter, gets a match with McCoy and wins the admiration of the heiress by knocking him out, only to be forced to run into hiding again by the appearance of the stranger he believed was from Scotland Yard.

Now the butler in the heiress's home discovers there are to be 13 people at the engagement dinner, and hastily calls an employment agency for someone to be another guest. Captain Gordon, seeking employment as a gentleman's gentleman, is sent there—the 14th man. After this, the fine common sense and logic of the drama vanish amid complications too involved to be followed, as the heiress confronts Gordon, whom she had previously known only as the victorious prizefighter, and Gordon, exposed as the man the butler has hired, meets his acquaintance, the jewel thief, his explanations becoming increasingly unconvincing as the safe is blown open and the police and the thieves put on an old-fashioned Mack Sennett chase around the premises while the hero and heroine tried to get things straight. *The Fourteenth Man* was directed by Joseph Henaberry, long an assistant of Griffith. Henaberry also played Abraham Lincoln in *The Birth of a Nation*. He became a well-known director in his own right, but the tangle of gags and mixed identities in *The Fourteenth Man* proved

too much for him. The best *Film Daily* could say of the picture, in its
advice to exhibitors was, "might go over with a low-brow crowd."

Type casting in McCoy's case was carried to ridiculous extremes.
He played only the part of a detective or prizefighter (or both) in
movies about jewel thefts. The next that came along was *The Great
Diamond Mystery,* a weird concoction produced by Fox, starring
Shirley Mason.[19] She was a cute little girl with a boyish figure and
manner, a favorite actress of Tourneur, who starred her in *Treasure
Island.*

*The Great Diamond Mystery* was a sad come down for Shirley
Mason and, for that matter, for McCoy. Shirley played the part of a
writer, the author of a mystery novel called *The Great Diamond
Mystery* who is lustfully coveted by the book publisher, a thoroughly
bad egg named Murdock. Her sweetheart (Buster Collier) works for
another bad egg, a crooked diamond merchant. When the diamond
merchant is murdered, Buster is convicted of the crime and sentenced
to death. One of Shirley's theories is that a murderer always returns
to the scene of his crime; by renting the house where the murder took
place, and setting a trap, she discovers that the real murderer is not
after the jewels, but instead hopes to get her by having her sweetheart
executed for a murder he did not commit.

In only a few months McCoy had made the transition from quality
productions such as *The House of Glass* to lower Grade B in *The
Great Diamond Mystery.* His final movie effort seems not to have been
released, if it was ever produced. It was another jewel theft mystery,
the inside story of the robbery of the gems of the Princess of Thurn
und Taxis 10 years before, called *The International Mistake.*[20] The
only record of it is a note that McCoy persuaded a writer to base a
melodrama on the events of the case and that McCoy played the lead,
some $200,000 being realized by the venture. How much of this went
to McCoy—if he got any—is not known. No film by that title is copyrighted and no report of its cast or director can be located. Like much
else in McCoy's life, it may have been set aside and forgotten. *The
Great Diamond Mystery* was released on October 26, 1924; by that
time McCoy had been arrested for murder. If there was another
jewel robbery film in the works, nobody wanted to know anything
about it.

# 7. The Real Norman Selby

Wednesday morning, August 13, 1924, was warm. A man named William Ross was the only stroller along West 7th Street in Los Angeles near Mors' art and antiques shop. He was the first customer when the store opened for business. It was a prosperous looking establishment with a dignified sign—Mors, Inc. Located west of the downtown center of the city, a block off Wilshire Boulevard, it was in what was then a district of good shops. Four people were in the store when Ross entered: the manager, N. C. Emden; the secretary, Miss Gladys Barberi, whose sister Grace was the secretary of Mors, Inc.; an office worker, Miss Frances Pearlstein; and another employee, Lewis Jones.

Ross looked over the stock which consisted of objects of art and antique jewelery and other valuables of the sort that were used in furnishing the mansions of movie stars. He did not have an opportunity to buy anything, if, indeed, he intended to. Soon after he entered the store, a tall, untidy person with black tousled curly hair came in abruptly, locked the door, and drew a .45 calibre revolver.[1] The man was dressed in a pinstripe blue suit of good quality, which however, was somewhat rumpled. He was haggard, and needed a shave. Apparently he had been up all night. His manner was desperate; when he ordered the men to go to one side of the store and the women to the other, Ross hastened to do as he was told.

Ross must have been one of the least fortunate of shoppers for bargains in antiques, for the next five months—after he got out of the hospital—he was a key witness in the trial of Kid McCoy for the murder of Mrs. Theresa Mors. He became a public figure. What happened in Mors' store and what happened to McCoy during the period before he held it up, became a matter of immensely detailed investiga-

135

gation. The reason was not so much the violent death of Mrs. Mors; it came during a series of movie-colony crimes.

Violence was by no means unknown in the early days of the movies, but the murders and the mysteries were widely spaced.[2] Francis Boggs, the leading director of Selig, was the first; he was shot and killed on the set by a Japanese gardener soon after the first movie company moved to Los Angeles in 1909. Bobby Harron, one of Griffith's early stars, left his Los Angeles home for the New York premiere of *Way Down East*. In what was ruled an accidental death, his pistol fell from the pocket of his dinner jacket and fired. By now murder mysteries in the movie colony were frequent. In 1921 the worst of all its scandals exploded when Virginia Rappe died during a party of motion picture stars in San Francisco, and Fatty Arbuckle, then on a salary of $7,500 a week, was tried for manslaughter. In 1922 William Desmond Taylor, a prominent silent film director, was murdered in a case that became doubly sensational because it involved two celebrated actresses and because Taylor's death revealed that he had been leading a double life for many years. He was originally William Deane-Tanner, born in Ireland, who became an antiques dealer in New York and married one of the original *Floradora* girls. After Taylor disappeared from New York and created his new identity, he prospered in the movies and was living in Alvarado Court near Westlake Park (not far from Mors' store) when he was shot and killed on the night of February 2, 1922. Mabel Normand was brought into the investigation of Taylor's death because she returned a book she had borrowed, a volume of Freud, and was the last person known to have seen him alive. Mary Miles Minter became a figure in the scandal because a packet of her uninhibited love letters to Taylor was found in one of his riding boots.

Another scandal broke on January 1, 1923 when Mabel Normand attended a New Year's Eve party at the home of Edna Purivance, Chaplin's leading lady, and her chauffeur was discovered with a pistol in his hand and Cortland Dines, a young Denver millionaire, lying shot on the floor beside him. Dines recovered, so the sensation in the case was short-lived. That same month Wallace Reid died as a result of narcotic addiction, and in 1924 the director and producer, Thomas Ince, a figure of prominence second to Griffith, died under mysterious circumstances on the yacht of William Randolph Hearst.

McCoy was a minor figure compared to the celebrated people

who were mixed up in Hollywood scandals, but the McCoy murder mystery was nevertheless almost on an equal scale of sensationalism, partly because it came in the midst of so many others, and partly because the image of Kid McCoy was in its own way comparable to the carefully cultivated images of movie stars movie producers had created. There were banner headlines in most metropolitan newspapers, and front-page stories everywhere, such as the restrained account in the New York *Times*:

KID McCOY ARRESTED
IN DEATH OF WOMAN
SHOOTS 3 OTHERS

McCoy was famous, as famous as the most famous stars, but in an unusual way: only his name was famous. The old phrase "the real McCoy" had been revived. Alcoholic beverages became illegal in the United States on January 17, 1920. While there was a period of secret consumption of hoarded supplies of genuine liquor, it soon became necessary to distinguish between a good drink of real whiskey and the various forms of bootleg hooch. Nostalgia returned with Prohibition. Older drinkers with fragrant memories of happier days and better booze were the first to revive the phrase, "the real McCoy."[3] The sight of these ruddy-cheeked oldsters putting down a glass of genuine bonded scotch, saying with resonant satisfaction, "That's the real McCoy!", inspired a younger generation to use the phrase, though only the older generation remembered Kid McCoy the fighter. The phrase still meant anything genuine, but it began to be applied to something genuine in liquor, as opposed to something cut, adulterated, bad-tasting, unsafe, mislabeled, toxic, or otherwise false. The most common phrase was, "It's the real McCoy—just came in from Canada," implying high praise and meaning liquor produced under legal conditions, aged, bottled, bonded, and smuggled, and thus could not only be consumed safely but with pleasure.

Nostalgia was not a sentimentalized idealization of the past; in this respect, the past *was* superior. Nostalgia flourished. So did expatriation. Hemingway and Fitzgerald were glamorous literary figures, not only because of their literary ability, but because their characters ordered pernods and other drinks unavailable to their readers. Bootleg hooch, no matter how it was disguised in whiskey sours, lime rickeys, or gin fizzes or the Jack Rose cocktail (lime juice, grenadine, and applejack) was awful. At its very best it had a medicinal, rancid, or spoiled taste. If one knew only bootleg liquor a drink of genuine whiskey was a revelation. "It's the real McCoy!"

Few of the many people who said this remembered Kid McCoy, the fighter. In the age of the Dempsey-Carpentier fight, or Dempsey-Firpo and Dempsey-Tunney, he belonged to ancient history. His opponents were likewise forgotten. Tom Sharkey had long since been dragged from his saloon when the police closed it down as a disorderly haunt of hoodlums with an illegal back room for women. Sharkey was working as a guard at a race track. Joe Choynski was a boxing instructor in an athletic club in Pittsburgh. Mysterious Billy Smith ran a Turkish bath in Tacoma. Tommy Ryan owned a gymnasium in Syracuse. Corbett lived quietly in Bayside, Long Island, still connected with the theatre—he appeared in an act in the 1923 *Ziegfeld Follies*—and wrote a newspaper column of fight dope (in which he never once picked the winner of a fight).

There were only a few references to McCoy's prizefighter past in the many articles on the death of Mrs. Mors, and they referred to his knockout of Peter Maher (likewise altogether unknown to the younger generation) as his major fight. One student of American speech suggested in a scholarly journal that McCoy might be asked, while in jail, if he was the real McCoy. An element of unreality in the Mors murder stimulated interest in it; the word most frequently used was "bizarre." It was as if a mythical figure, a slang phrase, had suddenly materialized and shot people. McCoy did not help to make his own image more real. He talked in stiff and artificial phrases that suggested something from a movie scenario. He seemed to be acting, not from overpowering emotion, but from a lack of emotion. "I loved her more than I ever loved any woman," he said of Theresa. "When she fired that shot all the lights in the world went out for me."

The police, however, did not believe she fired that shot. They were convinced that McCoy fired it. Twenty detectives were assigned to unearthing McCoy's past and reconstructing his actions up to and including the shooting. As for his past: if he really made $200,000 from *The International Mistake,* the money was quickly spent, for by 1923 he was bankrupt.[4] He worked briefly dealing in motion picture shares, for a warrant was once issued for his arrest on a charge of selling in his own name stock that belonged to a film company, but the charge was dropped. Early in 1924 he worked briefly as a guard for Chauncey C. Julian, an eccentric oil promoter who took $11 million from some 40,000 stockholders—it was the time of the Signal Hill oil boom, with 300 wells in Los Angeles producing a fifth of the world's petroleum. Julian, who later fled to China where he committed suicide, was thus responsible for McCoy's possession of the murder weapon; it had previously belonged to a special police officer, stunt man, and aviator who committed suicide. Apart from his five movie roles, McCoy's record of employment in Hollywood was not impressive.

On February 18, 1924, McCoy was in New York. There, according to Mrs. Schapps, who was with her at the time, he first met Theresa Mors.[5] Mrs. Mors was having both business and emotional difficulties. She had some property of her own, estimated at $125,000, apart from her share of Mors, Inc. and not including a good deal of jewelry. An insurance policy of $80,000 gave her husband as the beneficiary. One of her problems was related to her jewels. Gems known to have been in Europe were appearing in the movie colony with no record of customs duties having been paid on them; while the investigation was still unpublicized, Mrs. Mors was nervous about the stones she owned. The penalty for bringing in undeclared gems was high. Pola Negri was assessed $57,000 for her failure to declare jewels valued at $37,000.

Early in March 1924 Arthur Mediansky, a New York jeweler previously referred to, was indicted by federal authorities. He was charged with heading a ring that for years had successfully smuggled gems from Germany, Austria, and Russia into the United States. Stones valued at more than $250,000 were seized by the government as part of these shipments. Medinansky had been associated with both Albert and Theresa Mors since they bought jewels from refugees in Vienna in 1919. The investigation of the smuggling ring was uncomfortably close to the house of Mors, Inc.

Five persons were named with Mediansky in the indictment: Louis Kraus, the head of the ring's European operation, operating in Vienna; his wife Emma who lived in the United States; and their son and daughter, Fritz and Ada; and a Victor Reich.[6] Kraus died in Europe. Reich, who was arrested in Florida, jumped his $5,000 bail and was in hiding in Vienna. Mrs. Kraus and her son and daughter likewise fled, reportedly to Austria, which left Mediansky to stand trial alone. The name of Mors had not yet been brought into the inquiry, but it seemed almost certain that it would be. Relations between Theresa and her husband were strained at best. Mors was a suave, worldly individual who appeared to be younger than his 42 years; Theresa now seemed older than her 39 years. Mors liked the company of younger people, especially younger women, and he enjoyed a lively social life in the kind of company in which Theresa did not appear to advantage. But in more practical terms, the separation of husband and wife in this case involved the division of stocks of jewelry, some items of which had been smuggled, with the difficult problem of each trying to foist off on the other (while still receiving credit for) the more dangerous pieces.

Anna Schapps was astonished when Theresa became greatly interested in McCoy. She exerted herself to be charming, openly sought his company, flattered him, and behaved like a young girl instead of the middle-aged businesswoman she had become. Mrs. Schapps' displeasure was increased by McCoy's not seeming to understand her own importance in the situation and ignoring her. Because McCoy and Theresa were "frequently seen together," as Mrs. Schapps put it, she felt compelled to tell her friend that she hated to see her throwing herself away on a man like that. The result was the end of her lifelong friendship with Theresa. But it wasn't just a matter of ending a friendship. Theresa was too subtle, or perhaps too interested in gathering information, for that. She arranged a meeting between McCoy and Mrs. Schapps, where, while McCoy sat stony-faced and silent and Mrs. Schapps went white, she told McCoy what Mrs. Schapps had said about him.

McCoy told Mrs. Schapps that she was a "bitch." "If you were a man," he said, "I'd knock you down." They were in an unidentified public place, and Mrs. Schapps, embarrassed, was fearful of a worse scene. She began to talk about other things, trying to act as though nothing had happened. Theresa tried to get McCoy to apologize. After this meeting Theresa's connection with Sam and Ann Schapps was broken, and they became partisans of her former husband when Albert and Theresa were divorced.[7]

Back in Los Angeles with Theresa, McCoy again dropped out of sight, or at least kept away from the places where he was ordinarily seen. In May 1924, using the name of Shields,[8] he rented an apartment at the Nottingham Apartments, six blocks from Mors' store.

There he lived with Theresa as Mrs. Shields until the night of her death.

2

The inquiry about everyone involved in the death of Theresa Mors did not include Sam Schapps. Nothing of his background was reported. He appeared only as the husband of Anna, a friend of Mors, the operator of a millinery shop next door to the store, a man whose only importance was that McCoy inexplicably shot him after McCoy killed Mrs. Mors. Nor was anything heard of Schapps after the trial. McCoy's lawyer tried to prove that his real name was Schepps, not Schapps, but the judge refused to permit evidence on that point.[9]

Conceivably it could have made a difference. Whereas Sam Schapps was unknown, Sam *Schepps* was a well-known underworld figure. He had been a major prosecution witness in the first trial of Lientenant Becker for the murder of Herman Rosenthal. As has been said, there was no question in that case as to the identity of the actual killers of Rosenthal. The four gunmen were plainly identified by customers and waiters at the Hotel Metropole. They had acted so openly that their conduct had embarrassed the underworld. "What was the matter with that bunch?" asked Charles Plitt, Becker's press agent. "From the way they were acting you would think they were setting the stage for a motion picture show." Nor was there a question as to who paid the killers. Jack Rose, Bridgie Webber, and Harry Vallon, having been granted immunity, confessed they had done so. The question in the trial was whether the gamblers had done so on Becker's orders. Their testimony on that point was invalid unless corroborated by witnesses not directly involved in the plot, and it was Sam Schepps who supplied much of the corroboration needed to convict Becker.

This Sam Schepps was 37 at the time of the Becker trial, a short, slender, good-looking, well-dressed man, a friend of actors and a member of the New York sporting crowd, who listed his home as the Lafayette Baths and his business as real estate. In fact, he was an employee of Jack Rose, the principal figure in the plot to kill Becker. He was a gambler, fight promoter, and former operator of houses of prostitution, who had known Sam Schepps since childhood. It was Schepps who bailed Jack Zelig out of the Tombs to make a deal with the gunmen. After Rosenthal's murder Schepps became a center of national attention when it was discovered that he was hiding out in Hot Springs, Arkansas, and the district attorney and police of New York became involved in a wild conflict to extradite him. Schepps testified that on two occasions he had been present when Rose and Becker were arranging for Rosenthal to be murdered.

Much of Schepps' testimony was discredited. He was not called as a witness in Becker's second trial. After prospering as a jeweler in Vancouver, Canada (and after Becker died in the electric chair in 1915), Schepps returned to New York where he ran a jewelry store in the Times Square area. He was known as a fence and as a police informer. During World War I he came under investigation because of his connection with a woman known as Grace Leslie, whose real name was Marie von Schill, who was believed to be an enemy agent. She was charged with trafficking in drugs at U.S. Army posts. On April 2, 1918 Schepps was involved in the murder of Harry Cohen, known as Harry the Yot, considered one of the cleverest jewel thieves in the country. Harry the Yot was shot in the foyer of his apartment house an hour and a half after a meeting in the district attorney's office in which he agreed to cooperate with the district attorney.

Sam Schepps sold his New York jewelry business shortly before Sam Schapps started his millinery business in Los Angeles. In 1926, to move ahead a little, Sam Schepps was reported to be engaged "in the antique furniture business." Wherever he started that, he was presently back in New York operating Maison Cluny, an art and antiques shop on Madison Avenue, while Schapps simultaneously disappeared from the millinery business in Los Angeles. From 1912 to 1932, Schepps was periodically in the crime news in New York.[10]

But to go back to Sam Schapps, the milliner: for a man with no interest in Mors' art and antique shop he appeared to be unusually interested in keeping McCoy out of it. Theresa Mors, believing her former husband was stripping the business of its assets, was alarmed about the property settlement following her divorce, and began to appear there with McCoy. She spoke of him as her protector. On her part, she managed to carry away from the store objects which she felt were rightfully hers. In order to avoid legal complications in the property settlement, she rented safe deposit boxes in McCoy's name, which soon became stuffed with platinum and gold novelties, antique vases, miscellaneous figures and objects of art, and even a tapestry estimated at $20,000, though it was possible that the safe deposit boxes had contained more before the inventory was made. McCoy believed that Mrs. Mors would have possession of the store after the property settlement—after Mors had taken out his share. In anticipation of this, and in order to give himself some status during his visits to the store, McCoy had business cards printed identifying him as Mrs. Mors' associate in the enterprise.

Mors was highly indignant. He said the objects Mrs. Mors had taken belonged to him. He maintained that the jewels alleged to have been smuggled were his former wife's personal property, that in his own case the jewels he had bought with Mediansky in Vienna had been sold in France and Holland and had not been brought into the United States. As McCoy's visits continued, Mors wrote to Roy Davis, identified as a lawyer, asking him to find out how much Mors would have to pay McCoy to get him to leave Theresa alone. (Davis happened to be the name of McCoy's brother-in-law, the husband of his sister, Georgia.) After his offer to buy McCoy off had been rejected, Mors wrote to Davis again. This time, after threatening to kill McCoy if he did not stay out of his affairs. Mors wrote an explanation of Theresa in the highbrow, psychological vein popular in the twenties. She was a dual personality, half-good, half-evil. He had known her for 17 years—since 1907, when she went to work as a stenographer in the family metal-importing business. He admitted that she had been a factor in their business success, but they were often at odds and there was much about her that he did not understand. As a wife, she was sometimes loving and sometimes distant—all in all, "a curious mixture of saint and sinner."

But in the case of McCoy, he had no doubts. McCoy was a "moral leper." Neither letter was effective in preventing Theresa and McCoy from continuing to appear at the store. In mid-July 1924 Theresa was visited by federal officers and questioned for the first time about some smuggled jewels that had come to light in the discovery of the Mediansky ring. After several sessions she was in a highly nervous state. On the night of August 4 she decided to go to Mors' home—her former home—on Ira Circle and have a showdown with her former husband. McCoy went with her. As the New York *Times* discreetly phrased it, "The trouble started when Mrs. Mors, accompanied by McCoy, entered her home and found her husband and another man entertaining two women." She attacked Mors; when he pushed her roughly away, she demanded that McCoy come to her defense and retaliate. McCoy refused. As the husband-and-wife fight developed, he suddenly realized that he was in a very dangerous situation. If he touched Mors, nothing could prevent the action from being interpreted as an assault—*and* as the assault of a trained fighter on a husband with whose wife he was living, plus an assault in front of witnesses who were the husband's friends, in the husband's home, where he was present without an invitation. In the comedy, *The Fourteenth Man* the hero took the part of the wife in a husband-and-wife squabble only to find that he was battling his superior officer. But the situation in Mors' living room was not funny. Overriding everything was the obvious fact that anything Mors might do would automatically be considered self-defense.

Mors called the police who quickly arrived. Mors tried to have Theresa arrested for assault, but the officers refused to intervene in what they interpreted as a fight between a husband and wife. Mors ordered McCoy out of the house, but McCoy refused to leave without Theresa. Mors called on the police to eject McCoy and they did so vigorously, one of them hustling him down the stairs and into the street.

Back in the hideout of the Nottingham Apartments he tried to calm Theresa down and persuade her that his failure to come to her aid did not means a loss of regard. He was, however, keenly aware of the ominous implications in the affair as it now stood. It was not a new experience for McCoy to try to keep from becoming involved in a fight; but at none of those times had his opponent been manhandling the woman with him. It would be news of a sort in Hollywood, and while it was a small matter compared to other items of gossip, it would be another hard blow to the image of the real McCoy.

More than his own debts and a regard for proprieties accounted for McCoy masquerading as Shields and concealing his affair with Theresa. He had always been linked with beautiful and glamorous women, suitable consorts of Kid McCoy. He had been seen with Lillian Russell, Marie Dressler, the Princess of Thurn und Taxis, Maxine Elliott, Clara Kimball Young, Pauline Stark, Anna Q. Nilsson, as well as the dazzling creatures from the casts of the musical comedies in the old days at the Casino Theatre and, for that matter, his many wives. Theresa might be unusual and interesting, or even dangerous, but she did not figure in that company. In his days in the ring McCoy had been known for his willingness to fight anyone, without regard for the opinion of the fight crowd about the ability of his opponent, but now Kid McCoy was an actor in the movies, an occasional escort and companion of stars, a role that carried with it a kind of negative selectivity. Theresa spoiled the image.

She spoiled Mors' image even more effectively. He had barely begun to enjoy the victory in his living room when she filed suit, charging him with misappropriating her share of their joint property, including the theft of $50,000 in securities that belonged to her. The domestic squabble never reached the gossip columns, but Mors in court was news. He was released on bail of $62,000, and a hearing was set for August 16, 1924.

In the meantime, Sam Schapps had made a hurried trip to New York. He returned on Sunday, August 10, more than ever convinced that measures had to be taken immediately to break up the relationship of Theresa and McCoy. His argument, and that of Anna Schapps, was that if Mors and Theresa could sit down together and discuss their differences they could work out an agreement, free of the interference of their lawyers and the trouble-making of interlopers. But the meeting had to take place soon, before Mors appeared in court to answer Theresa's charges. The negotiations took some time. It wasn't until Tuesday morning, August 12, that the couple got together. Schapps' contribution to the discussion was to detail what he had learned of McCoy's past. McCoy's greatest admirer, if one could be found, or McCoy himself, could hardly deny aspects of that past which seemed less than admirable; to Schapps, they looked downright sinister. Anna Schapps pleaded with Theresa on the basis of their long friendship. She said McCoy had always lived on the money of women; he made a career of marrying women for their money, squandering it, and then deceiving them and leaving them. "Tess," she said, "you will be the laughing stock of the country if you marry McCoy."

Or it may have been Schapps who said that; recollections on the point were not precise. Whoever it was, Schapps' testimony was that, as a result of the meeting and the revelation that McCoy was a blackguard, Theresa agreed to stop seeing McCoy. There remained the original purpose of the meeting: an agreement between husband and wife. Among the points of tentative agreement was one that Theresa, in return for not seeing McCoy and dropping her charges against

Mors, would have possession of the store after Mors removed his own possessions from it.

McCoy was not informed about the agreement, if he knew of the meeting at all. Tuesday afternoon he drove Theresa and her lawyer to a meeting with Emden, the store manager. When McCoy tried to enter into the conference he was told that he could not do so because of the agreement Theresa had made with Mors. McCoy was mystified and then, as the door was closed on him, enraged. Anna Schapps, who seemed always to happen by at critical moments in his life, said that he was so angry he struck her, but her account of this meeting became increasingly violent each time she repeated it, and she eventually testified that he spat in her face.

When Theresa came out of the conference McCoy took her for a long drive. They returned to the apartment in the early evening. She was depressed and uncomfortable. She repeated that things were in a terrible shape, and she thought that everything, including the property settlement, was going to fall through. McCoy left her to buy a bottle of scotch and some sandwiches. When he returned, they sat on the sofa in the living room of the apartment, drinking scotch and soda and eating the sandwiches. It was a dreary talk, going over and over the events of the day. What concerned McCoy most was Theresa's agreement that he was to stay away from the store. In the scene in Mors' living room he had found himself almost at the point of being charged with assault, and was down on the police record as having been forcibly ejected from a home where he had no business being. Now he was on record as being excluded by the husband and wife from the business they still jointly operated. He was unable to think clearly—or to think at all. A sense of how things would look began to expand and take over. He was Kid McCoy, a great fighter, a celebrated figure, a Broadway playboy, a spender, a friend of princes and poets, a champion, the creator of a legend of his own life, as other creative spirits wrote novels and plays or directed movies. There was no place in the legend for the grotesque reality of squabbles over pieces of china and old rugs and chairs. His memory became confused between a knowledge of what was happening and what should be happening in accordance with some aloof, more important, standard, in the course of which, the only certainty was that the reality was false.

In a moment of clarity he said, "Suppose I go to New York until this blows over?"

She said, "Would you leave me?"

The scenario took over again, the stagey voice, the clichéd response, the assumption of unfelt emotion. Every image corresponds to an idea, Balzac said, or more exactly, to a sentiment which is a composite of ideas; but the public image was passive, something seen, and incapable of emotional response on its own. No more than a collection of newspaper clippings or a set of publicity stills could an image formulate an answer in the face of an emotional need, or generate anything more than a formula response that echoed the poses that went into its creation.

He said that it would only be for two weeks. By that time everything would be all right.

She said, "I have nothing left." Mors would take her property out of the store. The government was going to take her jewelry. And now he was going to leave her. He remembered her saying, "I am going to end it all." How did she get the cut on her lip? He could not remember. He remembered struggling for a pistol, a .32 calibre, but no, it was a knife he had brought from the kitchen to divide the sandwiches, and he remembered struggling with her until the shot was fired.[11]

3

McCoy said: "I was covered with blood. I just stood there." He covered her with a sheet and wrote his will, leaving all his possessions to his mother. Before he left, he saw a blood-splattered picture of himself on an end table; he placed it on her folded arms.

A neighborhood druggist saw him as he walked away. He said McCoy was sober. When he got her car from the garage the attendant also thought he was sober. About two o'clock in the morning he awakened his sister Jennie at her home and handed her a platinum wristwatch studded with diamonds and fixed with a diamond clasp, a large black pearl ring, a jeweled bird covered with canary yellow and white diamonds, and other jewelry. "I killed her," he said.

She said, "Did you kill him too?"

Later Jennie denied that McCoy said he had killed her. When she was reminded of her statement to the grand jury, she said, "He just said that she was dead and he had nothing more to live for . . . I can't remember what I said."

McCoy next appeared at the Hollywood police station. He said he was too drunk to drive and asked for an officer to drive his car home. He appeared to be drunk, and a patrolman named Young agreed to have an officer drive his car and another follow in a police car to bring him back to the station. The arrangement took time. McCoy asked for the officer who had thrown him out of Mors' house. The officer wasn't on duty. McCoy said, "It's lucky for him he's not here."

At the apartment he started to let the two officers follow him through the door, but at the last moment stopped them. He said, "I'll be in the can tomorrow," and closed the door.

The night wore on. At about 3:45 a.m. Jennie telephoned Roy Davis and told him that McCoy had been to her home. As Davis remembered it, she said: "He said, 'I think I killed the woman.'" Davis decided to wait until later that morning to phone the police.

Shortly after nine in the morning William Ross was in Mors' store when an apparition burst through the door. The transformation of McCoy's appearance was complete: his eyes wide and staring, his black curled hair rose in masses over his high forehead, his lips were set in a firm line of determination. McCoy locked the door, waving the revolver in his hand as he motioned the men to one side of the store and the women to the other. As frightened as Ross was at the sight of the gunman he got the impression that the others were more afraid of him than he was. To add to the impression of unreality, everyone seemed to know everyone else, gunman and victims alike.

There were antique padded chairs in a row on one side of the aisle; the men in the store were ordered by McCoy to sit down on them and take off their shoes, which they did. McCoy told them to stand up and take off their trousers. Later, tabloid stories claimed that the gunman planned an orgy of some sort, but nothing was further from his mind, or that of his victims, than sex: the disrobing was to delay pursuit. Ross took it for granted that the gunman meant to rob the store.

McCoy asked for Mors. He was not in the store. McCoy looked around, but made no attempt to take anything. He ordered the men to empty their pockets; he piled their money on a table. Then he directed Miss Pearlstein to telephone Mors at home and tell him he was needed at the store at once.

Ross's sense of what was happening became confused as time

passed and Mors did not appear. The recollections of others were also uncertain. As Emden remembered it, Sam and Anna Schapps came to the door and were brought inside under the gun.

McCoy said to Schapps, "Do you have any money?"

Schapps replied, "No."

McCoy said, "You shouldn't go through life like that," and gave Schapps the money he had taken from the other men.

Sam and Anna Schapps recalled it differently. They were never inside the store. The San Francisco *Chronicle* reported Emden's account; the Los Angeles *Times* quoted Schapps. It seemed a strange thing to make up, if someone invented it. If the Rosenthal murder seemed unreal to Charles Plitt, if it seemed to be the product of people who had seen too many movies, the sequence of the Mors affair was ahead of its time, a fantasy movie, deliberately irrational.

Only, Mrs. Mors was really dead. The gun was really loaded. The phone rang repeatedly at Mors' house. There was no answer. To William Ross, the Mors store had become filled with too many incomprehensible people for him to feel any sense of security there, and the air was charged with hatreds beyond any recognizable cause in the old carved bureaus and glasswork around them.

Ross managed to get his trousers on. When the gunman opened the door and stepped outside, he ran to the entrance. McCoy turned and fired, hitting Ross in the leg, and he fell to the sidewalk. Anna and Sam Schapps ran into the street. McCoy shot both of them. About 20 people were standing around, motionless, as he walked away holding the revolver, leaving one victim near the doorway and two others lying on the sidewalk.

McCoy got in Theresa's Ford and drove down Alvarado to Westlake Park. There he left the car and hurried into the park. It was later surmised that he wanted to throw something in the shrubbery where it couldn't be found, for he made no attempt to escape. At the far side of the park McCoy saw a police officer, Patrolman Kritzer. He approached Kritzer peacefully and handed over his gun. McCoy was suddenly shambling, bleary-eyed, and mumbling incoherently.

Kritzer thought McCoy said, "It's a good thing Mors didn't show up."

McCoy was not taken immediately to the police station. There was a little Mexican cafe near the park, where Detective Herman Cline questioned him. Yes, he was Kid McCoy. Yes, he had been

living at the Nottingham Apartments under the name of Shields. The
woman known as Mrs. Shields was really Mrs. Theresa Mors. He
knew that she was dead. "I did not shoot her," he said. "She shot
herself."

About nine in the morning the janitor at the Nottingham had
found Mrs. Mors' body. Around 10, Roy Davis notified the police of
McCoy's visit to his sister. When Cline finished his preliminary questioning of McCoy, he and McCoy rode with a police guard to the
station in Mrs. Mors' car. There was not enough room inside for
everyone, so the policeman rode on the running board, after the
fashion of the cops in the old Keystone comedies. On Alvarado the
car became overheated and stalled. It was late in the morning before
McCoy got to the station house, where McCoy was questioned for
several hours by Lieutenant Kreig and Lieutenant Jarvis and then
charged with the murder of Theresa Mors.


4


McCoy's trial began on December 9, 1924 and lasted until
December 31. He was charged with the murder of Theresa Mors,
with assault with a deadly weapon in the shooting of William Ross,
and with assault with intent to murder Anna and Sam Schapps, who
recovered.

A defense fund for Kid McCoy was organized immediately after
the report of his arrest, headed by Tex Rickard, with the names of
Corbett and Jeffries on the list of contributors. But when the confused
background of his involvement with the Morses became public, nothing more was heard of his support by eminent figures of the ring. The
retreat of his supporters was no less than panic-stricken; soon it was
nearly impossible to find anyone who would admit to having known
him well. When Maeterlinck made his triumphal way across the
United States in 1920 he freely discussed with reporters his friendship with McCoy, and the boxing lessons he had taken from the
former welterweight and middleweight champion ("He's a pretty
good boxer," McCoy had said, "and a mighty good sport"); and
William S. Hart a little later told that on one of his personal appearances in New York, when he was engulfed by a crowd of admirers
and nearly smothered, he was rescued by McCoy fighting his way

through the mob with experienced calm. Nothing like this was heard about McCoy after his arrest. As jewel theft and smuggling because somehow related to murder, the absence of McCoy supporters became an open avoidance of him. Even as a fighter his name all but disappeared. He was no longer referred to as a great fighter. The implication remained that he had never been more than a showman. The details of his best fights evaporated from the record, leaving a residue of suspicious battles, such as his fight with Corbett, in which there now appeared to be no question but that he had been guilty of the frame-up all along.

McCoy's defense was insanity. For a few days after his arrest he attempted to play the part of a man who had lost his mind, behaving erratically and talking incoherently when he said anything. He spent one night unwinding some of the springs of his jail bed, and constructed from the wires a piece of sculpture, a kind of mobile, with strips of toilet paper woven among the wires. But he was in full possession of his faculties when he shouted warnings and helped save the life of a prisoner in an adjoining cell who tried to commit suicide by hanging himself. Analysts hired by his lawyers pronounced him insane; state analysts pronounced him sane. A brain specialist, Dr. Cecil Reynolds, reported: "McCoy is now in the stage of incipient paresis, and will be a total paralytic and a madman within three years." Dr. Paul Bowes for the state found McCoy in good physical and mental health, and moreover, intelligent, suave, diplomatic, and cooperative. At a hearing on August 20, 1924, McCoy made a shamefaced attempt to act foolishly, but the hearing was at once adjourned. McCoy was told that his mother had died the night before. He was crushed. His erratic conduct stopped at once, and he never returned to it.

His lawyer was Jerry Giesler, then at the beginning of a career of representing movie celebrities in court. In the early days of Hollywood, Giesler represented Fred Mace, the first Keystone comedian, who persuaded Giesler to form a social club of people in the movies, the first of its kind in the film colony. From that connection Giesler became the one lawyer who was called on when a star got in trouble with the law, a career that led him into court on behalf of Charles Chaplin, Alexander Pantages, and, in later years, Lana Turner, Errol Flynn, Zsa Zsa Gabor, Marilyn Monroe, and many others, including 70 murder cases (not all of them movie people) conducted

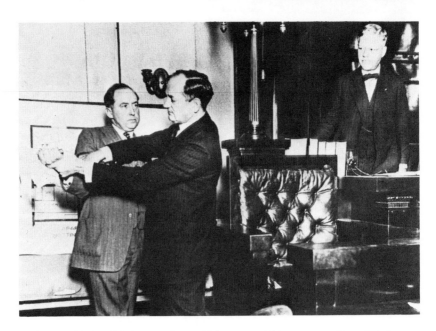

During McCoy's trial for murder in 1914, he and his attorney, Jerry Giesler, re-enact the struggle between McCoy and his girl friend, Mrs. Mors, for a knife. Courtesy United Press International.

A courtroom scene during McCoy's trial. Left to right: (1) Mabel Selby; (2) Albert Mors; (3) McCoy's Sister, Jennie Thomas; (4) McCoy; (5) an assistant of Giesler's; (6) the defense investigator; (7) Giesler; Courtesy United Press International.

so successfully that not one of his clients was executed. Jerry Giesler found the defense of McCoy difficult because, before he arrived on the scene, the fighter "had insisted to the police that he was guilty."

The district attorney was Asa Keyes, who later joined McCoy in prison. (He was found guilty of accepting bribes from the anti-Julian forces in a conflict involving the oil stock promoters of Los Angeles.) The courtroom was crowded with 300 spectators, most of them women, for the opening of the trial. They provided the rival attorneys with an appreciative audience before which, it was said, they had ample opportunities to display their devotion, not only to the great traditions of Anglo-Saxon jurisprudence, but to the great traditions of ham acting as well.

This last was appreciated in Hollywood by connoisseurs of ham acting more exacting and discriminating than anywhere else. Even among the spectators (photographers were permitted in the court-room) the impression persisted that the attorneys were leading figures in the courtroom drama. Among the spectators was the young dancer, Dagmar Dahlgren, one of McCoy's ex-wives, who repeatedly asserted her belief in his innocence and was repeatedly photographed in a pose of youthful concern as she did so.

McCoy was carefully made up as the leading man — well-groomed, composed, and confident. He had the appearance of successful middle-aged businessman. He had always taken good care of himself; now at the age of 51, he looked 10 years younger. Occasionally he smiled at the well-wishes of the spectators or, as the Los Angeles *Times* put it: "he basked in the glances of numerous women admirers, a lot that has been his since the day he first sprang into prominence as a crafty ring fighter."

The jury consisted of nine men and three women. As the defense outlined its case it became evident that what was really on trial was the image of Kid McCoy. What the jury would eventually consider in the jury room was the character of the man behind the myth and whether the many fights, the many marriages, the many fortunes were part of an adventurous and romantic career or whether the death of Mrs. Mors revealed an evil reality that had existed behind the facade from the start. If McCoy had not appeared at Mors' store and shot William Ross and Anna and Sam Schapps he might have been freed if only because of the legend of his life. But his behavior after her death was inexplicable if he was the real McCoy; there had either

McCoy at a prosperous point in his career, c. 1900. *The Ring.*

McCoy being arraigned on the charge of murdering Mrs. Mors, August 1924. Courtesy United Press International.

been a remarkable change in him or the image was false. The defense maintained that the image was a true reflection of McCoy's real character up to the time of Theresa Mors' death, but that after her death he became insane and was out of his mind with his determination to kill Mors, whom he held to be responsible.

The prosecution's case consisted largely of a patient recital by police officers of McCoy's actions, words, and manner, together with Jennie Thomas's account of his arrival at her house with Mrs. Mors' jewelry, and the testimony of Anna and Sam Schapps concerning the background of McCoy's relations with Mr. and Mrs. Mors. Mors himself, reportedly threatened with pneumonia, was not called to appear in court. Little that was not already known was brought out by the testimony of the police, and an alleged confession by McCoy when he was arrested was contradicted by the statement of Lieutenant Jarvis that McCoy, shambling and bleary-eyed, repeated that he had not shot Mrs. Mors. But the police testimony covering McCoy's ejection from Mors' home, his drunken arrival at the station, the shootings at the store, and McCoy's behavior after his arrest built up a vivid picture of a violent and cunning individual at variance in all respects with the public image of McCoy. The most puzzling figure involved was McCoy's sister, Jennie, frail and pallid, who was called to repeat the testimony she had given to the grand jury in August. She denied that McCoy had said that he killed Theresa: "He just said that she was dead and he had no more to live for."

All this detailed courtroom testimony lacked excitement. The case was also overshadowed by the greater sensation of the murder in Chicago of Bobby Franks by Leopold and Loeb. The audience was restless, and the crowds dwindled. The witnesses were not glamorous. Sam Schapps took the stand to assert his belief that he and his wife were the ones McCoy had planned to murder all along. He said, "I never saw him before in my life until he shot me!" as though he felt the shooting would have been entirely understandable if they had previously met face to face. By some mysterious reversal of the chemical processes involved in publicity build-ups, everything that had gone into the making of the legend of Kid McCoy seemed now to be operating to destroy that legend, even the tedium of the words of the people associated with the tragedy. The death of Ed Ellis and McCoy's marriage to his widow took on a new light in the face of evidence that McCoy threatened to kill Mors and planned to marry

Mors' former wife; the arrest for the theft of the jewels of the Princess of Thurn und Taxis seemed different now that McCoy had given to Jennie the jewels of the dead Mrs. Mors; McCoy's many trips abroad, his interest in gems and jewelry stores, his practice of carrying large amounts of cash in his earlier days was another matter now that Mors and Mrs. Mors were known to be mixed up with a smuggling ring; even the confusion of identities involved in the ring name of Kid McCoy and his real name Norman Selby seemed different after his masquerading under the name of Shields and presenting Mrs. Mors as Mrs. Shields. The composite of public ideas and impressions that had gone into the image of the real McCoy was subject to an abrasive reality that destroyed what had been romantic and picturesque in it before, bringing it down to the shocking level of everyday life. The legend vanished; the wounded figures on the sidewalk were unforgettable.

The individual most affected was McCoy. He listened with pained attention to the destruction of his biography. He seemed older. Sometimes, when his head sagged, the jury saw an aging, beaten man, a gleaming skull showing above his clipped black curly fringe of hair. He revived when Mrs. Schapps took the stand, and at the start of her testimony was again composed, dignified, and confident, with an air that suggested someone cast as a prosperous banker or lawyer in the movies. She was the most damaging witness against him. Voluble and vituperative, she recollected in detail her efforts to warn Mrs. Mors against him, as well as the brutality of his attacks on her for doing so. She called him a love pirate, a deceiver, a predator who stalked vulnerable and emotionally disturbed women like Theresa, a bully who struck her and spat in her face when she interfered, and who struck Theresa, who was afraid of him, when she tried to free herself of his dominance. Her testimony was deadly, and at one point McCoy bowed his head, tears running down his pasty cheeks.

The defense introduced a miscellaneous scattering of evidence intended to create reasonable doubt: the inability to locate Grace Barberi, the secretary of Mors, Inc.; the possibility that Schapps was Schepps; the testimony of Mrs. Mors' attorney on the value of her property—estimated as at least $110,000—that passed to her husband; a number of unidentified persons seen skulking around the Nottingham Apartments in the period before the death of Mrs. Mors; a neighbor who had seen Mors, or someone resembling him, run from the building after the shooting. But in the end the defense rested on McCoy himself. The courtroom was again filled when he took the stand on December 20.[12] His story was a compound of domestic touches and lofty sentiment. He seemed to be engrossed in each stage of the hypnotized progress of the night toward disaster. "She said her feet hurt," he said, "and I suggested we both go to the davenport, and I would take her shoes off, which I did."

But his attentions cheered her only briefly. "I went out again and made a scotch and soda which we drank out of a silver loving cup. Both of us drank from the same cup." He brought from the kitchen a knife to cut the sandwiches. "She was sitting there on the davenport, toying with the knife in her right hand. . . . We conversed. We discussed the occurrences of the day, Mors' actions, and the government threatening to seize her jewels. She was very depressed.

"I said, 'Tess, suppose I go to New York until things blow over?' Because of her agreement that I was to stay out of Mors' antiques shop, which was coming to her, until Mors got his things out."

"Tess said, 'Norman, would you leave me?' and I saw a tear run down her cheek. I explained that I would be back in two weeks, but suddenly she said, 'I'm going to end it all.' "

He was asked to step down to the aisle between the jury box and the witness stand to demonstrate the struggle for the knife. He was breathing heavily as he went through the motions. "I seized her right wrist and with all my force wrestled to save her. In the struggle she stood up, the knife blade bent, and as I was able with my two hands to force it back from her bosom, the knife was gradually raised. Her left hand went forward, back of my shoulder, and she made another lunge, which brought the knife to her lip, which it cut.

"That was when she screamed," he said. "Just one wild scream."

His voice was so tense that a woman juror audibly gasped. "By that time I had her forearm twisted around, but Theresa was strong, and I was at the limit of my strength to hold her with my two hands. Just as I got her forearm twisted around and was prying the knife from her loosening fingers I looked around to where her left arm was free behind my right shoulder and saw she had my little gun directed toward our heads. I left the knife and grabbed her left hand, but I was too late, and the gun went off. I just stood there. I was covered with blood. My eyes cleared and I didn't know at first if I was shot or Theresa. But I felt her body relax; I knew it was all over."

He wiped the blood from her face with a towel. That was all; his face was pale and he seemed exhausted. Until this point his account was clear and detailed, as exact in its own way as were his descriptions of precisely what happened in some disputed round of one of his fights. But now the scenario took over, a muddled account of sorrow for the death of a loved one, straight out of a thousand movies. He walked slowly back to the witness stand and slid into it. "I kissed her," he said. "I poured a drink of scotch into a glass but half of it spilled all over before I could get it to my lips."

"What did you do after that?" Giesler asked.

"I kissed her again and begged her to speak to me and I decided to kill myself. So I got my other revolver, the big .45 and I thought it would look better if I put her in bed. I tried to carry her but I couldn't lift her. I just got her off the couch and laid her on the floor. Then I saw a picture of me that she had liked and I folded it on her breast and cocked the gun and lay down on the floor beside her to kill myself. Why I didn't I don't know."

The jury deliberated for 78 hours. That length of time set a record in California for deliberation in a murder trial. As the days passed one rumor after another came from the jury room—that the jurors were 7 to 5 in favor of acquittal; that two women were determined that McCoy be found guilty; that one woman alone demanded a complete acquittal for McCoy; that the deadlock came after a 10 to 2 ballot on some unspecified verdict. The delay and the rumors generated a good deal of sardonic comment. In fact, the jury revealed a seriousness of purpose and a concern for the central issue of the trial. In a confused but nevertheless genuine fashion, the jurors were trying to distinguish between the legend of McCoy and the human being whose fate they were deciding. After the trial it was disclosed that they spent most of the 78 hours arguing about the reality of McCoy's past—"McCoy's so-called romantic aura," as one newspaper disparaged it—because it was related to the question of whether or not he was the kind of person who acted as the prosecution said he did. His nine marriages, his love affairs, background, and publicity, hinged on the question of whether the death of Mrs. Mors had merely brought to the surface something that had always been present in his life but had heretofore been hidden. In its own way the jury tried to get at the question of what formed that composite of impressions that went into one's opinion of a human being, his image, and the belief that it carried with it of his capabilities. In that context, had there been only the death of Mrs. Mors, the jury would have found McCoy innocent. The jurors at length disclosed that McCoy's nine marriages and his past in general did not influence them, in effect saying that they did not believe in the picture of him as a predatory individual who had at last been caught. After the trial Giesler said rather bitterly that if McCoy had remained silent "another man" would have been tried for the death of Mrs. Mors. On the other hand, the jury could not find him altogether innocent in light of the shooting at Mors' store. Late in the afternoon of December 28, 1924, on their 24th ballot, the jury found McCoy guilty of manslaughter in Mrs. Mors' death. There was no question of his guilt in shooting Ross and Anna and Sam Schapps. He was sentenced to 10 years in prison for manslaughter, plus 10 years for assault with a deadly weapon in the shooting of Ross, plus 14 years for assault with attempt to murder Anna Schapps and an additional 14 years for assault with attempt to murder Sam Schapps.

There was in all this a curious reaction in McCoy. Whatever else happened, Kid McCoy was dead. The legend was over and done with, and the image that had been nurtured since his first fight with Pete Jenkins 30 years before was wiped out as completely as if it had never existed. He was, for a man on his way to serve 48 years in prison, in a remarkably unburdened mood. As he was being led to the prison van that was to take him to San Quentin, he happened to meet Charles Chaplin approaching down the hall from the other direction. Chaplin was on his way home after a session in court in connection with proceedings against an imposter, Charles Amador, who impersonated him. As a fight fan, Chaplin knew McCoy, though they had never been close friends, and shook hands with him. McCoy tried to put his arm across Chaplin's shoulder, but found it impossible, as he was handcuffed, and was led away. Chaplin stood for a long time at the top of the steps, with what a perceptive reporter called a curious or pensive expression on his face, as McCoy crossed the street, flanked by guards, and got into the van. It was a good fade-out, like a scene from one of Chaplin's movies—the end of an unreality, the jailing of a real man for the doings of an intangible image he had created.

# Epilogue

Norman Selby was a model prisoner at San Quentin. He kept in good physical shape, read a good deal, raised a canary he called Mike, and was given the task of serving as a guide or advisor to new prisoners when they arrived, charged with familiarizing them with prison ways and usage. One of his charges was Asa Keyes; he went to considerable pains to acquaint Keyes with ways to live amicably with his fellow prisoners. Norman Selby bore no grudge against the man who had convicted Kid McCoy.

Shortly before his release he became interested in a theory having to do with juvenile delinquency: he thought that many of the problems came from physical difficulties; young people did not know the proper carriage of the body or the right way to eat. He began to think that there might still be some worthwhile work that he could do, and he found some satisfaction, now that he had no hope of bettering his own fortune, that he might be able to better the fortunes of others.

He was 60 years old when he came out of prison, appeared to be much younger, and was trim, physically fit, and good-natured. Henry Ford befriended him by giving him a job in the vegetable gardens established for Ford employees during the Depression. He was good at this kind of work; he had grown up on a farm. As the Depression grew worse, the program was expanded. Ford provided more and more company land on which his idle employees could grow their own produce. The main problem involved each gardener keeping to his own plot, and seeing to it that the gardens were not pilfered. Soon there were 12,000 company gardens, and McCoy was placed in charge of the 85 guards who protected them.

From time to time Selby spoke for church groups to juvenile

delinquents, or to youngsters who might become such, talking as an authority on the dangers of a fast life. He came to know a number of Detroit sportswriters and people in the fight crowd, including Battling Levinsky, once a light heavyweight title contender and its most prominent figure. But for the most part, he lived quietly after he was established in Ford's welfare department, making only a trip to New York and Philadelphia. It was arranged by Ford's publicity staff, and resulted in a few newspaper interviews and photographs of McCoy playing pool with Philadelphia Jack O'Brien, and posing with the former heavyweight champion, Jack Dempsey, and Peter Maher, now a frail old man.

On August 2, 1937, McCoy appeared in the office of the Rush Circuit Court in Rushville, Indiana, with an attractive, dark-haired, middle-aged woman and applied for a marriage license. The deputy clerk, Wilma Hougland, wrote his name, Norman Selby, and asked if he was related to Ray Selby. He replied that Ray was his cousin. His wife-to-be was Sue Cobb Cowley, from Kentucky, a niece of the humorist Irvin S. Cobb. Generations passed swiftly: when Kid McCoy started his saloon in the Casino Theatre, Cobb's first musical comedy, *Funsabashi,* played there.

When Wilma Hougland asked Selby how many times he had been married, he said, "Eight or ten." She put down 1. A young lawyer, John Hughes, suggested that she ought to get an explanation as to the number of times he had been married. "It's according to how you look at it," Selby said. "This will be my tenth marriage, but I remarried one of my divorced wives."

In this fashion he was identified by Hughes as Kid McCoy. There followed a long newspaper interview, a wedding at the home of an old friend, and a photograph of the couple in the Rushville paper. Back in Detroit, Selby and his wife lived placidly for three years in semiseclusion. He still had ambitions of making some great contribution, working in a program to improve the physical fitness of young people as an aid to moral strength and a betterment of the world, though he spoke of it less and less. He was now known only as a kindly, gray-haired gardener.

While it might have seemed that no one in the country was more remote from events in Europe, he became increasingly depressed as the war news grew worse. He could not sleep. When the need for sleep became imperative, McCoy took sleeping pills, though he dis-

Norman Selby's wives: *top left:* Mrs. George Wheelock; *top right:* Mrs. Estelle E. Ellis; *lower left:* Mrs. Edna Valentine Hein; *lower right:* Dagmar Dahlgren and Kid McCoy. (All photos courtesy United Press International.)

liked doing so. He tried to free himself of dependence on them. Hitler and Stalin stunned the world with their Nazi-Soviet pact; Poland was divided. Early in April 1940 German troops overran Denmark and invaded Norway.

On April 17, 1940, Selby told his wife he had to go to Chicago on business. He went to the Hotel Tuller in Detroit, rented a room, and swallowed the contents of a bottle of sleeping pills. He left a note:

*For the past 8 years I have wanted to help humanity, especially the youngsters, who do not know Nature's laws. . . . I wish you all the best of luck. Sorry I could not endure this world's madness.*

He signed it Norman Selby.

# Notes

## Chapter 1

1. References to Kid McCoy as the origin of the phrase "the real McCoy" are in virtually all standard works: H. L. Mencken, *The American Language: An Inquiry into the Development of English in the United States,* ed. Raven I. McDavid, Jr., Knopf, 1963, p. 580; Paul Robert Beath, article in *American Speech,* February 1932; the *Random House Dictionary;* the *Dictionary of Americanisms;* and the *Dictionary of American Slang.* Other possible sources are Irish folklore, Prohibition, and the American underworld. One Irish usage *(Dictionary of Americanisms)* involves a song of the 1880s in which a wife declares herself the head of the household with the phrase, "I'm the real McCoy!" In the Irish comedy, *The Real McCoy,* by J. J. Mackoewn, the action revolves around a shiftless husband, Robbie McCoy, and his wife, Rose.

An article by the author, "The Real McCoy," *Sports Illustrated,* June 1, 1970, evoked from readers other sources of the phrase, which included references to the Hatfield-McCoy feud, as well as to outlaws of the American West. One concerned Elisha McCoy, a Negro inventor. Before the turn of the century he patented a self-acting grease cup which reduced the need for oiling locomotive bearings by hand. The grease cups were known as "McCoys," and when less effective imitations were marketed they were disaparged as inferior to the "real McCoys." McCoy was, however, an obscure individual, and the railroad use of the term was so specialized and technical that it does not adequately account for the popularity of the phrase in common American speech. At the time of Kid McCoy's death the obituaries in the Detroit paper (April 18, 1940) all emphasized the origin of the phrase in the events of McCoy's life recounted elsewhere in this volume.

2. G. Bagley, *From the Prize Ring to the Four Hundred,* Hearst's *American Weekly,* June 13, 1907; Nexola Greely-Smith, "How He Expects to Get into the 400," New York *Evening World,* June 13, 1907; "Mr. McCoy, Engaged, Now Reads Chaucer," New York *Times,* May 29, 1905; interview, Edward Smith with McCoy, Columbus, Ohio *Journal,* June 10, 1917.

3. New York *Morning Telegraph,* August 8, 1910.

4. New York *Times,* May 14, 1919.

5. The vital records of Rush County did not begin until 1887. However, through the kindness of Miss Isabelle Dill of the Rush County Public Health Service, Mrs. Fannie Connor, vital records clerk, and Mr. John Hughes, a Rushville attorney, I secured the marriage record of Norman Selby and Sue Ethel Crawley, August 2, 1937, in which Norman Selby gave the names of his parents. Concerning the Selbys

in Rush County, see De Witt C. Goodrich, *An Illustrated History of the State of Indiana*, Indianapolis, 1875, pp. 569, 572; *Indiana Gazetteer*, Indianapolis, 1844, pp. 225, 325, 342.

6. McCoy's obituary, Detroit *Fress Press*, April 18, 1940.

7. "Wily Kid McCoy," *The Ring*, November 1949.

8. New York *World*, January 13, 1900.

9. New York *World*, March 10, 1898.

10. J. Stoddard Johnston, *Memorial History of Louisville*, Louisville Young Men's Christian Association, vol. 2, pp. 279-284.

11. Homer Croy, *Star Maker: The Story of D. W. Griffith*, pp. 9-12; Lillian Gish, *The Movies, Mr. Griffith and Me*, pp. 44-48.

12. The Jack McAuliffe-Billy Myers fiasco is described in *Ten—And Out!*, Alexander Johnston, pp. 303-305.

13. McCoy's obituary, Detroit *News*, Detroit *Free Press*, April 18, 1940.

14. *The Ring*, November 1949, pp. 48-49.

15. New York *World*, March 10, 1898.

16. *The Ring*, November 1949: "in honor of Pete McCoy, then a well-known boxer." John Hughes, of Rushville, Indiana, in a communication to the author: "He was supposed to have left home, gone to Greensburg, Indiana, south of Rush County, and went on a train to Cincinnati. The conductor asked him his name, and he looked out the window and saw the sign "McCoy Station" and said "McCoy." This station was on the railroad between Greensburg, Indiana and Cincinnati, Ohio, and was located on the farm owned by my grandfather."

17. The pseudonyms of fighters have generally been taken from prizefight histories, most from the annual volumes of Nat Fleischer, *Ring Record Book and Boxing Encyclopedia*.

18. *Ring Record Book*, p. 131.

19. New York *World*, March 10, 1898.

20. W. Naughton, *Kings of the Queensbury Realm*, Continental Publishing, 1902, p. 279.

21. James J. Corbett, *The Roar of the Crowd*, Garden City, 1920, pp. 38-40, 60-68, 74-88.

22. Nat Fleischer, *John L. Sullivan, Champion of Champions*, Fleet Publishing Company, 1958, p. 179. "Mr. Sullivan was manly, and spoke his lines distinctly with good effect." Review of *A True American*, starring Sullivan, New York *Herald*, September 4, 1894. See also, William Brady, *Showman*, the autobiography of Corbett's manager.

23. Corbett, *Roar of the Crowd*, pp. 189-201; Thomas Ewing Dabney, *One Hundred Great Years: The Story of the Times-Picayune*, pp. 301, 309, 320. On Corbett and the sports crowd, see New York *Times*, February 19, 1933.

24. Maurice Golesworthy, *The Encyclopedia of Boxing*, pp. 210-211; Johnston, *Ten—And Out!* p. 256.

25. Johnston, *Ten—And Out!*, p. 256.

26. I was unable to locate contemporary newspaper accounts of McCoy's fights with Jim Dickson, Jim Connors, Frank Lamode, Frank Murray, Kid McCarthy, and Ike Boone. The present account is from McCoy's record as given in the *Ring Record Book*.

27. Golesworthy, *Encyclopedia of Boxing*, p. 182; Johnston, *Ten—And Out!*, pp. 269-270. *The Ring*, November 1949. "It has been said for Tommy Ryan that he was the greatest fighter for his weight boxing has known," quotation in the Boxing

Hall of Fame. As the trainer of heavyweight champion Jim Jeffries, Ryan is credited with having transformed Jeffries from a plodding slugger into an expert boxer, although his temperament was such that he later quarreled even with the easygoing Jeffries.

28. Wheeling *Intelligencer,* October 13-14, 1893.

29. Corbett, *Roar of the Crowd,* pp. 296-297; Johnston, *Ten—And Out!,* pp. 133, 145, 266; Nat Fleischer, *Fifty Years at Ringside,* p. 281; Damon Runyon, in Chicago, *Examiner,* May 24, 1917.

## Chapter 2

1. *New Republic,* October 11, 1933.

2. Edward Smith, interview with McCoy, in Columbus, Ohio *Journal,* June 10, 1917.

3. The New York *Morning Telegraph,* June 24, 1911, identified Lottie Piehler as a milliner. For her background see Columbus, Ohio *Journal,* June 10, 1917. McCoy's embroidered green belt was described in the New Bedford, Massachusetts *Evening Standard,* March 17, 1894.

4. See Fleischer, *Ring Record Book and Boxing Encyclopedia,* under "Welterweight Champions." McCoy's comment on quick knockouts is in his obituary, Detroit *Free Press,* April 18, 1940.

5. I am indebted to Mrs. Nina Regis, genealogical librarian of the Free Public Library of New Bedford for uncovering the forgotten contemporary newspaper accounts of McCoy's fight and Scully's background.

6. *The Ring,* November 1949. McCoy gave his own recollections of the fight with Billy Steffers in an interview in the Toledo, Ohio *Blade,* August 10, 1909.

7. "Barron Broke His Hand," Minneapolis *Tribune,* May 19, 1894. For Barron's background see Naughton, *Kings of the Queensbury Realm,* p. 57. R. N. Haldane, *Champions and Challengers,* London: Stanley Paul, 1969, p. 152.

8. *The Ring,* November 1949. For McCoy's record see Fleischer, *Ring Record Book.* McCoy's recollection of his second fight with Steffers is in the Toledo *Blade,* August 10, 1909.

9. "McCoy was behind Fitzsimmons when he fought Creedon. . . ." St. Louis *Post-Dispatch,* April 19, 1895. See also New Orleans *Times-Picayune,* September 27, 1894.

10. Fleischer, *Ring Record Book.* New York *World,* April 21, 1896.

11. Memphis *Commercial Appeal,* March 14, 1895; "The Australian Had No Show," New Orleans *Times-Picayune,* March 14, 1895. For Maber's background see Haldane, *Champions and Challengers,* pp. 152-153; Johnston, *Ten—And Out!,* p. 129.

## Chapter 3

1. St. Louis *Post-Dispatch,* April 19-20, 1895; *The Ring,* November 1949. "In his class the St. Louis boy [Wilkes] compares with the best of them, having fought a draw with Tommy Ryan, the acknowledged welterweight champion of America." *Post-Dispatch,* June 14, 1893.

2. McCoy's obituary, Detroit *Free Press,* April 18, 1940. On Wilkes quitting the ring after the fight, see *The Ring,* November 1949.

3. Fleischer, *Ring Record Book and Boxing Encyclopedia.*

4. Edward Smith, interview with McCoy, in Columbus, Ohio *Journal,* June 10, 1917. On Corbett's fights on his vaudeville tour see Corbett, *Roar of the Crowd,* pp. 152-159.

5. See essay on Stendhal in *Le Revue Parisienne,* September 25, 1840.

6. "Lottie and I were together until about 1897. Then I persuaded her to go west and get a divorce," McCoy to Edward Smith, interview in Columbus *Journal,* June 10, 1917.

7. "I went to work in a Louisville theatre, fighting all comers for $250 a week, until I got enough money to come east and fight Abe Ullman." McCoy to Edward Smith, interview in Columbus *Journal,* June 10, 1917. Ullman fought Mysterious Billy Smith twice. He lost a 20-round decision the first time, and the second fight was a draw. Ullman figures in ring history on the strength of a 10-round, no-decision fight with Jake Kilrain, who lost the 75-round battle that made John L. Sullivan the world heavyweight champion.

8. I was unable to locate any record for Walker.

9. "He made 66 trips to Europe—at least, he always claimed he made that many." McCoy's obituary, Detroit *Free Press,* April 18, 1940. "During his long and stormy career, Selby made 33 trips across the ocean, he said." The Rushville, Indiana *Record,* interview with McCoy, August 3, 1937.

10. In his interview with a reporter in Rushville in 1937, McCoy remarked that he had been defeated only twice by fighters in his own weight class, by Billy Steffers, when he was new to the game, "and he [McCoy] was beaten in London by an Englishman whose name he does not recall," Haldane, *Champions and Challengers,* p. 157.

11. Johnston in *Ten—And Out!,* lists Tommy Ryan, Kid McCoy, and Tommy West as the leading contenders for the middleweight championship when Fitzsimmons relinquished it. Haldane, in *Champions and Challengers,* p. 127, describes two of West's fights with Ryan as "old-time classics of the ring." West figures in ring history primarily because of his fights with Joe Walcott, the great West Indian fighter who held the lightweight and welterweight titles. In 1892 Walcott knocked out West in the third round. In 1895 the timer erred in the 19th round and the fight was called a draw. In 1896 West was awarded a 20-round decision over Walcott. In 1898 they fought a six-round no-decision bout. In 1900 (shortly after Walcott had scored an amazing knockout of heavyweight Joe Choynski) they met in New York, after the 11th round Walcott refused to continue. In 1902 they met in London, Walcott winning the decision. West's fight with McCoy and the scene in the ring after Frawley's loss in a preliminary bout were reported in all the New York newspapers. The account here follows that in the *World,* February, 1, 1896.

12. All accounts agree that McCoy was embittered by the beatings he had taken as Ryan's sparring partner, the emphasis varying according to the partisanship of the writers. The beating was merely a salutary lesson administered by a great boxer to a cocky beginner (Alexander Johnston), or was typical of Ryan's punishment of his sparring partners *(The Ring).* Haldane, in *Champions and Challengers,* says that McCoy was "an extremely shrewd customer, a dangerous puncher, and one of the few old-timers who had a disagreeably ruthless character." All accounts agree that McCoy concealed his feelings in order to get a fight with Ryan. *The Ring* states that McCoy carried off his appearance of naivete so successfully that Ryan did not train for the fight with his usual care. *The Ring* report is the most convincing of the various interpretations, but the weakness in all of them is that Ryan is presented as

possessing less than average intelligence in being so easily fooled; but whatever else he was, Ryan was certainly smart. Ryan must have known something of McCoy's ability. Both men fought Jack Wilkes. Ryan won a hard-fought, 17-round battle with Wilkes in 1892 and later fought a six-round, no-decision bout with him, whereas McCoy easily knocked out Wilkes in the second round of their fight. At the time he met Ryan, McCoy had had 39 fights in five years and had been defeated twice. Besides Wilkes, he had beaten Jim Barron, Shadow Maber, Abe Ullman, and Tommy West, who were near the top of their class. Ryan's partisans emphasized McCoy's craftiness for the elementary reason that the McCoy fight indicated Ryan was not as good a fighter as he was said to be.

There are comparable contradictions in the round-by-round accounts of the fight itself. The difference is merely one of degree, in making the fight seem closer than it was. The account here generally follows that in the New York *World,* March 2, 1896, with some details from other newspaper reports. Alexander Johnston's description of the fight as a double-cross was not suggested in the contemporary newspaper stories. *Ten—And Out!,* p. 288.

13. "The erstwhile hobo heard himself acclaimed middleweight champion of the world. He had $40,000 in his pockets." McCoy's obituary, Detroit *Free Press,* April 18, 1940.

14. *Broadway Magazine,* May 1, 1901; Buffalo *Enquirer* October 21, 1911; New York *World,* March 5, 10, 1898.

15. New York Morning Telegraph, June 24, 1911; Columbus, Ohio *Journal,* June 10, 1917; New York *Times,* November 11, 1900. At McCoy's trial for murder in 1924, the list of his wives was given as follows:

| | |
|---|---|
| Lottie Piehler | 1894 |
| Charlotte Smith | 1897 |
| Mrs. Julia Woodruff Crosselmire | 1897 |
| divorced | 1899 |
| remarried | January 1900 |
| divorced | Jan. 12, 1902 |
| remarried | Apr. 11, 1902 |
| divorced | June 9, 1903 |
| Indianola Arnold (annulled) | 1903 |
| Mrs. Estelle Ellis | 1905 |
| divorced | 1910 |
| Mrs. Edna Valentine Hein | 1911 |
| divorced | 1917 |
| Dagmar Dahlgren | 1920 |
| divorced | 1921 |

When McCoy applied for a license to marry in 1937, he listed himself as having been married eight times before, not nine. No contemporary account of McCoy's marriage to Charlotte Smith could be found.

16. *Broadway Magazine,* January 6, 1900; New York *Enquirer,* January 7, 1901; New York *Morning Telegraph, S*eptember 14, 1904; New York *Times,* November 11, 1900, January 12, 1902, June 9, 1903, May 25, 1905; New York *World,* May 28, 1905. On January 6, 1915 the New York *Times* carried an article on the later career of the actress, "the former Mrs. Kid McCoy," then married to George Wheelock who was described as a retired bookmaker.

17. Memphis *Commercial Appeal,* April 28, 1896.

18. There are marked differences in the reports of this confused event. I have followed that in the New York *Herald, January* 13, 1900, as the most objective and coherent.

19. Doherty's career is recounted in "Wily Kid McCoy," *The Ring,* November 1949. The other material is from McCoy's obituary, Detroit *Free Press,* April 18, 1940.

20. O'Brien's promising career was blighted by two knockouts by Joe Gans at the start of Gans's remarkable career, but he was a more than respectable opponent. He had a 10-round draw with Mysterious Billy Smith to his credit and later lost a close fight to Tommy Ryan.

21. The history of this famous showhouse is in *The Encyclopedia of the American Theatre.* See also Gene Fowler, *Father Goose: the Biography of Mack Sennett;* and DeWolf Hopper, *Once a Clown, Always a Clown.*

22. See Corbett's obituary, New York *Times,* February 19, 1933, for the partnership of the Considine brothers. Their ownership of the Hotel Metropole is in Andy Logan, *Against the Evidence: The Becker-Rosenthal Affair,* p. 5. The scene in Corbett's saloon before a big fight is in the New York *Times,* June 10, 1899. The article describes the betting before the Fitzsimmons-Jeffries fight, in which Corbett had $6,000 on Jeffries at 2 to 1 odds.

23. *The Ring,* July 1953; article by George Britt in New York *World Telegram,* May 4, 1934. That the Killers of Herman Rosenthal met in Sharkey's saloon is in the testimony at the trial of Lieutenant Charles Becker, New York *Times,* May 16, 1914, as is also the partnership of Tom O'Rourke and Jack Rose in the Delavan Hotel bar.

24. The friendship of Mrs. Corbett and Julia McCoy is in *Broadway Magazine,* December 1, 1900. McCoy's saloon is described in the same publication, May 1,

25. This list has been compiled from many ring accounts.

26. New York *Morning Telegraph,* November 28, 1911.

27. "They fought in Syracuse, Ryan's home town. McCoy never had a chance to win, the cards being stacked against him. He was having the better of the fight, much the better, in fact, when the chief of police stopped it and a draw was the official result." *The Ring,* November 1949.

28. Louisville, Kentucky, January 19, 1898. McCoy won by a knockout in the fourth round. The later partnership of Payne and McCoy is in the Indianapolis *News,* April 5, 1898.

Dayton, Ohio, February 15, 1898. Harry Long. McCoy won by a knockout in the second round.

Hot Springs, Arkansas, March 4, 1898. Nick Burley. McCoy won by a knockout in the second round. Burley was well known. His hard fight with Tom Sharkey in Honolulu in 1894, won by Sharkey, was an important start in Sharkey's career. Burley went north in the gold rush, defeating Joe Choynski in Dawson City in 1903.

29. Indianapolis *News,* March 8, April 5, 1898.

30. Ruhlin was a major contender for the heavyweight title. He fought Jeffries, Peter Maher (both a draw after 20 rounds) and had a second-round knockout of Maher to his credit. The McCoy fight, a crushing defeat by Fitzsimmons, and a 10th-round knockout by Tom Sharkey ended what little chance he had. His deliberate, plainly visible fouling of Fitzsimmons in their fight at Madison Square Garden, August 10, 1900 made the film of the fight an important event in early movie history. New York *Times,* August 11, 1900. Naughton's comment is in his

*Kings of the Queensbury Realm,* p. 151; Johnston on McCoy is in *Ten—And Out!,* p. 173.

31. Goddard's place in the Australian invasion is described in Naughton, *Kings of the Queensbury Realm,* p. 57. His fights with Choynski may be found in *Ring Record Book,* p. 302. A description of his fight with Jefferies on February 28, 1898 is in Haldane, *Champions and Challengers,* p. 132. In 1897 Goddard was knocked out by Tom Sharkey in the sixth round of a savage battle.

32. Naughton called this fight one of the greatest scandals of the ring. *Kings of the Queensbury Realm,* p. 141. He described the Corbett-Sharkey fight as almost as bad. Corbett's pained reaction to Naughton's charge is in Corbett, *Roar of the Crowd,* p. 272.

33. New York *Morning Telegraph,* January 6, 1900, April 11, 1902.

34. Sailor Tom, in *The Ring,* July 1953; Naughton, *Kings of the Queensbury Realm,* pp. 132-143. Corbett's comment on Sharkey is in Grantland Rice's syndicated column, April 24, 1953.

35. *The Ring,* November 1949, July 1953.

36. Naughton's part in arranging the match is in McCoy's obituaries in the Detroit newspapers, April 14, 1940; the source is Jack Rush, McCoy's former manager.

37. The six volumes of Mark Sullivan's *Our Times: The United States, Nineteen Hundred–Nineteen Twenty-five,* contain much material on synthetic reputations and exaggerated claims. McCoy's comments are in his interview with Edward Smith, Columbus *Journal,* June 10, 1917.

38. New York *Morning Telegraph,* May 28, 1905; New York *Evening World,* August 24, 1907; New York *World,* May 28, 1905; New York *Times,* September 20, 1904, May 29, 1905.

39. McCoy's fights with Tom Dugan, Jack Graham, and Jim Carter are in the *Ring Record Book.*

40. McCormick was also known as Texas Jim McCormick. Alexander Johnston's description of him is in *Ten—And Out!,* p. 150. McCormick twice fought Tom Sharkey and was knocked out on both occasions. According to Nat Fleischer, however, McCormick was no set-up. "He had once scored a knockout over Kid McCoy, one of the cleverest heavyweights of the era." Fleischer, *Sullivan,* p. 198. McCormick, who was knocked out by Sullivan, had the distinction of being Sullivan's last opponent. Augustus Thomas's recollection of the McCoy-McCormick fight may be found in detail in his autobiography, *The Print of My Remembrance.*

41. Ring Record *Book.*

42. Johnston, *Ten—And Out!,* p. 150.

43. New York *World,* March 5, 1898; Indianapolis *News,* April 5, 1898; Detroit *Free Press,* April 18, 1940.

44. *Ring Record Book,* under "Choynski."

45. "McCoy hit Billy Stift so hard that Stift did not come to for more than an hour." *The Ring,* November 1949. Stift had a victory over Mysterious Billy Smith to his credit, and five hard-fought battles with Tommy Ryan, all lost.

46. Maher, who was 31 in 1900, was the middleweight champion of Ireland before moving on to heavier divisions. He was a "terribly uncertain fighter" (Alexander Johnston), and "fragile-chinned but dangerous" *(The Ring).* Maher knocked out Nick Burley in one round, beat Peter Courtney (Corbett's opponent in second prizefight ever filmed), knocked out Steve O'Donnell in one round, and Joe Choynski in the sixth round of a scheduled 10-round fight. He fought a brutal battle with Tom Sharkey in New York in 1897 that ended in a riot that had to be stopped

by the police. Maher, who had previously been knocked out in a hard fight with Fitz-simmons, was Fitzsimmons' opponent in the fifth prizefight to be filmed, that of February 21, 1896, across the Rio Grande from Langtry, Texas. New York *Times,* February 22, 1896. Maher was, in short, a major opponent, and McCoy's victory is sometimes described as the best fight of his life (New York *Times,* December 31, 1924). An "impersonation" of the fight was filmed by a Philadelphia movie pioneer, Siegmund Lublin, who hired actors to portray McCoy and Maher and duplicate the action as described in newspaper round-by-round accounts. *Library of Congress Catalogue of Copyright Entries.*

47. Bonner was also beaten by such first-rate opponents as Joe Walcott and Jack Root.

48. *Broadway Magazine,* December 1, 1910; New York *Times,* June 6, 1915.

49. "I never tried harder than in this fight with McCoy. . . . This accusation [that the fight was fixed] hurt me more than anything that had ever been said about me or done to me in my life." Corbett, *Roar of the Crowd,* pp. 296-302. Samuel Hopkins Adams, *There's No Fraud like an Old Fraud; Sports Illustrated,* May 12, 1958. The New York *Times* reporter at the ringside (August 31, 1900) saw no evidence of a fixed fight.

50. McCoy's planned rest at Cedar Bluff: New York *World* (front-page story), September 9, 10, 1900. Corbett's disappearance: "Corbett Runs Away—McCoy Fight Fixed," New York *World,* September 9, 1900. While all New York news-papers featured the news, the *World's* is the clearest and most detailed. Much con-fusion was caused because Mrs. Corbett steadily denied that Corbett had gone to Europe, and after his flight was established, collapsed with nervous prostration, in-terviews with reporters then being carried out by her companion, Mary Bonner. McCoy's denial of the fix is detailed in the *World,* September 11, 1900. Julia McCoy's charge that McCoy had stolen her jewels and planned to flee the country is in the *World,* September 12, 1900. The fight of Julia McCoy and McCoy in their apart-ment is in the same newspaper, September 14, 1900. Corbett's arrival in London is in the *World,* September 16, 1900.

51. Considine's story of McCoy's bribe is in Smauel Hopkins Adams' recollec-tions, *Sports Illustrated,* May 12, 1958.

52. McCoy's three fights, all on the same night (December 2, 1901), scarcely de-served a place in his record. Although in his street clothes, he was persuaded to enter the ring, and fought three aspirants, knocking out Dave Barry in two rounds, Jack Scales in one round, and Jack Madden in four rounds.

53. The story that the farm became a roadhouse is in the New York *Evening World,* August 24, 1907.

54. New York *Morning Telegraph,* May 28, 1905; New York *Times,* September 20, 1904, May 29, 1905. A place "for overworked and overplayed men"—New York *World,* May 28, 1905.

55. New York *World,* May 28, 1905; *Morning Telegraph,* November 2, 1906.

56. New York *Times,* June 6, 1915.

57. On the friendship of Julia McCoy and Lillian Earle see the New York *World* and the *Morning Telegraph,* May 28, 1905. In an interview in the New York *Times,* May 28, 1905, McCoy took pains to correct the report: "It isn't true that Miss Earle knew Mrs. Selby when she came to Saratoga. They met each other there. . . . Ed was a dear friend of mine. He knew Miss Earle, and she came to my place to nurse him. When he got well, he married her. About that time my wife ran away with a man named Thompson, who knew Ed."

58. New York *World,* May 28, 1905.

Chapter 4

1. New York *Times,* September 20, 1904; New York *World,* May 28, 1905; Toledo *Blade,* April 4, 1905.

2. "The Last of the Ellises Is Dead," New York *Times,* September 20, 1904. The date of Ellis's mother's death is unclear in available records.

3. McCoy's drinking is mentioned in his interview in the New York *Times,* May 29, 1905: "I have been a changed man ever since Christmas. I have not taken a drink." New York *World,* May 28, 1905: "He has not touched a drop of alcoholic liquor." The *Morning Telegraph* reported (May 28, 1905) that McCoy left the Cedar Bluff farm and returned to New York, remaining silent while he sued for divorce.

4. New York *Times,* May 29, 1905. Julia McCoy's comment that there was no affection to be alienated is in the New York *Times,* June 6, 1915.

5. *Ring Record Book and Boxing Encyclopedia.*

6. Root, born in 1876, began fighting in Chicago at 21, and was undefeated in 42 fights until in 1902 he was knocked out by George Gardner. He fought such durable contenders as Billy Stift, Alec Greggains, Tommy West, Dan Creedon, and Tommy Ryan. Shortly before his meeting with McCoy he won a decision over Marvin Hart, later the world heavyweight champion when Jeffries retired. The history of the light heavyweight class is in Johnston, *Ten—And Out!* Root held the new title only two months, losing it to Gardner.

7. *Morning Telegraph,* September 14, 1904, May 28, 1905.

8. On McCoy's bankruptcy see the *Morning Telegraph,* November 28, 1911. The date of this first bankruptcy was June 29, 1904.

9. In addition to the account of *The Other Girl* in Thomas's the *Print of My Remembrance,* Thomas detailed the genesis of the play in a long introduction to the published version. Thomas, was, if not the leading American playwright at the time, one of the most successful. His career is included in *The Dictionary of American Biography* and in standard American theatrical histories.

10. Barrymore's imitation of McCoy is mentioned in the *Morning Telegraph,* May 28, 1905. In his *The Barrymores,* p. 96, Hollis Alpert says Barrymore's part "required him to do a take-off on Kid McCoy, a famous fighter with whom he became fast friends." In John Barrymore's autobiography, *We Barrymores,* and in Gene Fowler's biography of John Barrymore, *Goodnight, Sweet Prince: The Life and Times of John Barrymore,* the point is repeatedly made that McCoy remained friendly with the actors despite the satire directed at himself in the play. I was unable to find any similar comment from McCoy.

The played, which opened at the Criterion on December 26, 1903, was an immediate and overwhelming success. The audience included many celebrated sporting people. The New York *Herald* noted the presence of Mr. and Mrs. Stanford White, Mr. and Mrs. Richard Harding Davis, Mr. John Drew, Mr. Peter Cooper Hewitt, Mr. Arthur Kemp (the playboy son of the owner of the Buckingham Hotel), Mr. A. H. Hummell, the famous attorney, Mr. and Mrs. Egmont Schermhorn, and others equally eminent. Said the New York *World:* "A veritable knockout for Mr. Barrymore." New York *Herald:* "A real delight." *Morning Telegraph:* "The talk of the town." The *Sunday Telegraph:* "Mr. Barrymore has copied his make-up from a well-known young prizefighter, even to the plastered hair and the too-well fitting clothes."

The only sour note was directed against Augustus Thomas; the *World* complained that he rushed to make a curtain speech despite the lack of cries of Author!

Author! and added that the speech, consisting of sarcastic remarks about prize-fighters and newspapermen, was the longest and least witty curtain speech of the season.

*The Other Girl* established Lionel Barrymore as an actor. He said in an interview (*Morning Telegraph*, May 8, 1904): "I suppose I got my first real, good chance in *The Other Girl*, and I made the best of my opportunity. I learned boxing, of course. . . ." Playing to packed houses, *The Other Girl* moved to the Empire Theatre, which adjoined the Casino, and completed its long run directly next door to McCoy's bar.

11. *The Ring*, November 1949.

12. Ellis's regatta at Lake George is reported in the New York *World*, May 28, 1905; his death, in New York *Times*, September 20, 1904.

13. *Ring Record Book*. Mike (Twin) Sullivan, became the welterweight champion in 1907; his twin brother Jack, less successful but a more frequent contender, fought such durable figures as Steve O'Donnell, Tommy Burns (the future heavyweight champion), Nick Burley, Stanley Ketchel, Jim Flynn, and Marvin Hart.

14. Mrs. Ellis's move to the Hotel Dunlap is in the New York *Times*, May 29, 1905, interview with McCoy: "When I got back from the coast about six weeks ago she got apartments in the same hotel where I was staying."

15. New York *Times*, April 27, 1905.

16. New York *Times*, May 29, 1905; New York *World*, May 28, 1905; *Morning Telegraph*, May 28, 1905.

17. The annulment of the McCoy-Indianola Arnold marriage is mentioned in the New York *Times*, October 20, 1905, the marriage of McCoy and Mrs. Ellis in the *Morning Telegraph*, October 21, 1905.

18. Obituary, Detroit *News*, April 18, 1940. On McCoy's determination to change his image, see New York *Times*, May 29, 1905; on his poetry, New York *Times*, October 20, 1905.

19. New York *Times*, December 14, 1906. On his partners, see *Morning Telegraph*, December 15, 1906.

20. There are only passing references to the agency in New York newspapers. However, an extensive account appeared in the Grand Rapids, Michigan *Herald*, November 3, 1908. Frank Peabody's connection with the Howard Gould divorce case is in the *Evening World*, December 27, 1907.

21. The divorce is related in Edwin P. Hoyt, *The Goulds;* in Harvey O'Connor, *Gould's Millions;* and in Howard Gould's obituary, New York *Times*, September 15, 1959.

22. New York *Morning Telegraph*, December 16, 1906; Toledo *Blade*, August 10, 1907. The accident McCoy witnessed is reported in the *Morning Telegraph*, March 10, 1906, the fire that destroyed his car, in the *Morning Telegraph*, November 2, 1906.

23. The McCoys at lectures: *Morning Telegraph*, January 21, 1908; travels to Europe: *Morning Telegraph*, April 4, 1909; to Hot Springs: *Morning Telegraph*, November 4, 1906; to Florida, *Morning Telegraph*, January 21, 1908; to Detroit: *Morning Telegraph*, January 12, 1909; to England: *Morning Telegraph*, June 12, 1909. McCoy's racing stable in England: *Morning Telegraph*, April 4, 1909. Tod Sloan's career is discussed in William H. P. Robertson, *The History of Thoroughbred Racing in America*, pp. 168-171.

24. *Morning Telegraph*, December 15, 1906; for the dissolution of the detective agency partnership, see New York *World*, December 27, 1907.

25. Scranton, Pennsylvania *Truth*, June 20, 1907; New York *Evening World*,

June 13, 1907; Los Angeles *Examiner,* June 22, 1907. An unidentified newspaper clipping in the Library of Performing Arts collection of material on McCoy and Julia McCoy (dated June 12, 1909) says that McCoy and his wife had purchased furniture for their new home in England, leaving it in storage in Liverpool when neighbors objected to their moving into the house.

26. Toledo *Blade,* August, 10, 1909.

27. New York *Morning Telegraph,* December 20, 1910.

28. *Ring Record Book* Mrs. Selby's comment is in an unidentified newspaper clipping dated October 8, 1908.

29. *Vanity Fair,* November 6, 1908.

30. See *Almanach de Gotha* (1928 edition), p. 224. Marguerite-Christine, Baronnes d'Heeckeren d'Enghuizen, was born at Sonsbeck, Holland on July 21, 1878. The historical importance of the family in the Duchy of Gelderland is noted in *The Encyclopaedia Britannica,* 11th edition, vol. 11, pp. 555-557. Baroness d'Heeckeren married Count Adolph-Zeigger *(Almanach de Gotha).* Her arrival in New York to visit Mrs. Selby was reported in the New York newspapers on April 2 and April 4, 1909.

31. McCoy's comment on the McVey-Jeanerette fight and on Prince of Monaco were in a letter to Bat Masterson at the *Morning Telegraph,* dated May 7, 1909, from the Grand Hotel in Paris.

32. The *Morning Telegraph* reported on September 2, 1909, that McCoy had returned from Paris the night before. On September 4, 1909 Winchell Smith's comedy, *The Fortune Hunter,* with John Barrymore in the starring role, opened on Broadway. Lionel Barrymore's recollections, detailed at some length in Fowler's *Goodnight, Sweet Prince,* and in Alpert's *The Barrymores,* were that McCoy and Lionel Barrymore went to the opening night together. "Lionel and McCoy could get no seats for *The Fortune Hunter.* They stood during the performance. They saw Jack suddenly become a comedian of the first rank." Fowler, *Goodnight, Sweet Prince,* p. 137. After the performance they rescued John Barrymore from a crowd of hero worshippers "and went to a small cafe on the East Side to stay up all night." John Barrymore recollected that during the drinking McCoy told him, "Remember what Bill Mizner said, son—be awfully nice to them going up, because you're bound to meet them all coming down." Alpert, *The Barrymores,* pp. 131-132.

33. Buffalo *Enquirer,* October 11, 1911; *Morning Telegraph,* December 20, 1910.

34. Toledo *Blade,* December 21, 1909. Mrs. Selby's divorce, which was unopposed by McCoy, is reported in the *Morning Telegraph,* December 22, 1910.

35. New York *Morning Telegraph,* June 24, 1911.


## Chapter 5

1. Fowler, *Father Goose,* pp. 53-58; Fowler, *Goodnight, Sweet Prince,* p. 101; Croy, *Star Maker,* p. 137. That the license was in Elsie Rush's name is in the *Morning Telegraph,* April 10, 1911.

2. Logan, *Against the Evidence,* gives a graphic description of the Tenderloin area. Similar material is in F. A. Mackenzie, *Killing by Proxy* (in *Sins of New York,* edited by Milton Crane); and in Henry A. Klein, *Sacrificed, The Story of Police Lieutenant Charles Becker.* The most vivid picture, however, emerges from the testimony of the two trials of Becker for the murder of Herman Rosenthal in 1912 and 1914. William S. Hart's recollections are in his autobiography, *My Life East and West.*

3. In addition to Homer Croy's *Star Maker* and Lillian Gish's *The Movies, Mr. Griffith and Me,* Kenneth Macgowan's *Behind the Screen* and Kevin Brownlow's *The Parade's Gone By* provide material on Griffith's interests, including his interest in boxing. The location of McCoy's gymnasium is given in Trow's New York directory.

4. Robert Cantwell, "Sport Was Box Office Poison," *Sports Illustrated.* On the Leonard-Cushing fight film see Terry Ramsaye, *A Million and One Nights,* pp. 109-115. The filming of the Fitzsimmons-Maher fight was reported in the New York *Times,* February 22, 1896. Lubin's "impersonations" of major fights are described in Fred Balshofer and Arthur Miller, *One Reel a Week,* p. 9. The filming of the Jeffries-Fitzsimmons fight is described in the New York *Times,* June 10, 1899. The film of the Jeffries-Sharkey fight is described in the New York *Herald,* November 21, 1899.

5. Bronco Billy Anderson's fight promotions are mentioned in Charles Chaplin, *My Autobiography.* The relationship of Big Tim Sullivan and William Fox is discussed in Upton Sinclair's biography of Fox, *Upton Sinclair Presents William Fox.* Jeffries' bar is described in Fred Balshofer and Arthur Miller, *One Reel a Week.* Victor McLaglen's fight with Jack Johnson is in the *Ring Record Book and Boxing Encyclopedia.* Tom McCarey, the promoter, and his sons Leo and Roy McCarey, are in a series of articles, *Hollywood in Sport,* Los Angeles *Times,* February-March 1937. Adam Kessel and Charles Bauman are in Fowler, *Father Goose: The Biography of Mack Sennett;* and in Balshofer and Miller, *One Reel a Week.* The most valuable source, however, is a series of articles on Adam Kessel by Douglas Gilbert, in the New York *World-Telegram,* May 22-27, 1936. The experiences of Balshofer's movie crews in Brooklyn, New Jersey, and the Catskills are in *One Reel a Week.*

6. A wild, hilarious evening at McCoy's rathskeller was reported in the *Morning Telegraph,* May 17, 1910. McCoy's arrest, March 20, April 4, 1910.

7. McCoy's obituary, newspapers, Detroit, April 18, 1940; see also, Fowler, *Father Goose,* p. 58.

8. *Morning Telegraph,* April 10, 1911.

9. *Ring Record Book,* under "Welterweight Champions."

10. *Morning Telegraph,* November 28, 1911.

11. The Paris edition of the New York *Herald,* November 23, 1911, reported that McCoy won on points from Hubert Roe at the Cirque de Paris. The French sports daily *L'Auto* commented on McCoy's fight with Curran in an article before the fight, that 20 three-minute rounds "were perhaps too long for McCoy." But the *Herald* said of McCoy's victory over Curran: "The fight went the full limit of 20 rounds. McCoy forced all the pace, Curran contenting himself with covering up." The London *Times* reported McCoy's victory, January 22, 1912.

12. Maeterlinck's interest in sports and especially boxing, including his friendship with McCoy, is described in W. D. Halls, *Maurice Maeterlinck, A Study of His Life and Thought,* pp. 109, 133. The best account of life at the Abbey of St. Wandrille is in Georgette Leblanc, *Souvenirs, My Life with Maeterlinck.* The autobiographical volumes of Margaret Anderson—*My Thirty Years War, The Fiery Fountains,* and *The Strange Necessity,* Horizon Press, 1967-69—contribute some insights.

13. Hall, *Maeterlinck,* p. 133. McCoy's recitations of Maeterlinck's poetry are mentioned in his obituaries in the Detroit newspapers, April 18, 1940.

14. Georgette Leblanc's account of her reluctance to leave St. Wandrille and her distrust of the "new people" around Maeterlinck (no names were mentioned) are in her autobiography, *Souvenirs.*

15. Hall, *Maeterlinck,* pp. 131-133. The filming of *The Blue Bird* is described in articles on Maurice Tourneur, the director, in *Photoplay,* July 1918; *Motion Picture Magazine,* September 1918; and *Motion Picture Classics,* February 1920.

16. New York *Morning Telegraph,* June 21, 1912.

17. The most detailed study is that of Andy Logan, *Against the Evidence.* Logan, however, assumes Becker's conviction was the result of the political ambitions of the prosecutor. This account is derived from the testimony at Becker's two trials for murder, as reported in the New York *Times* and the New York *World* in 1912 and 1914.

18. New York *Times,* July 27, 1912.

19. The *Almanach de Gotha* (1928 edition) gives a partial genealogy of the family. The background of Lida Eleanor Micholls Fitzgerald is in the New York *Morning Telegraph,* July 27, 1912. Her 20-room suite in the Palace Hotel in Ostend is described in the New York *Herald,* Paris edition, July 28, 1912.

20. Arthur Kemp was identified as a "London industrialist" in the Belgian newspaper, *Independence Belge,* July 30, 1912, and as Squealer Kemp, a race track operator, in the Boston *Traveler,* July 27, 1912.

21. The statement of Godefray, the Ostend police official, was reported in the Paris edition of the New York *Herald,* July 28, 1912.

22. This was reported in *Petit Parisien,* July 24, 1912, New York *Herald,* Paris edition, July 27, 1912; New York *Times,* July 27, 1912; Cincinnati *Commercial Tribune,* August 2, 1912; New York *Morning Telegraph,* July 27, 1912; Boston *Herald,* July 27, 1912.

23. New York *Times,* September 2, 1912. *The Ballad of Buxton Jail* was printed in the same issue.

24. New York *Morning Telegraph,* September 14, 1912.

Chapter 6

1. Damon Runyon, Chicago *Examiner,* May 24, 1917.

2. New York *American,* December 28, 1913.

3. Author interview with Carpentier, January 1, 1970.

4. The most enlightening comments on motion picture production at the time are those of Adam Kessel, in Douglas Gilbert's series of articles in the New York *World-Telegram* in 1936. The sports interests of the movie pioneers are described in a series of articles by William Henry, "Hollywood in Sports," in the Los Angeles *Times,* 1937.

5. Muldoon's establishment is described in Augustus Thomas's introduction to *The Other Girl.*

6. Her testimony concerning Kid McCoy and Ralph Thompson was reported in the New York *Times,* June 24, 1917.

7. His appearance in court on a charge of striking a Western Union messenger was reported in the New York *Morning Telegraph,* April 21, 1916.

8. McCoy's record was supplied by the Department of the Army, Office of the Adjutant General, September 21, 1970. The department gave the name under which Kid McCoy served as Norman Shelby, not Selby. General O'Ryan's history of the 27th division contains an account of the athletic program of the troops in Texas. McCoy's exhibition bout is given in *Ring Record Book and Boxing Encyclopedia.*

9. New York *Morning Telegraph,* February 17, 1917.

10. Macgowan, *Behind the Screen;* Brownlow, *The Parade's Gone By;* the Mo-

tion Picture World, 1918-1920; *Wid's Magazine* (later *Film* Daily), March 7, 1918. The note on Leon Trotsky as an extra in Clara Kimball Young's film is in Brownlow, *Parade's Gone By,* p. 18. Material on Rida Johnson Young is derived from scattered references in reviews of her plays, and from the review of *The Girl and the Pennant,* by Rida Johnson Young and Christy Mathewson, in New York *Times,* October 24, 1913. See also the obituary notice of Clara Kimball Young in the New York *Times,* October 16, 1960.

11. New York *Tribune,* July 13, 1918. Chautard as the director of the film is in *Wid's Magazine,* March 7, 1918. For Chautard's background see Brownlow, *Parade's Gone By,* p. 140. For the background of Maurice Tourneur see Macgowan, *Behind the Screen;* and Andrew Sarris, *The American Cinema, Directors and Directions, 1929-1968;* also, magazine articles: Maurice Tourneur, "Stylization in Motion Picture Direction," *Motion Picture Magazine,* September 1918; "Motion Picture Classics," February 1920; Dorothy Nutting, "Idealist and Artist, Maurice Tourneur," *Photoplay,* July 1918.

12. *Wid's Magazine,* March 7, 1918.

13. Review, New York *Times,* May 14, 1919. "The noblest achievement yet vouschafed to the cinema," Edward Wagenknecht, *Movies in the Age of Innocence,* p. 78.

14. *Wid's Daily,* September 12, 1920. For the false report that McCoy was to marry Carmen Browder in Chicago see Chicago *Herald,* April 20, 1920. On McCoy's arrest: New York *Times,* May 25, 1920.

15. "Murder Discloses Big Smuggling Plot," New York *Times,* November 13, 1924.

16. Klein, *Sacrificed: The Story of Police Lieutenant Charles Becker,* pp. 27, 72, 74, 82, 164, 430. Additional details are in the testimony at the trials of Becker for the murder of Herman Rosenthal in 1912 and 1914, as reported in the New York *Times* and the New York *World.*

17. New York *Times,* August 14, 1924.

18. New York *Evening Post,* March 12, 1920; *Wid's Daily,* September 12, 1920.

19. *Film Daily,* October 26, 1924.

20. Obituary of McCoy, Detroit newspapers, April 18, 1940.


## Chapter 7

1. This account is taken from the testimony at the trial of McCoy for the murder of Mrs. Mors, as reported in the New York *Times,* the New York *World,* the Los Angeles *Times,* and, in some instances, from the San Francisco *Chronicle.*

2. Balshofer and Miller, *One Reel a Week;* Brownlow, *Parade's Gone By;* Colleen Moore, *Silent Star;* Fowler, *Father Goose.* See also contemporary newspaper accounts.

3. Mencken, *American Language;* Beath, article in *American Speech,* February 1932.

4. New York *Times,* December 28, 1924. On employment by Julian as a guard see San Francisco *Chronicle,* December 18, 1924.

5. New York *Times,* December 17, 1924.

6. New York *Times,* November 11, 13, 14, 1924.

7. Testimony of Mrs. Schapps, New York *Times,* December 17, 1934.

8. New York *Times,* August 14, 1924.

9. The refusal of the court to permit testimony on this point was reported in the

New York *Times,* December 17, 1924. The records of the McCoy trial are reported to have been destroyed. The following communications from the office of the county clerk of Los Angeles County suggest they are no longer available:

> Mr. Andre Averin
> Deputy County Clerk
> Hall of Justice
> 211 West Temple Street
> Hall of Justice
> Los Angeles, California 90053
> August 12, 1970

Dear Mr. Cantwell:

We have been able to locate our records on Norman Selby. These documents are presently on micro-film. . . . Transcripts and documents pertaining to the trial may be obtained at the rate of 50¢ per sheet per side. If you could now direct specific questions as to what actual information you desire we could save you some time and money. In future correspondence please refer to Norman Selby: 23260 and 23261.

Hoping that we can be of service to you:

> I remain:

> William G. Sharp, County Clerk
> by Andre Averin, deputy

> August 25, 1970

re:  Superior Court Case No. 23260 & 23261
     The People vs. NORMAN SELBY

Dear Sir:

We are sorry to inform you that the documents are destroyed after a period of ten years, and the documents you are requesting for 1924 are no longer available.

Very truly yours,

> William G. Sharp
> County Clerk
> by P. J. Talmachoff

> Chief
> Criminal Division

10. Klein, *Sacrificed,* p. 430, says Sam Schepps was prospering in "the antique furniture business" in 1927. Sam Schepps' connection with the inquiry into the murder of Harry Cohen, known as "Harry the Yot," and his operation of a jewelry store in 1918, were reported in the New York *Times,* April 2, 1918; his involvement in the investigation of Grace Leslie was reported at the same time. His arrest on charges of forgery at his antiques store, Maison Cluny in New York, was reported in the New York *Times,* October 4, 1934.

11. This account is abstracted from the newspaper reports of the testimony at McCoy's trial, December 13 through December 31, 1924; January 3, 9, February 20, 21, 1925.

12. New York *Times,* December 20, 1924.

# Bibliography

ALBERT, HOLLIS. *The Barrymores*. New York: Dial Press, 1964.

ANDERSON, MARGARET. *My Thirty Years' War: Beginnings and Battles to 1930; The Fiery Fountains: Continuation and Crisis to 1950; The Strange Necessity: Resolutions and Reminiscences to 1969.* 3 vols. New York: Horizon Press, 1969.

BETTINSON, A. E. *The National Sporting Club.* London: printed privately,

BALSHOFER, FRED J., and MILLER, ARTHUR C. *One Reel a Week.* Berkeley: University of California Press, 1967.

BROWNLOW, KEVIN. *The Parade's Gone By.* New York: Knopf, 1968.

CORBETT, JAMES J. *The Roar of the Crowd; the True Tale of the Rise and Fall of a Champion.* New York: Grosset, 1930.

CROY, HOMER. *Star Maker: The Story of D. W. Griffith.* Des Moines, Iowa: Duell, Sloan and Pearce, 1959.

FLEISCHER, NATHANIEL. *Fifty Years at Ringside.* Fleet Publishing Company, 1958.

————. *John L. Sullivan, Champion of Champions.* New York: Putnam's, 1953.

————, ed. *Ring Record Book and Boxing Encyclopedia.* Published annually by *The Ring.*

FOWLER, GENE. *Father Goose; the Story of Mack Sennett.* Covici, 1934.

————. *Goodnight, Sweet Prince* [the life and times of John Barrymore]. New York: Viking Press, 1944.

GISH, LILLIAN. *Lillian Gish; the Movies, Mr. Griffith and Me.* Englewood Cliffs, N.J.: Prentice-Hall, 1969.

GOLESWORTHY, MAURICE, comp. *The Encyclopedia of Boxing.* London: R. Hale, 1960.

HALDANE, R. A. *Champions and Challengers.* London: Stanley Paul, 1969.

HALLS, W. D. *Maurice Maeterlinck: A Study of His Life and Thought.* New York: Oxford University Press, 1960.

HART, WILLIAM SURREY. *My Life East and West.* New York: Benjamin Blom, 1968 (first published 1929).

*History of Rush County, Indiana.* Chicago: Brant and Fuller, 1878.

HOPPER, DEWOLF. *Once a Clown Always a Clown.* Garden City, N.Y.: Garden City Publishing Co., 1932.

JOHNSTON, ALEXANDER. *Ten—And Out!.* Revised edition. New York: Washburn, Ives, 1949.

KLEIN, HENRY A. *Sacrificed: The Story of Police Lieutenant Charles Becker.* 1927.

LE BLANC, GEORGETTE. *Souvenirs; My Life with Maeterlinck*. New York: Dutton, 1932.

LOGAN, ANDY. *Against the Evidence: The Becker-Rosenthal Affair*. New York: McCall, 1970.

MACGOWAN, KENNETH. *Behind the Screen; the History and Techniques of the Motion Picture*. New York: Dell, 1967.

MACKENZIE, F. A. *Twentieth Century Crimes*. London: Christy and Moore, 1927.

NAUGHTON, W. W. *Kings of the Queensbury Realm*. Chicago: Continental Publishing, 1902.

SILER, GEORGE. *Inside Facts on Pugilism*. Chicago: Laird and Lee, 1907.

THOMAS, AUGUSTUS. *The Print of My Remembrance*. Scribner, 1922.

———. *The Other Girl* [a play]. S. French, 1917.

# Index

181